NOT I, BUT CHRIST

BY JASON HENDERSON

**This and other publications
are available <u>FREE</u> upon request
by contacting:**

MARKET STREET FELLOWSHIP
981 W. Market Street   Akron, Ohio 44313
email: MSFPrinting@gmail.com
phone: 330-419-1527

www.marketstreetfellowship.com

© *2013 – v.6*

Contents

Forward

This book is a complete re-write and a significant enlargement upon the previous booklet by the same title. The former booklet and corresponding audio series were put together quickly several years ago, and it has been my intention for some time to start over from scratch and attempt to present these things in a fuller and clearer way. Although I feel like my eyes are only just beginning to open, and I know that words always fall short of communicating spiritual things, this book represents my attempt to "speak the things which I have seen and heard." This is the gospel of life that the Spirit of God has made so real to my soul.

Like all of our publications, this book is available to all without cost and can be quoted, copied, and freely distributed so long as there is no alteration, deletion, or addition of words. The publishing company requires that I make copies available for sale on their website, but free copies are available through Market Street Fellowship and will be shipped to you at no cost.

Chapter I
Zeal Without Knowledge

I was close to finishing a degree in religion and philosophy and excitedly planning a future in Christian academia when the anxiety attacks began. I suppose it's more accurate to say the attacks *returned*, as I had had several bouts of irrational fear as a child. I remember lying awake at night as a boy, deeply concerned that minutes and hours were passing by while sleep continued to escape me. The large grandfather clock at the bottom of the stairs sounded every fifteen minutes. It was my greatest childhood enemy. The haunting chime caused my heart to race with the passing of every quarter hour and the realization that I was still wide awake. On some occasions, the anxiety snowballed into what I now understand to be panic attacks. Incredible fear would suddenly sweep over me and remain for hours or even days before eventually subsiding. These episodes continued on and off, perhaps occurring one or two times a year, until my junior year of high school when, after one particularly long bout, they seemed to disappear completely.

For those who are unfamiliar with anxiety attacks, they are like a sudden flood of irrational terror and dread that far exceeds any normal experience of fear. Sometimes they are triggered by events or circumstances; other times they seem to come out of nowhere and have nothing to do with one's experiences or outlook. Doctors describe them as a mysterious misfiring of flight neurons in the sympathetic nervous system. Sufferers say they are the most intensely frightening, upsetting, and uncomfortable experiences of their life. Usually these episodes stop on their own after twenty or thirty minutes. Some, like the ones I experienced, linger for days or weeks with little or no reprieve.

After my third year of high school, I was entirely panic-free for the next six years. However, on January 6th of my final year of college I experienced an anxiety attack that was incredibly intense and unbearably long. It lasted every bit of eight weeks. I had never in my life felt so desperate or known anything close to that kind of torment. In the winter of 1997 my world was destroyed in a great flood of fear. Hours felt to me like weeks, and weeks felt like years.

It was during this time, at twenty-one years of age, that I began to cry out with a genuine hunger and desperation to find what was spiritually real. In the turmoil of my emotions and instability of my mind, I longed to know something more real than my pain and more stable than my own thoughts. Despite my Christian upbringing and education, I doubted God's existence for the first time in my life. I doubted everything I had been taught and everything I had so easily believed and defended with my mind.

I knew so many Scriptures, facts, and strong arguments for the truth of Christianity. I had often debated my unbelieving classmates and defended the gospel against liberal professors. But now, in the midst of this storm, my collection of doctrines and proofs did nothing to help me. My spiritual house had obviously been built on sand because the wind and waves were sweeping it away. I remember beginning to realize that if God were real, I did not know Him, at least not in any meaningful way. I knew Christianity, but I didn't truly know Christ. This was a frightening realization that only added to my fear.

I remember walking around my college campus in the middle of the night calling out loud for God to make Himself known. I remember curling up under a desk in my room and fearfully confessing to the Lord that I didn't know what to believe or how I could ever be sure. The Bible seemed foreign and confusing, and my Christian platitudes felt powerless and empty. Of course my friends could not understand. I had no way to explain or even describe what I was experiencing. I was constantly terrified and felt utterly alone. Two months crept by with very little change. They were the longest two months of my life.

Even now, all these years later, I can find no words to describe the desperation that I felt during this time. Without God, the world seemed such an absurd and meaningless place. I could see the vanity of it. I saw humans running around chasing pretty shadows that never brought fulfillment. And even when men caught their dreams they could hold them for just a moment before time took them away. What was the point? What was real? Who was God and what did He really want? I was searching and groping for the truth. I needed it like my next breath of air. And then at last, after long weeks of confusion and darkness, the sun finally began to rise. The Lord began to prove Himself to me in a new and real way. In the words of Paul the apostle, He started to "open the eyes of my understanding"[1] and show me a truth that went beyond words and ideas. It was like I could see Him, though not with my eyes. In my heart there came an awareness of His presence and a peaceful certainty that Jesus was exactly who He claimed to be. It was simple but it was real, and the fear began to give way to the presence of His light.

A Wrong Turn

With a heart virtually bursting with gratitude, I dedicated myself anew to the kingdom of God. I was literally buzzing with excitement and zeal, and was determined to give myself to the Lord, whatever that meant and whatever the cost. It's impossible to overstate how consumed I was with the idea of knowing and walking with God. I had no understanding of God's eternal purpose in Christ or the true meaning of spiritual growth, so I did the only things I knew to do: I dedicated myself to prayer and fasting, spent long hours in the Bible, shared the gospel, and diligently tried to obey the Scriptures. As far as I knew, these were the essentials for any true walk with God, so I devoted myself to these disciplines with all my heart. I began to read the biographies of famous Christian ministers and

---

[1] Ephesians 1:18

missionaries. I devoured the stories of Hudson Taylor, David Brainerd, Jonathan Edwards, William Carey, Rees Howells, John G. Lake, and many others, and I did my best to imitate these men of faith. I wanted to have what they had and live as they lived. I wanted to walk and speak with God as the great prophets had done. I remember being captivated by Exodus 33:11 – "So the Lord spoke to Moses face to face, as a man speaks to a friend." *That* is what I wanted. I printed this verse, framed it, and it hung for many years on my living room wall.

In retrospect, the next seven years was a time of *zeal without knowledge.*[2] I didn't understand what it meant to know God, but I wanted it more than anything else. After graduating from college in the spring of 1997, I abandoned my plans for graduate school and looked for ways to give all of my time and energy to the Lord. I wanted to *experience* God and not just learn about him, and I found a large ministry that seemed every bit as zealous for God as I felt. I was soon involved with various branches of this ministry, was taking classes at their Bible school, and leading worship for various gatherings and prayer meetings. After a year I connected with a group who worked with the urban poor and I began to spend my days with drug addicts and homeless people, offering free meals and leading Bible studies. One of my friends was a chaplain in

---

[2] This is how Paul describes his Jewish countrymen in Romans 10:2-3 who were extremely zealous for the written word of God, but had rejected the living Word who had come to them as God's salvation. He says, "For I bear them witness that they have a zeal for God, but not according to knowledge. For they being ignorant of God's righteousness, and seeking to establish their own righteousness, have not submitted to the righteousness of God."

the county jail, and I joined him two afternoons a week sharing the gospel with inmates.

Before very long, I met and married my wife Jessie and immediately following our honeymoon we purchased an old three-story home in a part of the city renown for drugs and prostitution. After making a few essential repairs and giving it a fresh coat of paint, we filled our home with bunk-beds and opened *The Isaiah 58 Homeless Shelter* where we both lived and ministered for the first years of our marriage. Jessie cooked breakfast and dinner for all of our guests, and in the evenings we had group Bible study followed by a time of individual counseling and prayer. Our guests left the house between breakfast and dinner so that they could look for jobs and permanent housing, and so that Jessie and I could work to support the shelter. At this time, my day job was as a manager of a much larger homeless shelter not far from our home.

During these years I grew increasingly committed to prayer, fasting, and studying Scripture. I practiced these spiritual disciplines consistently, always motivated by a sense of the brevity of my time on earth and a gnawing fear of wasting my life. God was real, that much I knew, and I did not want to disappoint Him. I determined to sleep as little as possible and to always make the most of my time. Three hours each day were devoted to prayer, and another hour or two to the study of Scripture. For years I fasted a day or two each week, in addition to several much longer fasts each year.

As far as I knew, this lifestyle was not motivated by legalism or works theology. I wasn't trying to earn my way to heaven or punish myself for sins. The choices I made were constrained by a hunger for God and a strong sense of His reality that had stayed with me since my final semester of college. I wanted so badly to be a person to whom God would say, "Well done, my good and faithful servant."[3] If others had done it, why couldn't I? So with a combination of determination and desperation, I managed to continue this lifestyle for a number of years. In all of these things I was very sincere, but I understand now that I was also sincerely blind.

I realize that for many Christians this kind of zeal for the Lord and commitment to spiritual disciplines might seem quite commendable. Indeed, most of the time I was convinced that it was. I was devoted and consistent where others often failed, and in a number of ways my Christianity seemed to be "working." I had become very familiar with the Bible, and it was now easy for me to spend hours in worship and intercession. The ministries I was involved with appeared to be successful and growing, and I was recognized by some as a passionate young leader. Beyond that, I had even witnessed what I believed to be genuine miracles, healings, and movements of the Holy Spirit. Most of the time, the combination of these things seemed to be clear confirmation that I was on the right track.

However, there were other times, particularly towards the end of these seven years, when I became increasingly aware that something was wrong. When life slowed down a bit and I was less occupied with responsibilities and ministry activities, I could see things that deeply troubled and confused me. Regardless of my passion and determination, there was so much in my heart and in my life that

---

[3] Matthew 25:22

seemed to plainly contradict the Scriptures I had come to know so well. First of all, I continued to be plagued with fears. Some were the intense and irrational panic attacks that seemed to come and go throughout the years, but even more bothersome than those were the hidden insecurities and anxieties that motivated and controlled so much of what I thought and did. Along with this there was the uncomfortable realization that I did not love people. I loved the *idea* of loving people. And I loved the people that I naturally found lovable. But this seemed to be a far cry from what Jesus and the apostles described. Paul wrote, "And though I have the gift of prophecy, and understand all mysteries and all knowledge, and though I have all faith, so that I could remove mountains, but have not love, I am nothing."[4] The word *nothing* in this verse confronted and bothered me. It seemed so severe and unrelenting, and I couldn't help but wonder if it described me.

The most glaring problem of all, however, and the one that haunted me more than the rest, was the realization that I was a walking cesspool of pride, especially spiritual pride. In my heart, I knew that I wanted to be seen and recognized for my spirituality. I wanted to be exalted in man's eyes, known for my accomplishments, my wisdom, and my discipline. I could usually hide my pride from others and sometimes managed to justify it to myself, but I could never escape it. In fact, what bothered me most was that my pride seemed to be getting *worse* with every year that I served the Lord. I was respected as a committed Christian and even followed as a leader, but I secretly saw and hated all these things about myself, and no amount of

---

[4] 1 Corinthians 13:2

prayer and fasting had ever freed me from them.

Sometimes, when I was humbled by my hypocrisy and not trying to hide or justify these things, my heart became quiet and soft and more willing to see the truth. During these times, I would read passages of Scripture that seemed to be both familiar and foreign, verses like "out of your inner most being will flow rivers of living water,"[5] or "nevertheless I live, yet not I but Christ lives in me."[6] As I read Scriptures like these it was as though I could hear the Lord's voice in my heart saying, *"How long are you going to pretend you know what this means?"*

Eventually, my wife and I felt led to close our shelter and move back to her home state of Ohio. I took a job in home remodeling and though I continued my pursuit of the Lord and spiritual disciplines, for the first time since college I was not involved with ministry. For more than a year I had the opportunity to see myself apart from the busy Christianity I was accustomed to. What I saw deeply troubled me. Looking back now, I believe this time was a God-ordained reality check, but at the time it felt like my world was falling apart again. This time my problem wasn't primarily fear. It wasn't immorality, backsliding, or even burnout. This time, the great dilemma of my heart was that *there had to be so much more to Christianity than what I knew.* Somehow, the pages of the Bible were describing something I still did not understand because there was no way that my heart was experiencing the abundance of life and light that Jesus spoke so clearly about.

---

[5] John 4:14
[6] Galatians 2:20

I was discouraged and confused. I felt I had stopped at nothing in my pursuit of God. I had prayed, fasted, and disciplined my flesh. I had served the poor, visited prisoners, and fed the hungry. I had dedicated my life to His service, studied the Bible and the greatest Christian books, attended the most inspiring conferences and even served shoulder to shoulder with influential leaders in the body of Christ. But still, in moments of spiritual lucidity, I knew something enormous was missing. Despite my efforts, I realized I had no idea what it meant for a soul to be conformed to the image of Jesus Christ. I could fool others, but I had grown tired of fooling myself. My yoke was not easy, nor my burden light. And in the unseen places of my soul, I knew I was the exact same man who had begun this journey seven years ago.

Through discipline alone I maintained the outward appearance of spiritual life, but inwardly I had come to a crisis. I knew for certain that Jesus was real and I believed the Bible to be God's infallible self-revelation. So I concluded that one of two things had to be true: Either I was still lacking in my commitment, desire, or pursuit of the Lord, or somewhere at the beginning of my journey I had developed a foundational misunderstanding of the gospel and how it works in the soul of a believer. The difficulty with the first option was obvious. I had exhausted myself for years with the intensity of my pursuit of God and the practice of spiritual disciplines. I had always assumed that my devotion and effort were the issue, and in every way I had tried to address this. There was perhaps still more I could do, but at this point it seemed unlikely that a few more hours of prayer or an even greater commitment to discipline would be the catalyst for a spiritual breakthrough. The problem with the second option was simply that I had no idea what my foundational misunderstanding might be. But desperate and out of explanations, I began to turn my heart to the Lord in a way I had not done since the weeks of helplessness and desperation during my final year of college. I turned to Him like a little child who knew nothing at all, asking for His view of my problem as well as His understanding of the solution. I soon came to see that I had misunderstood both.

Chapter II

The Issue is Life

What I began to experience in the months and years to follow changed *everything,* but to make any progress I realized I had to start over at the very beginning. I've come to understand that knowing the truth always works this way. Truth destroys before it can rebuild. It questions, exposes, and removes so much that isn't real, in order to make room in our hearts for what is real. Even a glimpse of truth can tear down imaginations and create in the vacuum an awareness of our ignorance and a genuine *need* to know more. We grow very little until knowing the Lord changes from something that interests us into an absolute necessity. Only when we *need* the truth do we begin to ask the right questions and let the Lord show us Himself as the answer to every one.

There were so many foundational misunderstandings in my heart with regard to knowing God. There were wrong assumptions and hidden presuppositions buried underneath my beliefs. My problem was not complicated, in fact it was really quite simple, but to see it meant allowing the Lord to take me all the way back to the start.

He began to deal with my heart about some very simple questions – things like, *What is Christianity?* Or, *Why did Jesus come, and what did He accomplish?* For years I had held my own satisfactory answers to these questions. I felt I had settled these things long ago and moved on. But now, having watched my Christian world fall apart more than once, I was willing to revisit these fundamental questions; I was willing to start over with the right foundation.

Christianity is Not Religion

Before discussing what Christianity really is, it may do us some good to say a bit about what Christianity is not. Christianity is not a religion. It never has been a religion. What I mean is that Christianity has virtually nothing to do with intellectual belief in specific creeds, with changes made to human behavior, or with instructions regarding what man should do to be pleasing to God. Religion is generally understood to be an organized system of beliefs and practices, but Jesus' gift to the world was not correct doctrine, nor was His life as a man meant to be a mere lesson in morality. The letters of the New Testament were never intended to be crystallized into rigid theologies and passed along as articles of faith and lessons in Christian conduct. This is religion. I realize that Christianity is often presented in these ways by Christian leaders, but that is simply because we have created religion where God intended no such thing.

Although there are multitudes of different religions, nearly all involve man's attempt to be like God, to reach

God, appease Him, or perform in a manner pleasing to Him. Despite claims of divine origin and purpose, all religion has *man* as its true source, center, and goal. Religion is born when man interprets or defines God according to his own perspective and desire and then serves the god of his own creation. By doing this, we actually get to spiritualize our imaginations and worship our own ideas. In a very real sense, religion seeks to create God in the image of man, so that by serving God we actually serve ourselves.[1] This is precisely what happened in the infamous story of the golden calf. Israel believed in God and knew that He had freed them from slavery in Egypt. But wanting to define for themselves the character of God and the nature of their relationship to Him, they fashioned an image that corresponded to their opinions and desires. After melting their jewelry and forming the golden calf, they said, "This is your god, O Israel, who brought you out of the land of Egypt."[2] They then rose up to worship their creation with great celebration, feasts, and most likely fornication.[3] In this example the form of worship may have been openly immoral, but this is rarely the case. Religion most often wears a mask of virtue and piety, claiming to possess the beliefs and behaviors that are acceptable to God. But regardless how it looks to the eyes of man, religion is a

---

[1] This is the main idea behind the idols mentioned in the Bible. Whether or not they are given physical form, idols are inventions of the fallen human heart that allow us to worship our own ideas and imaginations.

[2] Exodus 32:4

[3] Exodus 32:6 says, "The people sat down to eat and drink, and rose up to play." According to some Bible scholars, the word "play" here implies fornication and adulterous intercourse or orgies.

human attempt to replace God's grace and revelation with a man-made counterfeit. The words of Karl Barth are helpful:

> *Religion is the attempted replacement of the divine work by a human manufacture... It is a feeble but defiant, an arrogant but hopeless, attempt to create something which man could do. In religion man bolts and bars himself against revelation by providing a substitute, by taking away in advance the very thing which has been given by God. It is never the truth. It is a complete fiction, which has not only little but no relation to God.*[4]

Religion is not simply the idea that man must work his way to heaven, or that God is served by human hands. It is not just our empty rituals, legalism, rules, and fleshly labors. Religion is any and every way that we replace God's gift of life in Jesus Christ with a human counterfeit, whether it be in our beliefs, efforts, understanding, righteousness, love, worship, fellowship, ministry, etc. In one way or another, religion introduces man and his resources where God has already given His Son.

Christianity is Life

Christianity is not a religion; *it is a life*. Specifically, it is the life of Jesus Christ given to the soul of man. It is not

---

[4] Karl Barth, *Church Dogmatics*. Vol. I, Pt. 2. Edinburgh: T&T Clark. 1956. pg. 302-303

a belief, although knowing this life will form and shape many beliefs. It is not a behavior or attitude, although experiencing this life affects all that we do. Christianity, at its very root and in every branch, is bound up with a very specific life that God gives, forms, and glorifies in the soul of man. *Christianity is Christ living in you.*

So Christianity is life, but we need to be careful how we understand this word. Assumption is always a great obstacle to knowing the truth. We should ask another question – *what is life?* What does life mean to God? For far too many of us, life is thought to be a collection of familiar things around us. It is the friends we have, the places we love, the environment in which we live, an environment that we create. We gather together people, things, emotions, places, experiences, jobs, and goals, and assemble them into an environment that surrounds and defines us, and we call that environment our life. And building upon this foundational idea, Christianity then becomes an attempt to bring God into that environment, to bring God into what we call life. Religion encourages us to include God in our lives, and then to give Him first priority among the many things that constitute our environment. We are told that we will be much happier and more fulfilled if we only invite God into our life! When God is a part of our life we can prosper and succeed, we can reach our potential and fulfill our destiny. And when at last our body dies, we begin the so-called *after-life,* which is often described as simply a new environment with even greater things, experiences, places, activities, and relationships.

With others, the concept of life is more internal, but is still entirely natural. Many believe that life is defined by a state of animation and consciousness, the presence of will, emotion, thought, and action. Naturally speaking this is true, but biological life is a mere shadow of the true life that God knows and offers to the human soul. Ignorant of the incredible difference between the two, we foolishly try to understand and appreciate spiritual life based upon our experiences of life in the created realm. We imagine that, because we live, surely we must understand a good deal about life! But this is simply not true. We do not naturally possess or understand what the Bible calls life. Obviously we exist, and are conscious and active beings with organic life. But when a disciple promised to follow Jesus just as soon as he had buried his father, Jesus replied, "Follow Me, and let the dead bury their dead."[5]   On another occasion, Jesus stood before an enormous crowd of Jews, all of whom had beating hearts and busy schedules, and told them, "Unless you eat the flesh of the Son of God and drink His blood, *you have no life in yourselves.*"[6] Evidently, whatever Jesus called life had nothing to do with man's natural environment or biological existence. From His perspective, life was something that humanity simply did not possess.

True Life is Foreign to the Natural Man

One of the most foundational and vital things that the Spirit of God seeks to make crystal clear in the heart of every believer is the fact that what God calls life is utterly

---

[5]   Matthew 8:22
[6]   John 6:53, emphasis mine

foreign to the natural man. Spiritual life is entirely *other-than* what we are and what we know by nature. To the human being, there is absolutely nothing familiar about it. Only when we are born of His Spirit do we possess true life, and even then, we begin like newborn babies who possess a life that we do not yet understand.

One night, a ruler of the Pharisees came secretly to Jesus so as not to be seen by his religious peers. He came with his heart full of questions and doubts, yet he was convinced that this Nazarene spoke and acted on behalf of God. He said, "Rabbi, we know that You are a teacher come from God; for no one can do these signs that You do unless God is with him." Jesus immediately responded, "Most assuredly, I say to you, unless one is born again, he cannot see the kingdom of God."[7] As He did with many others, Jesus set aside Nicodemus' comments and took him straight to the heart of the matter. It is as though Jesus said to him, "Nicodemus, I know that you have questions about Me, about My Father, and about His kingdom. I know that you are here because you are searching for something real. But things being as they are, there is nothing that I can do to help you. Nicodemus, although you see Me in this earthen vessel, we are operating in different realms and according to contrary lives. At this moment we have nothing in common. Flesh gives birth to flesh, spirit gives birth to spirit. I am from above, you are from beneath. In order to see and under-stand the answers to your questions, we must be on common ground. You must receive My life; you must be born again."

---

[7]   John 3:2-3

The gift of new birth is not a second chance, nor is it simply the forgiveness of sins. New birth is precisely what it says – *a new birth, a new life!* It is not new with regard to time, that is to say, it is not a newer version of you or me. It is not new in the sense that we are turning over a new leaf, or starting over with a clean slate. It is new with respect to nature, substance, kind, and origin. It is altogether new. It is not an addition to the old, an improvement, or a restoration. There is nothing old about it. Paul says, "Therefore, if anyone is in Christ, he is a new creation; old things have passed away; behold, all things have become new."[8] New birth is when the soul of man receives true life for the first time and is literally born of a different kind and into a different realm.

Partakers of Life

So Christianity is life, but life is not what we assume. Life is an attribute of God alone, and therefore our experience of life is the apprehension and experience of God Himself. Jesus says, "This is eternal life, that they may know You, the only true God, and Jesus Christ whom You have sent."[9] When we are born of His Spirit, Jesus Christ literally becomes the resident life of our soul. We are "made alive together with Him"[10] and become "partakers of the divine nature."[11] We never become God or possess divinity in ourselves, but we receive, know, participate in,

---

[8] 2 Corinthians 5:17
[9] John 17:3
[10] Ephesians 2:5
[11] 2 Peter 1:4

and enjoy all that He is. Standing before a crowd in Jerusalem, Jesus cried out, "I have come that they may have life, and may have it abundantly."[12]   John explains, "He who has the Son has the life. He who does not have the Son, does not have the life."[13] The very center and substance of the gospel has always been this issue of life.   One life (which was never truly alive) is lost at the cross and true life is gained. Jesus says, "Whoever desires to save his life will lose it, but whoever loses his life for My sake will save it."[14] To those who are born "dead in trespasses and sins,"[15] Jesus offers Himself as "the resurrection and the life."[16]

All of this may sound obvious, and certainly the *concept* of spiritual life is a familiar one in the body of Christ. Even so, I contend that our blindness to this reality is the origin of so much discouragement and confusion. If you are like me, many of you have invested much time and effort in an attempt to make *your life* more like that of Jesus Christ.   Much of what I did in the name of Christianity was an effort to somehow learn about the life of Christ and then put into practice the things I had learned. I sought to act like Christ, love like Christ, speak like Christ, and pray like Christ. But all of this represented a terrible misunderstanding, one that is spiritually and scripturally absurd but nevertheless extremely popular in the church: I believed that with the appropriate teaching, discipline, and effort, I could become more like Jesus Christ. This is a common idea, but it is absolutely impos-

---

[12]   John 10:10, LitV Translation, Jay P. Green
[13]   1 John 5:12
[14]   Luke 9:24
[15]   Ephesians 2:1
[16]   John 11:25

sible. No amount of learning, effort, or discipline can transform death into life.

According to Jesus Christ, "Flesh gives birth to flesh, spirit gives birth to spirit,"[17] "The Spirit gives life, the flesh profits nothing."[18] Flesh and spirit are opposite and contrary things that operate with incompatible natures and aim toward completely different goals. Human effort and devotion are not the issue. Bible study and self-discipline will never bridge this gap. The solution is not asking what Jesus would do as we go throughout our day or following a seven-step plan to become more like Christ. In the words of British pastor and author T. Austin-Sparks, "When you have come to your best, there is a gulf between you and the beginnings of Christ that cannot be bridged. If you attain *your* best, you have not commenced Christ."[19] Humanly speaking, this is an insurmountable problem, and one that demands a far greater solution than many have considered.

When we misunderstand the nature of the problem, we unknowingly search for a solution that is far less than what we need and what God offers. This was a big part of my problem for many years. If we assume, for example, that our primary spiritual dilemma consists of wrong thoughts and actions, then we will look to the Lord for forgiveness of sins and freedom from a guilty conscience. If we see ourselves as lacking direction or wisdom or in need of a lifestyle change, we may find exactly what we are looking for in the ever-popular seven steps for spiritual

---

[17] John 3:6

[18] John 6:63

[19] Sparks, T. Austin, *The School of Christ*. Emmanuel Publishing, Chapter 1

living. However, when we begin to recognize ourselves to be entirely *without life and contrary to God by nature*, and when this has become not only a theology but a deep and inescapable heart-realization, then we are driven to find a much fuller understanding and experience of God's salvation in Jesus Christ.

This is exactly what began to happen in me. As I started to see the great divide between life and death, between flesh and spirit, I recognized the frightening distinction between trying to live *my* life for God, and God Himself "working in me both to will and work for His good pleasure."[20] Like so many, as a young Christian I had assumed that with my sins forgiven I was now meant to live my life for Him. But after years of attempting exactly that, it was both a shock and a relief to discover that God desired no such thing. The Christianity of the Bible is not forgiveness of sin followed by human devotion, self-discipline, and religious zeal. True Christianity is not the imitation of Christ in the flesh, but rather the impartation of His life in the soul.

The Farmer and His Seed

Consider the following analogy. Imagine there was a farmer who purchased 100 acres of land in order to plant corn. He cleared the land, plowed his field, and finally planted the highest quality seed with great expectation for a harvest. With patience he awaited the increase of what he had planted, but at the end of several weeks the seed

---

[20] Philippians 2:13

had not grown at all. Instead, to his great surprise, the soil around each seed had risen up and begun to take on the form and appearance of the missing stalks of corn. Can you imagine the disappointment of the farmer when his anticipated harvest was nothing more than altered soil mimicking the increase of his quality seed?

Obviously this analogy makes little sense in the natural realm, yet we somehow fail to recognize its absurdity in the spiritual realm. Christ is the only "incorruptible Seed."[21] We are the soil, "God's field."[22] The Father is the farmer who has an expectation for the increase of His implanted seed unto a full expression of its life. The harvest of the farmer is the increase of the seed, and not the increase of anything else. God's expectation for us, the soil, is to be the "good ground" that receives the seed and "yields a crop: some one hundred, some sixty, some thirty fold."[23] The soil is the habitation of the seed, the "earthen vessel" that both experiences and displays its increase. God is not looking for our attempt to mimic the life of Christ any more than the farmer was looking for the soil to impersonate the corn. Our calling is much greater: to be the vessels of honor in which the very life of Christ Himself is formed and made manifest. Christ is one of a kind, a precious seed with no equal. And as far as any farmer is concerned, apart from bearing the increase of the seed, the soil can do no good thing.

As Christians we invest a tremendous amount of time and effort in various misunderstandings of spiritual growth, most of which are the direct result of not under-

---

[21] 1 Peter 1:23
[22] 1 Corinthians 3:9
[23] Matthew 13:8

standing this issue of life. We give ourselves to the transformation of the dirt and consequently experience very little of the increase of God's Seed. We receive the gift of life by faith, but then imagine that spiritual growth comes through our own effort and discipline. In other words, we receive Christ's life when we are born again but continue trying to live our own life for God. In response to this exact misunderstanding, Paul reprimanded the Galatians saying, "Are you so foolish? Having begun in the Spirit, are you now being perfected by the flesh?"[24] In my case, I was indeed that foolish.

---

[24] Galatians 3:3

Chapter III
The Weakness of Words

Before we move on, we need to grapple with something that is often overlooked by believers. As strange as it sounds, one of the greatest hindrances to truly knowing the Lord can be our familiarity with biblical words and spiritual concepts. Understanding this now will help immensely as we move on. In my case, most of the ideas and Bible verses mentioned in the previous chapter had long been familiar to me. In fact, during the years of spiritual frustration and confusion following college, I had committed many of these Scriptures to memory and even taught some of these concepts. Had I somehow then been able to read the second chapter of this book, I'm certain I would have insisted that I already knew these things. And as a matter of fact *I did already know the words.* However, I've come to realize that, for much of my life as a Christian, I was far more acquainted with the words them-selves than with the spiritual realities that these words described. To say it another way, I've learned that the Bible is like a window. Its purpose is to open up to our heart a view of Jesus Christ and all that is real in Him. Nobody looks *at* a window. Rather we look *through* a window to see something else. Reading the Bible should be a similar experience. The words of Scripture are a wonderful and essential gift from God, but we are meant to see past the words and behold the Lord Himself. When the Bible is studied and memorized for any other reason it is unavoidably misunderstood and misused. Jesus once rebuked the Pharisees saying,

> *You diligently search the Scriptures, for in them you think you have eternal life; and these are they which testify of Me. But you are not willing to come to Me that you may have life.*[1]

The Pharisees and Scribes of Jesus' day were extremely knowledgeable of the Old Testament Scriptures, more so than we often realize. Not just their religion, but every aspect of their daily lives – their laws, education, relationships, morals, and customs – were governed by their meticulous study of Scripture. But despite their great knowledge, the vast majority of them were unable to see, and consequently would not receive, the One who was being described on every page. The words of Scripture were familiar and revered in all of Israel, but the Person behind these words seemed foreign and offensive. John says, "He came to His own, and His own did not receive Him."[2] When He walked through their streets and taught in their synagogues, the great majority of Jews dismissed Him as a glutton, a sinner, or a demon-possessed deceiver.

---

[1]   John 5:39-40
[2]   John 1:11

In this way, words can be both wonderful and dangerous. Though they are used of God as a vehicle through which truth is proclaimed and described, they affect us in the way God desires only when we come to know and experience the reality that is behind them. If you think about it, all language works the same way. When we speak to each other, we intuitively understand that our words are merely attempts to explain and communicate something that is real *within us*. We speak and write in order to express our emotions, understanding, personality, and ideas. With words we try to give, reveal, or explain who we are and what we know; we seek to pass along to another person something of ourselves. This is perhaps our greatest form of communication, and yet we have all experienced the weakness of our words. We have all chosen words that seemed plain and clear to us, only to be completely misunderstood by our listeners. We have also mistakenly heard and believed things that others never meant to communicate.

The tricky thing about words is that they have no fixed meaning or reality. Of course we have dictionary definitions for all of our words, but when it comes to actual conversations, the meaning behind a word is very often supplied by the listener and not by the word itself. The same word can mean ten different things to ten different people. It can make one person laugh and another feel insecure. One sentence might be frightening to you and yet comforting to me. This happens because, despite the accepted meaning of words, it is our own understanding, experience, and imagination that often determine the impact that words have on us. The weakness of words is the fact that every speaker and listener, writer and reader, has the freedom to give meaning to the words that they use or encounter.

If this is true with human words that describe natural things, how much more true must it be when we read or hear the words that God uses to describe spiritual realities? If ten Christians were to hear the same sermon about grace, it is entirely possible that all ten could have conflicting understandings of this word along with different experiences of God's grace that support their ideas. How do we know who is correct? How can we ever know what grace really is? This is an important question that deserves some thought, and again, acknowledging our ignorance or uncertainty is a huge step in the right direction. We should never be afraid to admit to ourselves or to the Lord that we have no idea what is real and true. God's desire is not that we identify correct biblical concepts and cling to them with our mind. He wants us to receive, know, and experience the resurrected life of His Son! It is far better to be ignorant and teachable than firmly attached to dead concepts or satisfied with a sterile belief in the correct Christian doctrines. Familiarity with the Bible very often does not lead to a real knowledge of God. Familiarity with God, however, always leads to a great knowledge and understanding of the Bible.

Words Are a Package

While reading a familiar passage of Scripture, it is not uncommon for a believer to suddenly see something altogether new and different. We say, "It was like the words jumped off the page!" Why does this happen? Why did it *not* happen the last time we read the same Scripture? I think the answer to these questions lies in the fact that knowing God's words and knowing God are two very different things. We can read God's words as much as we like, but real spiritual communication begins when the reality behind these words, the actual substance of which they speak, is shown to us.

Words are like a package. Somebody can hand you a box that is filled or empty and either way the box is exactly the same. The package is merely the transportation or communication of something else inside. Words function in a similar way. They are meant to be the carriers or vehicles of something else that is far more real. The words of God in the Bible are like a collection of packages that seek to convey realities of spirit and truth to the human soul. They carry a description or testimony of something that is much greater than language. The words themselves are never really what God is trying to make known to us. Rather, God uses words to describe spiritual realities in the hope that hungry hearts will turn to experience their Author.

Imagine that somebody handed you a box with the word "disgusting" written on top. That would not be too bad. It's just the word "disgusting" on a box. There is nothing terribly disgusting about the *word* "disgusting." There is nothing disgusting about the box. And considering that one man's trash can be another man's treasure, you begin to wonder if there might actually be something valuable inside. As long as "disgusting" is just a word on a box, your imagination gets to define the contents. It could be anything at all, until you see it. So you stare at the box until curiosity gets the best of you, and then finally decide that you must have a look inside. As you tear into the box you uncover a bucket of the most revolting substance you have ever encountered. It is vile beyond description and offensive to all of your senses. You gag, throw the box as far as you can, and run the opposite direction. *Now the contents have defined this word.* Experiencing what was behind the word has cast down your imagination and replaced it with the truth. And the next time you encounter a similar box, the word *disgusting* will be far more than a word to you. This word has now been defined and filled with meaning because of your encounter with the substance behind it.

All words are like this, and Scripture even more so. The Bible is a collection of packages that cannot be truly known until you are confronted with their contents. Suppose now that somebody hands you a package with the word "glory" written on it. That's an exciting word! Or maybe it's a scary word. Or maybe it's a boring word, and you set the box aside feeling confident that you already know exactly what's inside. As long as glory remains a word on a box it can be whatever you want. And until you see the reality behind the word, it will be defined by your own understanding, experience, and imagination.

Our relationship is not with true words, but with the Lord who is described by them. Though we rarely admit to it, most of us would much prefer relating to God in the security of words and concepts. Words can be learned with the mind, defined, and thereby controlled, so that learning

Christ, like learning math, feels systematic, predictable, and therefore safe. In this way we get to decide what it is that we believe, what it means, and how it applies or doesn't apply to our lives. We decide which Christian books are of interest, which denomination best fits our personality, which theological camp best corresponds to our views. As long as the words of Scripture are largely unopened packages, we will inadvertently interpret and manipulate them to align with our interests, our felt needs, and our man-centered ideas. In this way we can be "always learning and never able to come to the knowledge of the Truth."[3]

The danger with words is that we can amass an enormous collection of familiar packages and unknowingly forbid the Lord to open a single one. For the Christian, the issue is not usually whether we believe in the inspiration and authority of the written words of God. Nearly all Christians hold Scripture in high regard. The real issue is always the willingness of our heart to see the One of whom these words speak. Will we allow the Lord to open up these packages and show us what's inside? Believers are quick to say yes, but curiosity is not the same as a real willingness to know. Asking questions is not the same as seeking truth. Truth comes at a cost. Knowing the truth will always cost us our familiar definitions and favorite imaginations. Very rarely do we realize how much we cherish our own ideas and cling to them in our heart. In my case, it took nearly eight years of diligently pursuing God before I realized I was inwardly resisting the very thing I was begging God to show me.

---

[3] 2 Timothy 3:7

Often the most helpful and important counsel I have to offer a believer is the simple admonition that we do not know what we think we know. Paul says, "If anyone supposes that he knows anything, he has not yet known as he ought to know."[4] This realization must become the continuous posture of our heart. Although we grow in the Lord, we must never cease approaching Him with a child-like heart that is deeply aware of its need for God to open all of our boxes. The importance of this cannot be over-stated. The sad alternative is often a lifetime of busy Christianity that amounts to little more than vain imaginations built upon empty words.

The Word of God

Long before there were words in the Bible that described Jesus Christ, there was the eternal reality of God the Word. The apostle John writes, "In the beginning was the Word, and the Word was with God, and the Word was God."[5] Christians understand that the Word mentioned here is a reference to the pre-incarnate Son of God, but oftentimes we fail to ask *why* He is given this name. We have mentioned how human words are what we use to convey and communicate who we are and what we know. Despite their limitations, our words reveal and present to others the things that are very real within us. I believe this is precisely the sense in which Jesus Christ is the living Word of God. He is, in His very being, what is real and

[4] 1 Corinthians 8:2
[5] John 1:1

true of God, and what God desires to make known to us. Christ the Word is "the radiance of God's glory and the express image of His person."[6] He represents all that God is, and all that He knows, wants, understands, and loves. He is the manifestation of God in bodily form. To see Him is to see the Father; to receive the Word is to receive the One who sends Him. He is called the wisdom of God, the truth of God, the love of God, the righteousness of God, and God is using *this* perfect Word to communicate Himself to the human soul. "No one has seen God at any time. The only begotten Son, who is in the bosom of the Father, He has declared Him."[7] God unveils and communicates Himself to the human heart through this one perfect Word. When the Father reveals His Son, He is saying all that there is to say.

As such, Jesus Christ is the sum total of all spiritual words. He is the perfect meaning and the defining reality behind every word that God has spoken. He is the substance inside of every package. In Revelation, the angel tells John that "the testimony of Jesus is the spirit of prophecy."[8] All prophetic utterances in the Old Testament came out from Him, and in one way or another, all pointed back to Him as well. Peter explains that the Spirit of Christ was in the prophets "testifying beforehand of the sufferings of the Christ and the glories that would follow."[9] On more than one occasion, Jesus told the Jews that the Law, Psalms, and Prophets all bore witness of Him.[10] Clearly

---

[6] Hebrews 1:3
[7] John 1:18
[8] Revelation 19:10
[9] 1 Peter 1:11
[10] John 5:39, Luke 24:27

these spoken and written words could never truly define or contain Him, but with them God opened many windows and put His eternal Son on display.

I emphasize these things because for years I was unknowingly just like the Pharisees, diligently studying the Scriptures and thinking that "in them was eternal life."[11] I may not have stated it quite like that, but I assumed that by studying and learning the Bible I would thereby come to know the Lord. Let me be very clear that I believe the Bible to be the only God-given, Spirit-inspired word of God. All 66 books are a gift to us from the Lord, and at no point, and in no way, should we stray from what God has revealed in Scripture. However, having understood that, we must also understand that the words of the Bible cannot truly define or explain Jesus Christ. Rather, Christ Himself is the one who gives definition and meaning to all biblical words. The distinction here is critical. Righteousness, for example, is not a thing in itself. It is not a concept, behavior, or moral standard to which Jesus always adheres. Righteousness is defined by a *Person*; it is the nature of Christ Himself which He gives and forms in the members of His body. In the same way, love is not an emotion or an action that characterizes or describes God. God *is* love, and only in Him and as Him can love truly be made known. Truth is not correct doctrines, creeds, or theologies. Truth is the Person who is described by these things. Jesus said plainly, "*I am* the Truth."[12] The reason this is so important is because God does not want us to read the Bible and walk away with right definitions and accurate spiritual concepts.

---

[11] John 5:39
[12] John 14:6

He is not primarily interested in correcting our theology. God's desire is that, while reading His words, our hearts will turn to see and know the Person of His Word. There is a living Person who fills every spiritual word with its true meaning and reality. God gives us His words in the form of the Bible, but then desires to open every package and show us Who is inside. Paul says something very similar to this in 1 Corinthians chapter two.

> *For what man knows the things of a man except the spirit of the man which is in him? Even so no one knows the things of God except the Spirit of God. Now we have received, not the spirit of the world, but the Spirit who is from God, that we might know the things that have been freely given to us by God. These things we also speak, not in words which man's wisdom teaches but which the Holy Spirit teaches, comparing spiritual things with spiritual.*[13]

Paul explains that to truly know another person one would have to participate in or somehow partake of what is *inside* of them. With natural relationships in physical bodies this is only somewhat possible. We can never fully see or know the inner life of another human. When we hear somebody's words, we often have no idea what is really behind them. But this is not the case in a Christian's relationship with God! The Lord has granted us access to the deep things of God by giving us His very Spirit. We not only have His words, but we also have the Spirit of Truth

---

[13] 1 Corinthians 2:11-13

resident within us, and He wants nothing more than to show us the things that have been freely given to us by God.

Chapter IV

The Eternal Purpose

To reach the destination in any journey, a person must at least begin by facing in the right direction. In our journey of faith, this means starting with an understanding of the eternal plan and purpose of God. As those who have been born of His Spirit, it only makes sense that we should also come to know and share His purpose, aligning our hearts with the thing that He truly wants. Wrong presuppositions lead to wrong conclusions. When we don't recognize God's purpose, we naturally become confused about our involvement in that purpose, and the sad consequence is often a life spent wandering in the vast wilderness of man's religious opinions.

Types and Shadows

Even as far back as the first chapters of Genesis, God has been seeking to make known his purpose for creation. Unfortunately, Christians often fail to recognize this purpose because we don't understand the language He consistently uses to describe it. One of the principal ways that the Spirit of God speaks to us through Scripture is by first illustrating something using the natural realm and then bringing it to a spiritual fulfillment and realization in Jesus Christ. This is often referred to as typology, or the use of types and shadows. The Lord uses types and shadows throughout the Bible in a similar way that we use blueprints for the construction of a house. The blueprints are obviously not the actual house; nobody lives in a blue-print. But these detailed representations are useful in defining and portraying something that is going to be made. The house is built in accordance with the plans and comes to be their perfect fulfillment and realization. And even after we've moved into a new home, we can look at the blueprints and come to a greater understanding of where we live.

The Old Testament is filled with types and shadows of God's one eternal purpose in Christ. From Genesis to Malachi, it is as if God was compiling an enormous collection of blueprints, land surveys, descriptions of building materials, zoning regulations, electrical wiring maps, etc., all describing the house He would build through the death, burial, and resurrection of Jesus Christ. He filled history with a testimony of His eternal dwelling place, and then, through the work of His Son, He completed the house and invited us in to live with Him. Yet even for us who have found our true home in Him, these God-given descriptions are still used by the Spirit of God to teach us the One in whom we live. For example, the Passover lamb in Exodus chapter 12 is clearly a type of the true "Lamb of God that takes away the sin of the world,"[1] and paints a picture for us of the death of Christ and our participation in it. King David was mentioned over and over in the prophets as a type of the coming Messiah, the King of Kings. Reading about David's natural kingdom in Israel reveals a great number of things that God wants us to understand about the spiritual and eternal kingdom of Christ. Aaron, the first high priest, is said in the book of Hebrews to be a picture of Christ our great High Priest who not only fulfills this priestly office, but the corresponding sacrifices, offerings, and feasts as well. There are innumerable types and shadows in Scripture. They are the people, institutions, places, ceremonies, stories, etc., that paint a natural, physical picture of something that is altogether spiritual and eternal.

Biblical types and shadows are extremely important. In fact, the authors of the New Testament reference them constantly and tell us that they were intentionally recorded and preserved for *our* benefit. Writing to the Corinthians about the story of Israel's exodus from Egypt, Paul says, "Now all these things happened to them as examples, and they were written for our admonition."[2] The entire Old Testament was inspired by the Spirit of God and written for this express purpose. The people were real and the stories true, but through them God deliberately spoke beyond their day, beyond their covenant, even beyond their creation. The books of the Old Testament are diverse in many ways, but they are united in this one purpose – Jesus said, "these are they which testify of Me."[3] After the

[1] John 1:29
[2] 1 Corinthians 10:11
[3] John 5:39

resurrection, "Jesus opened [the disciples'] understanding, that they might comprehend the Scripture,"[4] and "beginning at Moses and all the Prophets, He expounded to them in all the Scriptures the things concerning Himself."[5]

Although these books span a period of many centuries and differ with respect to their theme, style, and historical setting, together they form an interconnected and harmonious collage of pictures that testify of God's eternal purpose in His Son. We say that a picture is worth a thousand words, and for the same reason the living pictures that God created through types and shadows are worth countless millions. They are like an earthly canvas on which God masterfully painted His own perspective of spiritual realities, and showed us how these things would come to pass. For thousands of years these pictures served as a promise and prophecy of a coming fulfillment, until at last the living Substance arrived. In the fullness of time, the One who had filled God's heart from the beginning and cast every Old Testament shadow, presented Himself as the perfect fulfillment of all that God had ever described.

The First and the Second

The Bible can therefore be understood as the story of the *first* and the *second*. Though Scripture is infinitely profound, it is not complicated. It is the proclamation of God's purpose in the first, and the realization and fulfill-

---

[4] Luke 24:45
[5] Luke 24:27

ment of this purpose in the second. From the creation of the world to the coming of the Son, God spoke of, testified to, prophesied, illustrated, promised, and proclaimed a salvation that was to come. In numerous and varied ways He required that His people live out a natural testimony of a spiritual relationship that He would one day offer the world in Jesus Christ. Their sacrifices, priesthood, feasts, and laws, together created a living illustration of a far greater covenant to come. This was all part of the first. It was the first man, the first creation, and the first covenant. It was the shadow, the promise, the prophecy, the picture. It was not God's true purpose, but it foreshadowed that purpose. It was not God's perfect salvation, yet in every detail it spoke loudly and clearly of the eternal salvation that has now come in Christ.

In contrast, the *second* is the one glorious Son of God in whom all of the types and shadows become spirit and truth. In Him God has established a new man, a new creation, and a new covenant. He has brought us to the administration of the Spirit where God "gathers together into one all things in Christ."[6] The second is the substance, the person, the fulfillment, and the reality to which everything of the first pointed. It is what God saw from the beginning, "Christ all and in all,"[7] now filling the souls of the redeemed and perfectly fulfilling His eternal purpose. Notice how the author of Hebrews describes the mission of Christ:

Sacrifice and offering You did not desire, but a body you have prepared for me. In burnt offer-

---

[6] Ephesians 1:10
[7] Colossians 3:11

ings and sacrifices for sin You had no pleasure. Then I said "Behold, I have come - in the volume of the book it is written of Me, to do your will, O God"... <u>*He takes away the first that He may establish the second.*</u>[8]

There is a new covenant reality that corresponds to every old covenant shadow. The tabernacle of Moses testified of "the true tabernacle which the Lord erected."[9] The natural seed of Abraham spoke of the Seed to Whom we are joined by faith.[10] The Jerusalem below was an earthly foreshadowing of God's true city, "the Jerusalem above,"[11] the "heavenly Jerusalem"[12] to which we are said to have come in Christ. The natural land of Canaan is where Joshua brought the people to rest in the bountiful provision of the Lord. Yet the author of Hebrews tells us that "there remains a rest for the people of God,"[13] who find in Christ the true and eternal provision of the Lord. Sinai is the mountain where God met with his people and established the old covenant. Yet the New Testament says that we "have come to Mt. Zion and to the city of the living God"[14] and to the greater covenant of which all the prophets spoke. Paul explains, "For if the first had been faultless, then no place would have been sought for a second."[15] But

---

[8] Hebrews 10:5-9, emphasis mine
[9] Hebrews 8:2, see also John 2:19
[10] Galatians 3:16-29
[11] Galatians 4:26
[12] Hebrews 12:22
[13] Hebrews 4:9
[14] Hebrews 12:22
[15] Hebrews 8:7

in making "a new covenant, He has made the first obsolete."[16]

Understanding the difference between the first and the second is absolutely vital. The one is the mere shadow, the other is the spiritual reality, and the cross stands between them as a fixed and eternal boundary. The first and the second are not separated by *time*. They are not equivalent to B.C. and A.D. Although the crucifixion of Christ certainly happened in time and space, we shouldn't understand the cross as a mere dividing point between eras or dispensations. Rather, the cross is the division between the shadow and the substance, the promise and the fulfillment, old and new, flesh and spirit, Adam and Christ. We have much to say about this division, but for now it is important to understand that, through the work of the cross, God took away the first to establish the second. The first was the testimony and proclamation of the Christ who was to come. The second is the revelation and experience of the Christ who has come.

Adam: A Shadow of Purpose

It is with this understanding of the first and second that the apostle Paul tells us Adam "was a type of Him who was to come."[17] In other words, the stories recorded in the book of Genesis with regard to the first man, though literal and historical, have also a divinely intended purpose of *typifying* or prefiguring something that was coming in

---

[16] Hebrews 8:13
[17] Romans 5:14

Christ. The first man testified of the "Second Man."[18] The first Adam painted a picture of the "Last Adam."[19] We see this not only in the epistle to the Romans but in a number of other New Testament Scriptures as well. Another example is found in Ephesians chapter five. Here Paul speaks of the union between Adam and Eve and explains that this natural covenant was an intentional foreshadowing of Christ and His bride, the church.

> *For this reason a man shall leave his father and mother and be joined to his wife, and the two shall become one flesh. This is a great mystery, but I speak concerning Christ and the church.*[20]

In these and other similar Scriptures, we see that the authors of the New Testament unquestionably saw in Adam a series of God-given shadows that pointed to a coming spiritual fulfillment. Shadows never paint a perfect picture, but they do reveal certain characteristics about whatever is casting the shadow. If you were to look at my shadow on a wall you would obviously not see the color of my eyes or the expression on my face, but you could discern my general shape, my movements, and perhaps get an approximate idea of my size. No single type and shadow in the Old Testament tells the entire story of God's plan and purpose in Christ, but each one serves to bring something specific into view.

What is it then that we see of God's eternal purpose when we look to the story of Adam? At the outset, we see

---

[18] 1 Corinthians 15:47
[19] 1 Corinthians 15:45
[20] Ephesians 5:31

that all living things were created according to their *kind*. Every plant and animal was unique, and each was able to reproduce according to its specific species. The first two chapters of Genesis are filled with the language of growth and increase. The earth was bringing forth grass and fruit. The waters were abounding with living creatures. Each of the plants and animals that God created were made to be fruitful, to multiply, to fill the waters, land, and sky. All created life had the capacity to bring forth an increase of itself, a harvest, so to speak, of its own seed. This was God's desire for the first man as well, but, unlike the rest of creation, "for Adam there was not found a partner comparable to him."[21] For a short time Adam was alone in the earth, the only one of his kind. Without the means to bring forth his increase, man was unable to be fruitful, multiply, and fill the earth with his seed.

Until Genesis 2:18, everything in creation had been declared good. The light was good; the land was good; the plants and animals, the stars and moon, all was said to be good. But then, in stark contrast to the beginning of this story comes the sudden proclamation that it was *not good* for the first man to be the only one of his kind. Eve was the answer to this situation, the miraculous provision for Adam's increase and glory. God declared, "It is not good that man should be alone; I will make him a helper comparable to him."[22] Because such a partner could not be found in all of creation, God created the woman *from the very life of the first man*.

---

[21] Genesis 2:20
[22] Genesis 2:18

It is crucial that we pay special attention to both the reason why God created this partner and the means by which she was made. The woman was created because God desired an increase of Adam's kind in the earth. And how was she made? Eve was not formed from the dust as Adam was, nor was she made from a plant or from any other living creature. Eve was taken from Adam's side. God caused Adam to fall into a deep sleep, pierced his side, took a rib from his body, and fashioned his suitable companion. In other words, Eve was generated from the very life of Adam, and given back to him as his own increase. Awaking from his sleep and recognizing what God had done, Adam said, "This is now bone of my bones and flesh of my flesh; She shall be called Woman, because she was taken out of Man."[23] Adam called his companion Eve, but God, "in the day that He created them, blessed them and called them Man."[24] God called them both by one name, knowing that the two shared one life.

The Increase of Christ

There is far more to this story than the history of man's beginnings. Looking through the window of the creation story we can see an even greater story unfold. We can understand, for example, that in God's heart it was really Christ, the Last Adam,[25] who did not have a partner

---

[23] Genesis 2:23

[24] Genesis 5:2 The word man is the English translation of the Hebrew word Adam. Other translations read, God "blessed them and called them Adam."

[25] 1 Corinthians 15:45

of like kind, nor the means to bring forth an increase of Himself. In the New Testament, Christ is said to be the true Seed of God,[26] the only incorruptible Seed,[27] and it was the Father's desire to fill creation with His increase, glory, and dominion. Even as the first man was meant to multiply according to his kind and fill the natural creation, God foresaw a new creation that would bear the image and fullness of the Second Man.[28] He foresaw a harvest of His Son, a harvest which does not consist of many Christs, nor many people trying to act like Christ, but rather the one and only begotten Son formed in and magnified through a corporate people – His bride.

In the beginning, the Father looked beyond Adam and spoke of His Son when He said, "It is not good for man to be alone." We can hear an echo of this same declaration in Jesus' words, "Most assuredly, I say to you, unless a grain of wheat falls into the ground and dies, *it remains alone*; but if it dies, it produces much fruit."[29] In His death and burial Jesus was planted like a solitary seed into the earth. But when He rose from the dead, Christ offered Himself as the resurrection and life to a people who could now be joined to Him and bear the fruit of His Spirit. Perfectly paralleling Adam's experience with Eve, Paul explains that Christ's life was bestowed upon His bride so that we, in turn, might be presented back to Him as His "glorious church, not having spot or wrinkle."[30] Through the resurrection of the Lord Jesus Christ we were "made alive

---

[26] Galatians 3:16
[27] 1 Peter 1:23
[28] 1 Corinthians 15:47
[29] John 12:24, emphasis mine
[30] Ephesians 5:27

together, raised together, and made to sit together with Christ in the heavens."[31] Thus the fulfillment of Adam and Eve's union is the new covenant reality that "he who is joined to the Lord is one spirit with Him."[32] Speaking now of our union with Christ, Paul says, "We are members of His body, of His flesh, and of His bone."[33]

Centuries before Christ, Zechariah had spoken of this day, saying, "Many nations shall be joined to the Lord in that day, and they shall become My people. And I will dwell in your midst."[34] But in order for us to be joined to Him and produce a harvest of His kind, the perfect Seed had to die alone. There could be no bride, nor any increase, if God did not first cause a deep sleep to fall upon the Last Adam. Again in perfect fulfillment of Adam's experience, Christ was put to death, His side was pierced, and out from His side poured forth the blood and water by which we are made partakers of His life. Not one thing in all of natural creation was a fitting companion for this perfect Man, so a new creation was born of His very Spirit. Through the work of the cross, we become "partakers of the divine nature"[35] and are thereby made to be the "wife of the Lamb,"[36] the increase of His Seed, and the ones called by His name. In the death, burial, and resurrection of Jesus Christ, God fulfilled every type and shadow from the creation story. The first was perfectly fulfilled in the second; the shadow gave way to the substance.

---

[31] Ephesians 2:5-6
[32] 1 Corinthians 6:17
[33] Ephesians 5:30
[34] Zechariah 2:11
[35] 2 Peter 1:4
[36] Revelation 21:9

Adam was indeed "a type of Him who was to come."[37] The parallels between the first and the second here are too perfect to deny, and with them God has begun to describe for us His eternal plan and expectation. From the very beginning, God has desired the increased expression and glory of His one and only Son, and He accomplished this purpose through a newly created people who receive His life and bear His image.

It is significant to note that this particular shadow of purpose takes place *prior* to man's involvement with sin. In other words, the story that we have been considering in Genesis was intentionally given to us before the fall, thus introducing us to God's purpose *before* we see man's need for redemption and reconciliation to God. This is meaningful because, contrary to our often man-centered views of God's involvement with humanity, His purpose for mankind was not a reaction to our rebellion. The plan existed before any of our failures, and it did not budge one inch when Adam and Eve ate the forbidden fruit. God's objective was not simply to provide a solution to the problems created by sin. That would be like an automobile mechanic intentionally building a defective car just to be the one who knew how to repair it. Man's problems are undoubtedly resolved and all of his needs are met through the cross of Christ, but we need to recognize that God's purpose was decided and set into motion well before Genesis chapter one. God never once considered a plan B. From the very beginning His objective was Christ-centered, not man-centered; it was purpose-centered, not provision-centered. Humanity is very much involved in

---

[37] Romans 5:14

the purpose of God, but Christ has always been the center. Sadly, this was another foundational reality that I failed to appreciate for much of my Christian life.

God's highest thought for humanity involves our transformation into the living corporate body in which He is glorified, and the story of Adam and Eve is only one of many descriptions of this purpose. There are countless other stories, ceremonies, events, miracles, and laws in the Old Testament that reveal this same intention. In some Scriptures the focus is upon a land that God is filling with the seed of Israel. The idolatrous land of Canaan is being transformed and occupied by God's kingdom of righteousness. In other Scriptures, the spotlight shifts to a temple that is filled with the glory of God, or to fields that abound with 100 times what was sown. Elsewhere we read of God's vineyard that bears His fruit in season, or a bride that is adorned with the beauty and riches of her Husband. Each of these descriptions offer a natural testimony of the same eternal purpose, and the New Testament clearly proclaims their spiritual fulfillment to be in the person and work of Jesus Christ. Jesus announces the arrival of a kingdom within us,[38] and the apostles describe Christ's formation and government in the land of our soul. Paul tells the Corinthians, "you are God's field...I planted, Apollos watered, but God gave the increase."[39] Later he asks, "Do you not know that you are the temple of God and that the Spirit of God dwells in you?"[40] In the gospel of John, Jesus describes the fulfillment of the vineyard that Isaiah and Jeremiah saw long ago, saying, "I am the true

[38] Luke 17:21
[39] 1 Corinthians 3:9,6
[40] 1 Corinthians 3:16

vine, and My Father is the Vinedresser."[41] These biblical analogies are different in many respects, but the message behind them is single and it is clear. God's desire for creation has always been to fully give Himself through Jesus Christ to a redeemed and purified people who, in turn, become the increase of His Seed, the temple for His glory, and the land that is filled with the kingdom of God. This is "the eternal purpose which He accomplished in Christ Jesus our Lord."[42]

Provision or Purpose

In my own experience, one of the unpleasant realities that I needed to face was the fact that I had centered my relationship with God on His provision rather than His purpose. Like all of my misunderstandings, I wasn't able to recognize this until His light made it visible. But with even a small spark of divine perspective I began to understand that my love for the Lord was primarily based upon my purposes for Him, and not His eternal purpose for me.

I have a young son named Miciah who has always been fascinated with mud.[43] One morning I wanted Miciah to come with me to the store.   I had some important errands to run, and I wanted his company for a few hours. I told him to find his shoes because we would be leaving in just a few minutes. Somehow, in the amount of time it took me to find the car keys and grab my coat, Miciah

---

[41] John 15:1

[42] Ephesians 3:11

[43] This is an adaptation of an analogy used by DeVern Fromke in *The Ultimate Intention* (Sure Foundation, March 1999) pg. 38

managed to run to the backyard and throw himself into a large, black puddle of mud. So, before we were able to leave for the store, I found myself having to go out to the yard, carry Miciah back into the house, remove his filthy clothes, and give him a bath. Bath-time in our house can be quite an adventure. As I attempted to hold him down and clean the mud from his little body, he giggled and splashed and squirted me with bath toys. While I washed the dirt from his hair, he sculpted a bubble-beard on his face and then some bushy white eyebrows. Finally I finished, rinsed and dried him, picked out some clothes and once again got him dressed. In my mind, this bath was a necessary means to arriving at my original purpose; I still wanted to go to the store. But judging from the look of contentment I saw on Miciah's face, I could tell that, for him, bath-time with daddy was about as good as life got. In his three year-old mind, my plans to run errands were far from his thoughts, and could never compare with splashing in the tub and playing with dad.

We are often very much like Miciah in our relationship with the Lord. In fact, I believe we all begin with this mindset. We assume the greatness of our salvation to be the ways that we personally benefit from knowing the Lord. Like my son, we imagine that our individual experience of God's provision is the only purpose in His heart, and so we are content to splash around in rivers of revival proclaiming the forgiveness of sins and various other personal benefits of being a Christian. This is normal and even appropriate for a believer who is newly born of the Spirit. But if I told you that the aforementioned story took place when my son was eighteen years old, you would no doubt think something was wrong.

Israel's exodus from Egypt is an important type and shadow that the Lord used to demonstrate this very problem. Among other things, the books of Exodus through Numbers tell the story of a people who rejected purpose in favor of provision. As they wandered in the wilderness, the people of God failed to see that the greatness of their salvation was not what they escaped from, but rather what they had been brought into. God's purpose for them was not realized in the judgment of Egypt or even in Israel's freedom from slavery and oppression. God's involvement with His people was bound up with a desire to have an eternal dwelling place, a house and family who were called by His name. Israel was not merely a nation whom God delivered from evil men and difficult situations. Israel was a people joined to the Lord with the expectation of bearing His glory.

God's dealing with Israel was filled with purpose from the very beginning. Even as they painted the blood of the lamb on the doorposts of their homes, the Lord looked beyond the shadows and saw a people who would be baptized into Christ and conformed to His image. He saw "Zion, the perfection of beauty where God shines forth."[44] Redemption was not God's purpose for Israel; Israel was redeemed *for a purpose.* They were saved by the outstretched arm of God with terrifying judgments and awesome miracles, but from the very beginning the heart of the Lord was set on a land filled from corner to corner with the glory of God. Moses said, "He brought us out

---

[44] Psalm 50:2

from there, *that He might bring us in*, to give us the Land of which He swore to our fathers."[45]

When the first generation rebelled against God's purpose in the wilderness, Moses cried out to the Lord to forgive them. The Lord responded, "I have pardoned, according to your word; but truly, as I live, all of the land shall be filled with the glory of the Lord."[46] Israel's persistent unbelief and disobedience did not affect God's plan; it only affected Israel's experience of it. God would be glorified in His people. Israel would one day become the manifestation of God's victory over uncircumcised flesh, the expression of God's righteousness in the law, the declaration of God's grace through sacrifices and offerings, and so much more. All of these old covenant shadows now find their fulfillment in a new and spiritual Israel, but our objective for the moment is understanding that freedom from slavery and death was never God's highest thought for Israel. Israel was a kingdom of priests, taken out of Egypt to bear the image and greatness of their God.

God certainly provides for His people, and provision is a wonderful thing. The problem is simply that we, like the Israelites before us, are quick to assume that God's provision is the extent of our inheritance as well as the center of God's purpose. Israel loved and worshipped the Lord when He fought their battles, fed their stomachs, and met their expectations. But they rejected Him when it became

---

[45] Deuteronomy 6:23, emphasis mine

[46] Numbers 14:20-21. The Hebrew word ארץ 'erets can be translated either earth or land, but the immediate context (see verses 3, 6, 7, 8, 9, 14, 16, 23, 24, 30, 31, etc. of the same chapter where the same Hebrew word is translated land) and God's reference to the promises made to the Fathers (vs. 23) make clear that the promised land of Canaan is what God has in view.

apparent that He had an expectation of His own. Just like Israel, everyone starts their journey of faith fleeing to the Lord for deliverance and looking to Him for provision. But we begin to encounter the true purpose for our salvation when the Lord finds in us a land for His increase, a kingdom for His glory.

Chapter V

The Problem

Understanding something of God's purpose for creation, the next question that confronts us is what it means to align with and experience this purpose. This is not something that happens automatically. Just like the generation that was delivered from Egypt by the arm of the Lord, we too can be saved from death for the purpose of God and yet live our lives in unbelief and opposition to Him. This is easier to do than one might think. It's clear in Scripture that the vast majority of men and women in the exodus generation died in the wilderness with bellies full of God's provision but hearts still ignorant of His eternal purpose. Speaking of this generation in the Psalms, the Lord said, "They are a people who go astray in their hearts, and they do not know my ways. So I swore in My wrath, 'They shall not enter My rest.'"[1] This is not just a tragic story from ancient history. These Israelites were not uniquely blind, nor were their hearts abnormally stubborn. These were men and women exactly like you and I, and the story of their failure to enter God's rest is

---
[1] Psalm 95:10-11

often our story as well. Israel was given so much but they experienced so little, and Paul, writing 1500 years later about this same story warns the church, "Now all these things happened to them as examples, and they were written for our admonition."[2]

Why does this happen? Why do so many of us fall short of experiencing the purpose for which we were saved? I believe a large part of the reason has to do with a profound ignorance of our natural condition. In other words, failing to recognize the depth of our problem, we fail to turn and see the greatness of God's solution. This was certainly the case with the Jews in the days of Jesus' earthly ministry. Jesus offered Israel a salvation from bondage and freedom from the rule of sin and death. But in their incredible blindness the Jews could only respond, "We are Abraham's descendants, and have never been in bondage to anyone. How can You say, 'You will be made free'?"[3] Unaware of their inward slavery to sin and death, the majority of them turned their back on God's incredible gift. In this case, ignorance of the problem resulted in their total rejection of salvation. But even as Christians, this same ignorance often prevents us from seeking to know and experience the fullness of the salvation that we have already received.

The Fall of Man

To understand the seriousness of man's natural condition we need to return to the Garden of Eden and revisit

---

[2] 1 Corinthians 10:11
[3] John 8:33

the man who defines the nature of our problem. It is there that God shows us how we fell from His created design and the unfortunate consequence of man's choice.

The nature of Adam's infamous fall is something that is not well understood in the Lord's body. There are many mistaken ideas about what man fell from, why he fell, and what changed as a result. We should start by asking from where, or from what, did humanity fall? Adam and Eve did *not* fall from a true relationship of union with God like the one we are given now in Jesus Christ. It is a common idea in the church that God is seeking to restore humanity to Adam's pre-fall condition. This is absolutely not true. Adam never had a relationship with God like the one the church can now enjoy in Christ. In the garden, God walked with man in an *external* relationship unhindered by sin, but God did not reside in man. God spoke His words *to* Adam and Eve, but humanity did not know the living, implanted Word that is now the life and light of every believing soul. Adam's experience of God in the garden was an illustrative natural shadow of our salvation in Christ, but it was not the actual substance. It painted a visible picture of a spiritual relationship and reality, but Adam never knew the indwelling spiritual life that God now offers us in His Son.

It is true that God breathed the "breath of life"[4] into the first man. Many believe this to be evidence of a true spiritual union. However, we should notice the following two things: First, although receiving the "breath of life" certainly testified to what God would one day offer

---

[4] Genesis 2:7

humanity in Christ[5], this same phrase is used three times with reference to the animals in God's creation as well.[6] Second, in 1 Corinthians 15, Paul makes a deliberate contrast between the soul-life given to the first man, and the spiritual life offered to the believer in "the second Man."

> *And so it is written, "The first man Adam became a living soul." The last Adam became a life-giving spirit. However, the spiritual is not first, but the natural, and afterward the spiritual. The first man was of the earth, earthly; the second Man is the Lord from heaven.*[7]

When Adam fell, he did not fall from spiritual life, *he fell from purpose*. He fell short of what God had created him to be and to do. He lost his ability to bear in himself the image and likeness of Christ, and to fill the earth with the testimony of a greater Man to come. In other words, in the Garden of Eden, man fell short of the glory of God.

The Cause of the Fall

How did this happen? When God created Adam and Eve, He instructed them to take and eat freely from any of the trees in the garden, but added, "Of the tree of the knowledge of good and evil you shall not eat."[8] Many have

---

[5] See especially John 20:22, "And when He had said this, He breathed on them, and said to them, 'Receive the Holy Spirit'"
[6] See Genesis 6:17, 7:15, 7:22
[7] 1 Corinthians 15:45-47, emphasis mine
[8] Genesis 2:17

read this story and seen only a test of obedience. It is often assumed that mankind's test and subsequent transgression was a simple matter of not keeping the rules. I believe there is far more involved in this story. We often forget that "the tree of life was also in the midst of the garden along with the tree of the knowledge of good and evil."[9] With these two trees God presented man more than a test of obedience. We are meant to see in these two trees an immeasurably significant *choice*. Man could live by the tree of life – a picture of the Life of God offered to the soul of man. Or man could believe the Serpent's lie, and declare his independence from God.

Therefore, man's fall from glory was not merely the consequence of picking a forbidden fruit. Something significant had already transpired when Eve reached for the tree of the knowledge of good and evil. The Serpent was not selling apples; he was selling a lie. First he deceived the woman, and only when she *believed the lie* did the fruit take on a new appearance. First she ate the lie, then she ate the fruit because it then appeared "good for food, pleasant to the eyes, and desirable to make one wise."[10] Eating from the tree was an outward indication of something that had already transpired in her heart. She fell from glory, not because she touched something with her hands, but because she accepted something into her heart.

This was far worse than merely falling for a trick. Eve did not simply confuse two trees or get duped by a talking lizard. Something much more significant happened here

---

[9] Genesis 2:9
[10] Genesis 3:6

and the result can be clearly seen in the transformation that immediately ensued. At once, Adam's perception was permanently disfigured. Something shifted in his soul, and this man became entirely self-aware, self-consumed, and self-condemned. Adam and Eve were not just misled by words. They swallowed a lie that permanently altered and entirely corrupted the way they viewed themselves and their Creator. They exchanged God's perspective and purpose for their own. They could no longer see God's creation according to truth because all things were now viewed and comprehended through the darkened and perverted lens of self.

Immediately Adam and Eve were aware of themselves, their lack, their need, their shame. Nothing is clearer in the story of this man and his descendants. A new day had begun where all things in the natural creation were known, understood, and used, not according to God-given perspective, but entirely with respect to self-interest. *This* was the effect of the Lie, and the resulting corruption has been passed to every son and daughter born in the "image and likeness of Adam."[11]

Fear entered into this otherwise perfect testimony. Anger, pride, shame, and murder soon followed. Why? Because man's relationship with all things now found its root and reality in the awareness of self and the all-consuming obsession of self-preservation. This is precisely what Paul describes in the first chapter of Romans. Man exchanged the glory of God for his own darkened understanding. He "exchanged the truth of God for the lie."[12]

---

[11] Genesis 5:3
[12] Romans 1:25

Consequently, he became the center of his own story and a purpose unto himself. Immediately he found himself compelled to hide from God and to disguise his nothingness. He feared God's wrath, blamed others for his own guilt, and soon his sons filled the earth with violence and murder. These are the fruits of self-love. This is how the Lie corrupted the soul of the first man. It became the perverted lens, the twisted mirror, through which all things were seen. Man had contracted a virus of self-obsession. Man had become a lie.

T. Austin-Sparks writes this: "With the Fall, an entangling with another nature and order took place. It became organic, therefore constitutional."[13] This is a brief but accurate way to summarize the result of man's fall. As a race, we have fallen. We have fallen *from* something. We have fallen from the glory of God, fallen from purpose. But we have also fallen *into* something. We have fallen into an entanglement with a nature and order that maintains deep control over our soul, one that has total jurisdiction over our being.

Man was created a living soul, and that soul was meant to become the eternal dwelling place of God, the perfect and only environment for God's life and glory. In some ways, the human soul is like a sponge that has the capacity to take into itself, to bear, hold, and carry, pure water. Imagine now that this sponge fell short of its created purpose. However, in falling from purpose it didn't just fall *out* of a bucket of water, it also fell *into* a swamp of sewage and sickness that saturated every crevice

---

[13] T. Austin-Sparks, *The Centrality and Universality of The Cross*, Chapter 3

and pore. This is something like the nature of man's fall. As Sparks says, we fell into an organic entanglement with all that is contrary to God. Despite our objections to the contrary and our utter blindness to the reality, the human soul is born twisted and knotted up in a nature and order that now constrains all that we think, want, and do. It is a nature and order that is without God, and therefore without glory. It is the profound and overpowering relationship that the New Testament calls slavery to sin.

The First Break in Purpose

Therefore, although Adam's choice involved the willful disregard of God's command, it was far more significant than a simple transgression. It was a decisive moment where Adam rejected the tree of life and consented to the Serpent's idea that, independent of God, man's eyes could be opened, and he "could be like God, knowing good and evil."[14] From that day forward, Adam became a source unto himself. He lived his own life and walked by his own light. Centuries later Jesus spoke of this false light saying, "If therefore the light that is in you is darkness, how great is that darkness!"[15]

Before the fall, everything in God's creation was declared "good" because it bore an image and carried a testimony of God's eternal purpose in Christ. We have mentioned this with respect to the old covenant with all of its laws, ceremonies, sacrifices, etc., but it is true of the old

---

[14] Genesis 3:5
[15] Matthew 6:23

creation as well. Every aspect of natural creation was a physical reflection or representation of some spiritual and eternal reality in Christ. Fruit trees, rivers, light, grain, growth, etc., all of these created things in their own way declared the glory of God and testified of their spiritual counterpart. In a multitude of natural pictures and shadows, the physical heavens and earth pointed to the One who would one day come and declare Himself to be their fulfillment, saying, "I am the true Vine, the true Light, the Living Water, the Bread of Life."

Foreshadowed in the natural creation are incredible pictures of growth, transformation, redemption, darkness and light, death and life, love, increase, power, and wisdom. And Adam, as we have seen, was the crown of all types and shadows. All was good in God's eyes, all was in harmony with its created design, until Adam believed he could be like God and live by his own knowledge of good and evil. At that moment, the world made its first break from created purpose, its first contradiction to the glory of God.

There was a sliver of truth in Satan's promise – Adam's eyes *were,* in a sense, opened. He saw in a way that he was never meant to see. He saw a contrast between good and evil, between God and all that opposed Him. However, he came to understand this distinction only by *becoming* that which opposed God's created design. When he stepped away from God's purpose and perspective, he saw himself alone, contrary to God, naked, and needing to hide from God's holy eyes. And in the first act of religion, he covered himself with something other than Jesus Christ. We discussed religion in a previous chapter, but right here in the garden is where it all began. Religion is nothing more than men and women living according to a personal assessment of good and evil, and attempting to cover their shame with something less than Christ. Through religion, man perpetuates the age-old story of Adam and the two trees, seeking to be like God independent of the life that only He can impart. And to whatever extent Christianity is anything less than a genuine experience of the Tree of Life, it is no different than any religion.

Man's Condition Illustrated by the Two Trees

Having forfeited the offer of life and become slaves to the nature of sin, God declared that "the imagination of man's heart is evil from his youth."[16] But even so, the proud adamic race became a people who sought to live and justify their lives according to their own knowledge of good and evil. As is still the case today, "Everyone did what was right in his own eyes."[17] The problem that they faced, and that we still face in our day, is that both what we call good and what we call evil fall vastly short of the life that God offers. Man's best is still not life.

Using the two trees in the Garden of Eden in a somewhat different context, the Lord once severely dealt with my heart on this issue. Looking at the diagram on the following page, I've drawn man's tree of good and evil on the left and the tree of life on the right. Fallen man seeks

---

[16] Genesis 8:21
[17] Judges 21:25. See also Jeremiah 16:12, 18:12, 23:16, 23:17, 23:26

to live by his own evaluation of good and evil. Judging by our own criteria, education, or values, we strive to increase our good fruit and eliminate the bad. But as I began to see the unspeakable contrast between Adam and Christ, death and life, I suddenly realized that the problem with the tree of good and evil is not the evil fruit; it is the *entire tree*. Even if you could remove all of the bad fruit from this tree, you would still have the wrong tree. It would still be *man's* tree, *man's* way, *man's* knowledge of good and evil. Every fruit on this tree, regardless whether it seems good or bad in the eyes of man, has fallen infinitely short of the tree of life.

Tree of the Knowledge of Good & Evil

Tree of Life

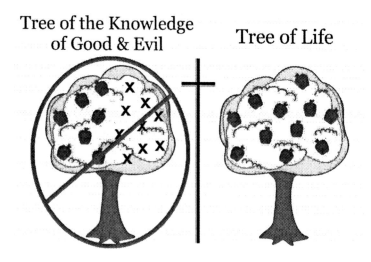

The Increase of Adam

Like all created things, the fallen adamic man was fruitful and multiplied, reproducing according to his kind. Soon the earth was filled with sons and daughters "in his own likeness, and after his image,"[18] who walked "in the futility of their mind, having their understanding darkened, being alienated from the life of God."[19]

When trying to understand man's inherent depravity, Christians are often told that the entire human race is punished for Adam's disobedience in the garden. This is commonly referred to as the doctrine of original sin, and in my opinion it is largely misunderstood and misapplied. Many object to the idea that they bear responsibility before God for a transgression that Adam and Eve committed thousands of years ago. But this is not a right understanding of the situation. It is not that we are being penalized for Adam's ancient fruit-picking transgression. It's simply that we are the *same likeness and image of Adam*. We are, by nature, the increase of his kind, the continuation of his seed.

Consider this analogy. An apple tree is capable of producing apples, and nothing else. Because all things were created to reproduce according to their own kind, even if a single apple tree were to produce a million apple seeds, each would be the same *kind* as the mother tree. Not one of them would be a watermelon seed. Not even one would be an orange. Furthermore, if each of the one million seeds produced a million of their own, the billions of third generation seeds would still consistently bear the image and likeness of the original tree. The many would be the increase or harvest of the one. And even if a number of those trees somehow failed to produce a single apple, they would still, by nature, be an apple tree.

[18] Genesis 5:3
[19] Ephesians 4:17-18

My point is that regardless of whether we transgress in a way similar to our forefather, we are still Adam by nature. Paul says, "Nevertheless death reigned from Adam to Moses, even over those who had not sinned according to the likeness of the transgression of Adam."[20] Having believed the lie and eaten from the forbidden tree, Adam's fundamental constitution changed. The lasting effect of what is often called "original sin" is not that we continue to be punished for Adam's mistake. The problem is simply that we are Adam. We are born of his seed, a partaker of his nature, the increase of his kind. Like all who came before us, we are a people who "conduct ourselves in the lusts of the flesh, fulfilling the desires of the flesh and of the mind, and are by nature children of wrath."[21] Speaking by the Spirit, David says "Behold, I was brought forth in iniquity, and in sin my mother conceived me."[22] Like it or not, we are all inherently a people who have rejected the tree of life and who live by the lie that Adam believed in the garden.

This is our problem, and we must face it. The bad news is that the problem is worse than we thought. The problem is worse than we *could* think, because our thinking is part of the problem. The good news is that God's solution is also beyond what we could think or imagine. Paul knew the Lord as One who "is able to do exceedingly abundantly above all that we ask or think, according to the power that works within us."[23] Nevertheless, if we are not willing to accept God's view of the

---

[20] Romans 5:14
[21] Ephesians 2:3
[22] Psalm 51:5
[23] Ephesians 3:20

adamic man (which is what we call our natural life), we will never turn our hearts to see the greatness of our salvation.

The Serpent's lie is still the underlying perspective of every adamic man and woman. It is a view of reality where man understands himself to have life, wisdom, purpose, and potential apart from God. It is not just one of our thoughts, it is the foundation for all of our thinking. Therefore, this lie isn't something that we must stop believing. It's too late for that. This lie is *someone* who must stop living.

The Flood – A Picture of God's Solution

It is no wonder that immediately following the fall, we read of the world filled with violence and corruption. We see God grieved in His heart, mourning over the state of the world, and preparing to destroy both man and the earth in a great flood.

> *Then the LORD saw that the wickedness of man was great in the earth, <u>and that every intent of the thoughts of his heart was only evil continually</u>. And the LORD was sorry that He had made man on the earth, and He was grieved in His heart. So the LORD said, "I will destroy man whom I have created from the face of the earth, both man and beast, creeping thing and birds of the air, for I am sorry that I have made them."*[24]

---

[24] Genesis 6:5-7, emphasis mine

The earth also was corrupt before God, and the earth was filled with violence. So God looked upon the earth, and indeed it was corrupt; <u>for all flesh had corrupted their way on the earth</u>. And God said to Noah, "The end of all flesh has come before Me, for the earth is filled with violence through them; and behold, I will destroy them with the earth."[25]

Why such remorse and wrath in the heart of God? Because the earth had fallen together with Adam – distorted and spoiled of purpose. Truth had been rejected and God's testimony in Adam was lost. Man had handed himself over to become an instrument of Satan's unrighteousness, and as a consequence, "all the earth lies under the power of the evil one;"[26] all of its inhabitants are under the dominion of the "Father of Lies."[27] The Serpent is henceforth known as the "ruler of this world,"[28] the "prince of the power of the air,"[29] the "god of this age."[30]

In the days of Noah, the judgment of God came upon the world of Adam as a great flood that wiped man off the face of the earth. This world-wide flood paints an incredible picture of what Christ would one day accomplish through His death, burial, and resurrection. It's too soon to deal with the cross in detail, but we should at least draw attention to the fact that, in the flood, Adam and his

---

[25] Genesis 6:11-13, emphasis mine
[26] 1 John 5:19
[27] John 8:44
[28] John 12:31
[29] Ephesians 2:2
[30] 2 Corinthians 4:4

creation were not repaired or improved; they were destroyed. Yet in the midst of this incredible judgment, God provided an ark that carried the seed of a new creation. In the ark was the only man that God had found to be righteous, together with the family that belonged to him. The ark was raised up and made to sit on top of the waters, high above death and destruction, until it came to rest on the mountain of God. When the waters had subsided, out from the ark came a type and shadow of a new creation, redeemed of the Lord, relating to God under a rainbow that God gave to demonstrate a new covenant with man.

Chapter VI

The Ministry of Condemnation

Although the flood of Noah testified of Adam's judgment and the salvation which is in Christ, it neither solved man's problem nor accomplished God's purpose. Noah and the ark were merely a shadow of the coming judgment and restoration accomplished in the cross. Consequently, it was not long before the earth was again filled with the seed that fell short of the glory of God. In fact, soon after the sons of Noah had multiplied and filled the earth, we once again see the adamic man exalting himself and together seeking to make their own way to heaven. They said, "Come, let us build for ourselves a city, and a tower whose top is in the heavens; let us make a name for ourselves."[1]

The Promised Seed

Despite man's fall and persistent disregard for the truth, God never lost sight of His purpose. The seed of

---

[1] Genesis 11:4

Adam had corrupted its way in the earth, but God called a man named Abraham and began to speak to him about another seed in whom God would truly be glorified. Abraham's promised son Isaac was a man like any other, but every detail of God's dealings with Abraham and Isaac foreshadowed the incorruptible Seed[2] to come, and the gospel of life that would be offered through Him.

To offer some examples, the birth of Isaac shows us that the seed of God comes by way of a promise and not by works of the flesh. When Abraham tried to fulfill God's promise through human effort Ishmael was born, of whom Sarah said, "the son of the slave girl shall have no inheritance with my son, Isaac."[3] In contrast, Isaac (like Christ) was born in fulfillment of the word of God, according to the power of God, and his life came forth from the dead womb of Sarah. As the story continues, we see Abraham, the father, willing to offer his only son[4] as a burnt offering, and then "receiving him back from the dead, in a figurative sense."[5] As a consequence for this obedient sacrifice, God promises Abraham an everlasting covenant, a great inheritance, an everlasting possession, and a blessing that would come to all nations through his seed. The increase of his seed would be like the stars in the sky and the sand on the seashore, and as it grew and filled the land the seed would experience victory over every enemy.

We know that all of these blessings and promises had

---

[2]   1 Peter 1:23
[3]   Genesis 21:10
[4]   See Genesis 22:2, 12, 16
[5]   Hebrews 11:19. See Hebrews 11:8-21 to see how Abraham and Isaac are clearly understood as living types and shadows of the salvation that has come in Christ.

a natural, temporary fulfillment through Isaac and his natural descendants. Israel experienced a physical picture or shadow of each of these things. But clearly the Lord saw beyond the natural seed, and looked toward the day when all of these promises would be yes and amen in Jesus Christ.[6] As always, the Lord used these Old Testament stories to point to a greater covenant, kingdom, and increase. Only in Christ, the spiritual Seed of promise, would man find his true inheritance and a victory over an enemy far greater than the Philistines. Paul is clear that every one of these blessings finds its true fulfillment as "spiritual blessings in heavenly places in Christ."[7] Through the work of the cross, Christ has made a way for "the blessing of Abraham to come upon the nations in Christ Jesus."[8]

The apostle Paul tells us in Galatians 3 that Abraham and his seed were intentional representations of Christ and those who would be joined to Him as His body. He says, "Now to Abraham and his Seed were the promises made. He does not say, 'And to seeds,' as of many, but as of one, 'and to your Seed,' who is Christ."[9] Later he adds, "For you are all one in Christ Jesus. And if you are Christ's, then you are Abraham's seed, and heirs according to the promise."[10] The thing that we must see and understand is that Abraham's natural seed was chosen by God to bear the image and foretell the coming of the true Seed who would

---

[6] 2 Corinthians 1:20
[7] Ephesians 1:3
[8] Galatians 3:14
[9] Galatians 3:16
[10] Galatians 3:28-29

fulfill God's ultimate intention. It is vital that we understand this. Natural Israel was not unique in the flesh. They had the same sinful nature and blindness found in every other son of Adam. Their uniqueness was found in the One whose corporate body they represented, the One whose testimony they were called to bear. The Bible speaks of them as a special people, but the Lord makes abundantly clear[11] that this was not for any inherent quality, righteousness, or unique bloodline. Israel was special because God used them as a physical representation, a living picture, of the true Seed of promise to come.

Though their calling was great, Israel proved time and again that they were no different than any other adamic men and women. They were redeemed from death and liberated from bondage, but Israel consistently grumbled against Moses and against God their Savior. They were called to be "Israel my son, even my firstborn,"[12] but they were a stiff-necked people, a disobedient son, and they refused to walk in faith like their forefather Abraham. Just like Adam in the garden, Israel forsook their true purpose and repeatedly lost the image and likeness that they were meant to bear.

Nevertheless, the true Seed was coming. The types and shadows described Him. The prophets, with one voice, proclaimed Him. The adamic man groaned in desperate need of Him. He was coming as the personification of God's purpose and the salvation of all who would be joined to Him by faith. But until that day, Israel was "kept under guard by the law."[13] Paul tells us that the law

---

[11] See, for example, Deuteronomy 9:4-5, Romans 2:28-29
[12] Exodus 4:22
[13] Galatians 3:23

was "added because of transgressions, till the Seed should come to whom the promise was made."[14]

Sin and Righteousness

Contrary to what the Jews came to believe and teach, the law was not given by God as a means by which Israel could actually escape sin or possess true righteousness. In fact, the prophets, the apostles, and Jesus Himself made it abundantly clear that inward obedience to the law was a complete impossibility for the adamic man. However, before we discuss the real reason for the law, we should take one step back and ask ourselves something even more fundamental: What is righteousness? What is sin?

Despite our incredibly widespread misunderstandings, sin is not a word that should be used merely to describe a certain kind of behavior. Sin is a *nature*, the nature that operates in the adamic man. Sin isn't simply something that we do. It's worse than that. Sin is actually what we *are* apart from Christ. Sin has to do with missing the mark, falling short of the glory of God, and this is what the adamic man *is* even before he thinks or does anything. This isn't pleasant, but we need to understand it about ourselves. We are not sinners because we sin. We sin because we are sinners. In other words, God does not reckon you a sinner because of what you do, think, or desire. You were a sinner before you did or thought anything. You are a sinner by nature, and as such you bring forth the fruit of that nature. You bring that nature

---

[14] Galatians 3:19

into expression through a multitude of individual *sins*. Jesus said plainly, "whoever commits sin is a slave of sin."[15]

We often fail to realize that our individual sins are not the reason that we are constituted sinners before God. Rather, our sins are the result and evidence that we are sinners. They are the proof that we are slaves to a nature that governs us from within. For example, we all know that dogs bark. Barking is simply what dogs do. However, barking is not what makes something a dog. I can bark, and I am not a dog. My point is that just as barking doesn't produce a dog, neither does sinning produce a sinner. But both barking and sinning are the outward expressions or byproducts of a particular nature.

In a similar way, righteousness should not be a word that we use to describe certain kinds of human behavior. Like sin, righteousness is a nature. It is the nature of Christ that can operate in those who are born of a new seed, those who become "partakers of the divine nature."[16] It is certainly true that as Christians we are called to righteousness, but this is not because God simply tells us how to behave. We are called to righteousness because the actual nature of Christ is given to us and meant to be formed in us. In Paul's letter to the Romans we read that we are alive from the dead in Christ and have become "instruments" and "slaves of righteousness."[17] We are the vessel and righteousness is the governing nature that works within us. In 1 Corinthians we are told that "Christ is made unto us righteousness."[18] So righteousness is not something that

---

[15] John 8:34
[16] 2 Peter 1:4
[17] Romans 6:13, 16-19
[18] 1 Corinthians 1:30

man can *do*, but rather something that Christ *is*. Righteousness is defined by a Person. Apart from Christ Himself working in us both to will and to work for His good pleasure, we have no righteousness to speak of. In fact, Isaiah says "all of our righteousness is filthy rags."[19] We have much to say about how Christ's nature comes to work within us, but in order to understand the true function of the law we must at least understand that sin and righteousness are not two kinds of behavior. Rather, they are two different natures, two different men – Adam and Christ.

Two Purposes for the Law

What was the law? How should we understand it? Usually, when Christians think about the law that was given to Israel, the first thing that comes to mind is a written list of do's and don'ts. We think of how Israel was permitted or commanded to act in certain ways, and strictly forbidden to act in other ways. This is true to an extent. The law certainly included many specific rules, but it was far more than a checklist of acceptable behaviors. Like everything else in the first, the law was a picture or testimony of the second. It was a detailed, written description of God's Son and what it meant for Israel to live and relate to God in Him. Every individual component of the law served as "a shadow of the good things to come"[20] in Christ. For example, the moral aspects of the law

---

[19] Isaiah 64:6
[20] Hebrews 10:1

described the nature and character of God's Son. Commands given to Israel like, "Thou shalt not covet," "Thou shalt not bear false witness," "Thou shalt love the Lord your God with all your heart," etc. were written descriptions of Christ's being and moral constitution. These laws forbade Israel to act contrary to God's understanding of Christ's nature. Other laws had to do with the priesthood, that is to say, with sacrifices, offerings, feasts, and ceremonies involving the tabernacle and its instruments. These laws also testified to Christ in unique and important ways. In the various sacrifices and offerings we see vivid pictures of Jesus' work on the cross and the way that the cross operates in the heart of the believer. In the tabernacle we see God's understanding of the church's relationship to His Son and what it means to draw near to God through Him. In the laws that dealt with purification, we see the work of our great High Priest in cleansing His body of all impurity.

In these ways, and so many more, the law created a physical testimony, a natural and temporary illustration, of God's eternal purpose in Jesus Christ. The law was an incredible gift because in every way it pointed to Christ and revealed God's righteous requirement and expectation for His body. However, when this written description of Jesus Christ was given to and demanded of Israel, the vast difference between Adam and Christ was immediately made manifest. Adam was utterly powerless to live up to God's righteous requirement. In their finest moments, the Jews managed to observe some aspects of the law in outward demonstrations of obedience, but they could never inwardly align with what the law described. They were simply the wrong kind. By nature they were contrary to God in thought and in action. Romans says, "For the carnal mind is enmity against God; for it is not subject to the law of God, nor indeed can it be. So then, those who are in the flesh cannot please God."[21]

From the days of Adam and Eve to the gathering of Israel at Mount Sinai, man had lived as a law unto himself, doing what was right in his own eyes. Paul says, "For until the law sin was in the world, but sin is not reckoned when there is no law."[22] Without the standard of the law, there was no way to measure the extent to which Adam had fallen short. But when God described His own nature, judgments, and ways in the words of the law, it was like shining a spotlight on the adamic man, causing all of his faults and shortcomings to be clearly seen. In the light of God's revealed righteousness, Adam was exposed, and the nature of sin began to manifest itself in a multitude of individual sins and transgressions. Paul says,

> *I would not have come to know sin except through the law; for I would not have known about coveting if the law had not said, "You shall not covet." But sin, taking opportunity through the commandment, produced in me coveting of every kind; for apart from the Law sin is dead.*[23]

For this reason Paul tells us, "Through the law comes the knowledge of sin."[24] All that the law could do was

---

[21] Romans 8:7-8
[22] Romans 5:13
[23] Romans 7:7-8
[24] Romans 3:20

make evident the weakness and corruption of humanity. In the words of the Psalmist, it demonstrated that, "all have turned aside, they have together become corrupt; there is none who does good, no, not one."[25] Although it was a strong proclamation of God's expectation, it was "weak because of the flesh,"[26] unable to impart the righteousness that it described. This is precisely what Paul explains in his letter to the Galatians.

> *Is the law then contrary to the promises of God? May it never be! For if a law had been given <u>which was able to impart life</u>, truly righteousness would have been based on law.*[27]

Thus, as strange at is sounds to Christians who have invested years of their lives attempting to obey God's written commands, God never expected Adam to find righteousness through works of the law. In Romans we read, "By the works of the law no flesh will be justified."[28] Sadly, many of us have sought to transform or tame the adamic nature by subjecting it to God's perfect commands and precepts. But how ironic that Paul, a scholar of the law and an apostle to the church, tells us plainly that "the law entered so that transgression would increase."[29] Instead of human lust being subjugated by the law, Paul informs us that just the opposite is true – "Our sinful passions are aroused by the law."[30] In no way does this

---

[25] Psalm 14:2-3
[26] Romans 8:3
[27] Galatians 3:21, NASB emphasis mine
[28] Romans 3:20
[29] Romans 5:20
[30] Romans 7:5

mean that the law was in some way bad. Paul completely rejects this idea, insisting that the law is indeed "holy and just and good."[31] Nevertheless, the goodness of the law contrasted with the fallenness of man became to us "a ministry of condemnation" and "a ministry of death."[32]

Therefore, in these two important ways the law served as "a tutor to lead us to Christ."[33] On the one hand it testified of Him in every commandment, sacrifice, and ceremony. On the other hand, it exposed man's spiritual bankruptcy, "shut up all the world under sin,"[34] and left the honest heart waiting in desperation for the righteous Seed of promise.

Misunderstanding the Law

The great majority of religious leaders in the days of Christ's earthly ministry failed to recognize God's purpose for the law. Worse than that, most of them found in the law a reason for boasting. Instead of allowing the righteous requirements of God to reveal their depravity, they claimed that possession of God's commandments and outward adherence to its demands made them righteous in God's sight.

Israel was indeed a unique people. They were unique among the nations as stewards of the promises of God. Only the Jews received the oracles of God, the types and shadows, the service in the temple, the prophecies of the

---

[31] Romans 7:12
[32] 2 Corinthians 3:7,9
[33] Galatians 3:24
[34] Galatians 3:22

coming Messiah. They were the ones "from whom, according to the flesh, Christ came."[35] But with regard to nature, they were still the fallen seed of Adam, every bit as enslaved to the nature of sin as the Gentiles that they held in contempt. Paul says, "What then? Are we better than they? Not at all. For we have previously charged both Jews and Greeks that they are all under sin."[36]

Jesus came and walked among a nation that had been created by God to testify of Him. Their laws, their religion, their very existence was meant to proclaim the coming of God's Messiah. Nevertheless, when He finally came they did not recognize Him. John says, "He came to His own, and His own did not receive Him." He came to a people who should have been hungering and thirsting for the true righteousness of God, but He found a people who were seeking to establish a righteousness of their own. Speaking of this same generation, Paul says,

> *For I bear them witness that they have a zeal for God, but not according to knowledge. For they being ignorant of God's righteousness, and seeking to establish their own righteousness, have not submitted to the righteousness of God.*[37]

Israel did not understand their calling or their relationship with God. They mistook the shadows for the substance, the natural picture for the spiritual reality. They boasted in being the physical seed of Abraham, but

---

[35] Romans 9:5
[36] Romans 3:9
[37] Romans 10:2-3

rejected the spiritual Seed to whom all of the promises were made. They thought that the blood of bulls and goats was sufficient to forgive their sins and cleanse them from all unrighteousness. They thought God's eternal purpose was found in a natural land, a physical temple, and a particular adamic bloodline.

Jesus was very aware of their misunderstandings and with his teachings He continually tried to expose their true condition. He told them plainly that beneath their ceremonially clean exterior, they still carried the pollution of the adamic man. He called them "whitewashed tombs" and dishes that were outwardly clean but inwardly filled with lawlessness and hypocrisy. And when they complained that He ate bread with unwashed hands, He said,

> *Do you not perceive that whatever enters a man from outside cannot defile him... But what comes out of a man, that defiles a man. For from within, out of the heart of men, proceed evil thoughts, adulteries, fornications, murders, thefts, covetousness, wickedness, deceit, lewdness, an evil eye, blasphemy, pride, foolishness. All these evil things come from within and defile a man.*[38]

Not understanding (nor wanting to understand) the true nature of their problem, their external rituals and traditions seemed a sufficient solution. But in their religious blindness, the Jews of Jesus' day had "strained out a gnat and swallowed a camel."[39]

---

[38] Mark 7:18, 20-23
[39] Matthew 23:24

God was requiring a righteousness that they could never produce. And for those who believed themselves to be accepted by God through keeping the outward form of the law, Jesus clarified the difference between modified behavior and a transformed heart. In the famous Sermon on the Mount, He explained God's law in a way that was meant to uncover and condemn even the most religiously devout among them. He said,

> *You have heard that it was said to those of old, 'You shall not murder... But I say to you that whoever is angry with his brother without a cause shall be in danger of the judgment... You have heard that it was said to those of old, 'You shall not commit adultery.' But I say to you that whoever looks at a woman to lust for her has already committed adultery with her in his heart... You have heard that it was said, 'You shall love your neighbor and hate your enemy.' But I say to you, love your enemies, bless those who curse you, do good to those who hate you, and pray for those who spitefully use you and persecute you.*[40]

In saying these things, Jesus was not raising the bar and demanding more from the adamic man. Quite the opposite is actually the case. By describing the true nature of God's standard, Jesus wanted Israel to face the *impossibility* of true obedience in the flesh, and accept the fact that "a bad tree cannot produce good fruit."[41] This is what Paul

---

[40] Mark 5:21-22, 27-28, 43-44
[41] Matthew 7:18

meant when he said that by the law comes the knowledge of sin. The law described a nature that humanity simply did not possess.

The religious leaders and the majority of the Jewish people would not accept this. Instead, they touted their birthright and boasted in the law of Moses – the very thing that condemned them in the sight of God. Jesus had strong words for those who asserted their own righteousness through works of the law. He rebuked and warned them time and again, explaining that they were relying upon a law that actually proved their guilt before God. He said, "Do not think that I will accuse you before the Father; the one who accuses you is Moses, in whom you have set your hope."[42] And, "Did not Moses give you the law, and yet none of you carries out the law? Why do you seek to kill me?"[43] For three and a half years Jesus declared Israel's true problem, and through His teachings and miraculous signs He showed Himself to be the only solution. They were dead in sin, but He could become their resurrection and their life. They were born blind to spiritual reality, but Jesus could give them sight. By nature they were contrary to the law, but He had come to give them a new spirit, and to write God's law on their heart.

This Same Misunderstanding in the Church

Regrettably, we in the church have proven to be very much the same as the Jews of the first century. Though we

---

[42] John 5:45
[43] John 7:19

have accepted Jesus as the Messiah, we have not accepted His view of the adamic man. We confess that He is the only righteous Son of God, yet we continue in our efforts to produce righteousness through deeds of the flesh. The Jews of Jesus' day claimed holiness and divine approval through obedience to the Old Testament. We often claim the exact same thing through our obedience to the New Testament. Though we believe that Jesus has forgiven our sins, we still imagine that God is satisfied with outward obedience and behavioral change. In many ways we, like the Jews, have failed to learn the lesson of the law. We have not allowed God's written requirement to work in us as a ministry of condemnation. And until the law has exposed and condemned the first man in our heart, we will never see or experience the New Man who fulfills every "jot and tittle"[44] of the law.

---

[44] Matthew 5:18

Chapter VII

The Otherness of Christ

Nearly every Christian will readily confess that they are fallen and sinful by nature. Relatively few, however, have seen the magnitude of what this really means. It is one thing to recognize sins in our lives. It is quite another thing to understand that our natural lives, in their totality, are expressions of the nature of sin. To most people this seems far too harsh an assessment of the situation. While we agree that sin is bad, and that Christ is entirely good, most of the time we see ourselves somewhere in between these two extremes. We certainly don't see ourselves on par with Christ, but neither do we think of ourselves as entirely contrary to Him in every way. In our minds we are somewhere in the middle, sometimes leaning one way, other times leaning the other way. The Bible, however, does not allow for this imaginary third option. Such an idea exists in our mind only when we haven't come face to face with the *otherness* of Christ.

Christ is, by nature, something entirely different, contrary to, *other-than* all that we are and think and do.

He is not just superior, He is a living contradiction to the nature and thought of the adamic man. The prophet Isaiah wrote, "For as the heavens are higher than the earth, so are My ways higher than your ways, and My thoughts than your thoughts."[1] Indeed, Adam and Christ live and move and think in two entirely opposite worlds.

For years of my life, I may have agreed with this as a theological concept, but my life and ministry were the proof that I had never truly seen this reality. I spent years trying to know and serve the Lord without understanding the great divide between all that is Christ and all that is man. But when at last a small flash of divine perspective shined in my heart, I knew with absolute certainty that all I had known and valued and accomplished for God was on the wrong side of the divide. There was no condemnation or guilt involved in this realization; it was simply a deep and shocking awareness of the truth. In this new light it was evident that Adam and Christ had nothing in common.

The School of Christ

When a ray of God's perspective shines in the darkness of our hearts, one of the first things that appears is this terrible and wonderful *otherness*. There comes a sudden understanding that absolutely no aspect of Christ's life, nature, or character could be produced or copied by a human being. In this light, all that we see of Christ is perfectly foreign to us in every conceivable way. We understand that the will of man, at its best, is another will

---

[1] Isaiah 55:9

and not the Lord's. Our greatest intentions and most spiritual ideas are seen to be Towers of Babel that rise up and contradict God's purpose and His ways. The mind of man, in its highest state of enlightenment and education, is still very much a contrary mind. The apostle Paul described the natural mind as "enmity with God"[2] and entirely incapable of knowing spiritual reality.[3] In the light of God's perspective we understand and agree that our purest thoughts are unclean, and that what we call wisdom is foolishness to God. Describing this reality in the strongest of words, Jesus said, "That which is highly esteemed among men is an abomination in the sight of God."[4] When we have submitted ourselves to the Holy Spirit's school of Christ, one of His very first lessons reveals that Jesus Christ is the only one of His kind. T. Austin-Sparks says it like this:

> *We have to come into a very severe school of the Spirit which eventuates in our coming to discover that our best intentions are defiled, our purest motives are unclean before those eyes; things we intended to be for God, somewhere at their spring is self. We cannot produce from this nature anything acceptable to God. All that can ever come to God is in Christ alone, not in us. It never will, in this life, be in us as ours. It will always be the difference between Christ and ourselves. Though He be resident within us, He and He only is the*

---

[2] Romans 8:7

[3] 1 Corinthians 2:14

[4] Luke 16:15

object of the Divine good pleasure and satisfac-
tion; and the one basic lesson you and I have to
learn in this life, under the Holy Spirit's tuition
and revelation and discipline is that He is other
than we are... When you have come to your
best, there is still a gulf between you and the
beginnings of Christ that cannot be bridged.[5]

As strange at it sounds, genuinely knowing the Lord begins with a Spirit-given comprehension of what we are *not*. This is a hard first step, but it leads to a wonderful place. In an earlier chapter we read God's evaluation of the post-fall adamic man. It is worth repeating here: "Then the LORD saw that the wickedness of man was great in the earth, and that every intent of the thoughts of his heart was only evil continually."[6] Undoubtedly, the majority of people living in Noah's generation would have disagreed with God's assessment. Like we do today, they would have pointed out a variety of good actions and causes, happy families, friendly neighbors, societal laws and acts of justice, and with these things in view, insisted that the human race had much to admire. Certainly they would admit some shortcomings, but mankind had some very good qualities and an exciting potential for progress! The Lord, however, did not share their perspective. From His point of view there were still just two trees, and the so-called good fruit of Adam's kind had nothing to do with the Tree of Life. The issue was not the appearance or outward effect of man's actions. God's assessment had to do with the *source, nature, and purpose* of all that man called

---

[5] T. Austin-Sparks, *The School of Christ,* Chapter 1
[6] Genesis 6:5

good. Regardless of appearances and effects, God saw clearly that the natural man had *self* as its only source and goal.

I emphasize the great difference between Adam and Christ because it is vital to all spiritual understanding and progress. Only when we clearly see and accept the great division between these two kinds do we realize that progress involves the increase of one Man and the decrease of another. Spiritual growth begins when our impersonation of Christ ends. And it is not safe to assume that we have learned the lesson of Christ's otherness until we have ceased trying to offer God the fruit of our own lives.

The "Dog Life" Analogy

Imagine you are at church on a Sunday morning when, much to your surprise, the pastor stands at the podium and announces to the congregation that he will be teaching a new series called '*How to Live the Dog Life.*' He then opens a thick book and begins to read aloud about all of the amazing characteristics and abilities that dogs possess. He starts by describing their strength and speed, noting how some breeds can run up to forty-five miles per hour and jump well over three times their own height. He mentions their capacity to endure harsh weather conditions, and their uncanny ability to find their way home even when they have been separated from their families by hundreds of miles. The pastor then turns the page and begins to describe the five canine senses and their amazing capabilities. Dogs can hear pitches up to 67 kilohertz, far higher than a human being. They can pick up a scent up to a mile away, then identify and track it with pinpoint accuracy. On and on the pastor continues until he finally concludes his sermon by saying, "Now that you know the nature, character, and capabilities of a dog, go and do likewise! Go and live the dog life! It will take practice and discipline, but it will be well worth the effort. And just in case you forget what you've heard today, I will be giving each of you a copy of this dog book to read and study for fifteen minutes a day."

When the congregation gathers together the following week, the pastor continues the 'Dog Life' series but this time concludes the service by pointing out some conspicuous areas of failure among the members of the fellowship. Several of the men, despite their efforts, have managed to jump only *a third* their body's height! This is obviously not an acceptable manifestation of the dog life. Even worse, some of the women were observed during the week running at an embarrassing *five* miles per hour. Things would have to improve. However, the pastor was prepared for these failures. He has taken the required classes in dog life burn-out, and knows just how to keep the congregation motivated. He turns on the overhead projector and begins to share the time-tested, seven step plan called '*Discovering Your Canine Potential.*' Fortunately, this plan comes with a practical workbook designed for small groups.

Obviously, all of this is ridiculous, and we can immediately see what is wrong with this story. It is very nice that a dog can do these things, but there are inflexible boundaries of *nature* that prevent humans from living the dog life. It really does not matter how diligently somebody studies a dog or how hard they try to mimic these abilities. We are humans, and for good or for bad, we are bound to and governed by human nature. The only hypothetical solution would be some sort of scientific breakthrough that allowed a genuine dog's nature to be implanted into a human being. With the actual life of a dog developing within the body of a human being, it is conceivable that men could accomplish some legitimately canine things. However, this being impossible, the dog life is entirely out of our reach.

If the above anecdote were true, there would be only two categories of people in this particular congregation. There would be those who had deceived themselves and believe they are making genuine progress. These ones share exaggerated testimonies of smelling food hundreds of yards away and hearing sounds that others cannot detect. They are proud and self-righteous, and fancy themselves well along the way in the journey of transformation. The other category would consist of those who realize, despite all prayer and discipline, that their efforts have been fruitless and they simply cannot do better. These people are filled with condemnation and hopelessness, and they eventually either withdraw from the church or grow accustomed to a life of pretending, hoping that nobody sees through their dog mask.

In a very real way, the Bible is like that dog book. It describes something that you could never be; it demands what you cannot produce. As we saw in the previous chapter, the law was given to Israel to prove this very thing. Sometimes Christians understand the impossibility of keeping the Old Testament law, but then we turn around and try to *do* Christ's teachings from the Sermon on the Mount. Or we read Paul's famous description of love from 1 Corinthians 13 during our wedding services, and we make vows to live accordingly. But these Scriptures describe an altogether different nature, something entirely foreign to us. They describe the nature and character of the Lord Jesus Christ. And if humanity cannot extend beyond its own abilities to accomplish things inherent in a dog's nature, how could we dream of reproducing the nature of Jesus Christ?

The only hope of experiencing what the Bible describes would be a miracle of grace whereby the actual life of Christ was implanted and formed in the soul of man. If the nature of Adam were somehow crucified and put away, and we were made actual partakers of Jesus Christ Himself, we might then rightly expect to experience something far greater than human nature. But this transformation would not be a change *of ourselves*, but rather a change *from* ourselves into something altogether new. It would not be an improved version of the natural man, it would be an altogether new creation in Christ where old things had passed away and all things had been made new. Obviously, this is exactly what the New Testament describes as God's offer to us through the cross of Christ. We will deal with this in more detail in the following chapter. What we must grasp right now is that the gift of life in Jesus Christ is unavoidably misunderstood and neglected if we haven't lost all hope in the natural man.

A Lesson in Despair

In a very real sense, the written words of God are divinely intended to bring us to despair. It is the realization of our inadequacy and the recognition of our spiritual nothingness that prepares in our hearts the way of the Lord. This was the heart of John the Baptist's forerunner message. For this explicit purpose, John was sent to Israel before the Messiah. The only hope that Israel had of recognizing and receiving their Messiah lay in their willingness to accept John's proclamation that all flesh was grass.

> *A voice of one crying in the wilderness; Prepare the way of the Lord; make straight in the desert a highway for our God... The voice said "Cry out!" And He said, "What shall I cry?" "All flesh is grass, and all its loveliness is like the flower of the field. The grass withers, the flower fades, because the breath of the Lord blows upon it; surely the people are grass."*[7]

We see here that Isaiah the prophet described Christ's forerunner as one who would proclaim Adam's weakness and contrariness to God. Only when this proclamation becomes distressingly real in our hearts is there ground in us "for the glory of the Lord to be revealed."[8] So much of the time, the Lord's highway in our hearts is obstructed by high places and crooked paths where we still have expectations in our flesh. Once again, T. Austin-Sparks says it so well.

---

[7] Isaiah 40:3, 6-7
[8] Isaiah 40:5

Have you not learned the lesson of despair yet? Is it necessary for the Holy Spirit to make you despair again? Why not have one good despair and get it all over? Why despair every few days? Only because you are still hunting around for something, somewhere, some rag of goodness in yourself that you can present to God that will please Him, satisfy Him, and answer to His requirements. You will never find it. Settle it today.[9]

The Only Acceptable Life

The idea that man can be like God, or that he can possess or produce something that is acceptable to God, has enticed and deceived us from the very beginning. It has spread throughout the entire world, creating thousands of religions, even infecting the body of Christ. In the church we are happy to give our talents, our time, and our money, so long as we feel that our contribution is valuable and appreciated. We are willing to invest our lives or even change our lives, but something inside us cannot bear to hear that *our* life is not what God is seeking. Very few Sunday sermons recount the New Testament's condemnation of adamic man, or repeat the words of Jesus that demand the loss of our life in order to experience the life that God offers. Something deep in our heart cries out, "You can tell me I am a sinner or tell me that I must work harder for God, just don't tell me that I have been crucified

---

[9] T. Austin-Sparks, *The School of Christ,* Chapter 1

with Christ and have nothing to offer except the measure of Christ that is real in my soul!"

Despite our strong opinions to the contrary, Adam is not fixable. He cannot be patched up and put back in the game. Seeking to end all debate on this issue, Paul compiled a list of Scriptures from the law, prophets, and Psalms, and with them exposed and emphatically condemned the heart of the adamic man.

> *As it is written, 'There is none righteous, not even one; there is none who understands, there is none that seeks for God; all have turned aside, together they have become useless; there is none who does good, there is not even one. Their throat is an open grave, with their tongues they keep deceiving, the poison of asps is under their lips; whose mouth is full of cursing and bitterness; their feet are swift to shed blood: destruction and misery are in their paths, and the path of peace they have not known. There is no fear of God before their eyes."*[10]

In one way or another, man is always seeking to avert the judgment of the cross by devising methods of Adam-repair. Some insist that, with the proper discipline, Adam can be made to behave. Others offer five steps or seven keys for pleasing God and meeting His expectations. There are Christians who suggest that a true sense of gratitude towards God will empower lives of obedience and purity, as though gratitude has the power to prevent flesh from

---

[10] Romans 3:10-18

behaving like flesh. Others seek to be like Christ by asking themselves what Jesus would do in the various situations that arise throughout their day. There is an endless smorgasbord of religious ideas that in one way or another seek to please God while sidestepping the cross. They are popular, but they are lies, and they produce plastic fruit. However, when we allow the light of God's perspective to shine in our hearts, we see unmistakably that nothing of the old can pass over into the new. There is nothing of the first that mixes together with the second. We live in a covenant where the only life acceptable to God is the life of His Son.

Immediately after the fall, God used the story of Cain and Abel to illustrate this very thing. Both Cain and Abel brought an offering to the Lord. Cain, the first, brought the best of the earth, the fruit of his labors, and God rejected his offering. Abel, the second, brought the life of a lamb, a picture of Christ, and he and his offering were accepted by God. So often we are like Cain, offering to the Lord the best of the wrong man, the best of the earth. We want Him to accept the work of our hands, the fruit of our efforts and ideas. And just like Cain, we are shocked and offended when the best of the flesh is not what the Lord desires.

Paul writes, "those who are in the flesh cannot please God,"[11] because "with the flesh we serve the law of sin."[12] Adam is like a bad tree. If you have a bad tree in your yard, one that consistently produces bad fruit, trimming the branches will not solve your problem. Throwing the rotten

---

[11] Romans 8:8
[12] Romans 7:25

fruit into your neighbor's yard or painting the ugly fruit pretty colors will not change the nature of the tree. Bad fruit is indicative of a bad seed. In one of His parables, Jesus described this problem and pointed to the only solution.

> He also spoke this parable: "A certain man had a fig tree planted in his vineyard, and he came seeking fruit on it and found none. Then he said to the keeper of his vineyard, 'Look, for three years I have come seeking fruit on this fig tree and find none. Cut it down; why does it use up the ground?' But he answered and said to him, 'Sir, let it alone this year also, until I dig around it and fertilize it. And if it bears fruit, well. But if not, after that you can cut it down.'"[13]

Though this parable was spoken with specific reference to old covenant Israel, their failures and infidelity manifested the condition of *all* fallen humanity. In order for God to truly deal with man's fruitlessness, He had to lay the axe to the root of the tree. When Jesus spoke this parable the cross was quickly approaching, and in the cross came God's appointed time to deal with man's problem at its source. It was time for Adam to die.

The Law Demands Death

Though we resist it in our hearts and duck it with our theologies, Adam was condemned by the law and

[13] Luke 13:6-9

sentenced to death. For this reason, Paul refers to the law as a "ministry of death" and describes his own experience saying, "For I, through the law, died to the law that I might live to God. I have been crucified with Christ."[14] To Paul the law was both judge and jury. It pronounced man's death sentence, and the cross of Christ became the instrument of his execution.

The law demanded the death of the adamic man, *not* the death of the natural body. The distinction here is vital. The end of biological life has nothing to do with the death of the cross, and is powerless to bring an end to the adamic nature. Believers often speak of physical death as though it were the great transition of the human soul, the doorway from sinful humanity to spiritual life. But the New Testament challenges this idea on every page. Physical death ends physical life, and that is all that it does. In fact, were a person to die a thousand physical deaths, they would still find their soul entirely bound to the nature of Adam. However, there exists another kind of death that offers the soul a true exodus out of one man and into Another. And this far greater death, the death of the cross, was a reality and an experience for the apostles long before their earthen vessels were executed by the enemies of the gospel.

Therefore, God's answer to the problem of the adamic nature was not physical death. It was not another flood that would again affect only human bodies. This time, the judgment that came from heaven was both the permanent solution to the condition of man's soul and the perfect manifestation of God's righteousness. The story of Noah and the flood was a type and shadow that found its fulfill-

---

[14] Galatians 2:19-20

ment in the death of Christ, where both sinner *and the nature of sin* were put away in one mighty judgment. And in the wake of what Jesus called "the judgment of the world,"[15] a new creation began to rise up from the grave, beginning with the Firstborn from among the dead.

---

[15] John 12:31

Chapter VIII

The Cross as an End

In one of the clearest pictures of the cross in the Old Testament, God commanded Abraham to sacrifice his only son as a burnt offering. For three agonizing days, Abraham walked towards the mountain that God had specified, knowing the awful task that lay before him. His son Isaac understood they had come to offer a sacrifice to the Lord, so when they began to ascend the mountain without a sacrificial lamb, he said, "My father, look, the fire and the wood, but where is the lamb for the burnt offering?"[1] And with a reply no doubt inspired by the Spirit and over-flowing with truth, Abraham answered, "My son, God will provide for Himself the lamb for the burnt offering."[2]

I doubt very much that Abraham understood the full significance of his reply to Isaac. But centuries later, when this story was fulfilled by the true Son and Lamb of God, Abraham's words proved to be incredibly providential. The more we comprehend the death, burial, and resurrection of Christ, the more we realize that truly, only God

---

[1]   Genesis 22:7
[2]   Genesis 22:8

could have provided a sacrifice that accomplished so much. To the unbeliever the cross is foolishness. To many Christians it is little more than a means to forgive sin. But to a man like Paul the apostle, whose eyes had been opened, the cross was both the wisdom and the power of God. In the cross Paul saw a door slammed shut on the adamic world, and the heavens opened by a new and living way. He saw God's righteousness revealed and all of His enemies vanquished. He saw the planting of a spiritual Seed, and the first fruits of an eternal harvest. He saw these things and so much more, and so he "determined not to know anything... except Jesus Christ and Him crucified."[3]

A Greater View of the Cross

How well do we know the cross of Christ? Is it as real to us as it was to Paul and the other apostles? Most Christians are very familiar with the story of Christ's death and resurrection. But there is a great difference between knowledge of the crucifixion and a true apprehension of the cross.

The crucifixion of Jesus Christ was an event that took place two thousand years ago. It was the single most important event in all of human history, but it was still an *event* that happened in time and space. Jesus was delivered over to the religious leaders of Israel, beaten and falsely accused, and then sentenced to die on a Roman cross. This is the crucifixion. However, when the apostles were sent out by the Lord to preach the cross, there was far

---

[3]   1 Corinthians 2:2

more to their gospel than the proclamation of these histor-ical events. To the apostles, the cross was a present, ongoing, and eternal reality established through Christ's death and resurrection. In their letters to the churches, the cross is presented as both a finished work of God *and* a perpetual experience in the believer. It is both a consum-mated judgment *and* a timeless truth needing to be revealed and made real in the hearts of every Christian in every age. The church must look to the pages of history to learn about the crucifixion, but we can look to the Spirit of God today and forever to learn and experience the power of the cross.

Perhaps the greatest need in the church today is a greater view of the cross of Jesus Christ. Were someone to survey Christian believers asking what God accomplished at the cross, a large percentage would mention only the forgiveness of sins. This is a problem. Although forgive-ness is certainly an important aspect of salvation, it is by no means the fullness of what God accomplished at the cross. In fact, taken by itself, forgiveness does nothing to solve man's true problem. A forgiven Adam is still Adam, and in many ways Jesus' earthly ministry demonstrated this very thing. Jesus walked through the cities of Israel forgiving many sins, but the people continued to transgress God's commands. He cast out countless demons, but the same spirits returned with seven more and again found the natural man to be a perfectly suitable home. Jesus healed their infirmities, but their bodies continued to grow old and die. He miraculously fed the multitudes, but their hunger returned the very next day. He spoke God's words to the swarming crowds, all the while lamenting the fact that they could neither understand nor obey. If Jesus was sent to fix the natural man, His mission was a failure. But He did not come to fix Adam. He came to "take away the first and establish the second."[4]

The natural man, governed by sin and obsessed with self, was a tree that would never bear fruit. Merely forgiving man's fruitlessness was not God's solution. Man needed a remedy that would address more than the symptoms of this adamic disease. He needed freedom from what he was, not just what he did, and the cross of Christ was the preordained instrument to accomplish exactly that. In the death, burial, and resurrection of Jesus Christ, God cut down one tree and planted another. He executed the offender together with the offenses, "putting off the old man together with his deeds."[5] Showing the disciples yet another illustration of what the cross would accomplish, Jesus approached a fig tree and searched for something to eat. When he found nothing but leaves, He cursed the tree saying, "Let no one eat fruit from you ever again,"[6] and immediately the fig tree began to wither from the roots upward. At the time of this miracle, the disciples did not understand its significance. But after the resurrection, they no doubt realized what the Lord had showed them. Adam is a fruitless tree and mere forgiveness is not the answer. That entire kind must be crucified with Christ, so that the human soul can be grafted into an entirely different tree.

For much of my life as a Christian, I failed to understand these things. I had learned that once my sins were

---

[4] Hebrews 10:9
[5] Colossians 3:9
[6] Mark 11:14

forgiven it was my responsibility to produce fruit accept-able to God.   I knew that the Holy Spirit was there to instruct and convict, but I believed that reaching Christian maturity would largely be the result of personal dedication and discipline. As I mentioned in a previous chapter, these beliefs together with my religious zeal initiated years of striving to be like Christ.   During this time I was grateful for being forgiven, thrilled to be a Christian, but I contin-ually wrestled with the realization that even my most diligent efforts were only producing a measure of outward change.   Very little, if anything, was changing inwardly. Like others around me, I became quite skilled at cleaning the outside of the cup, but over time the true condition of my heart became more apparent and more disconcerting.

Looking back, I understand the reason for my frustra-tion.   Trying to be like Christ is like holding a beach ball under water. For a moment or two it seems possible. But sooner or later, because of the very nature of water and air and the laws that govern their relationship, the ball always pops back up to where it naturally belongs.   In other words, during my years of misplaced zeal and human discipline, I was actually striving against my very nature. I was trying to defeat the adamic nature with the strength of the adamic man. And of course, I was failing.

For several years I was most concerned with my outward behavior because I thought that this was my primary problem.   With fasting and prayer, self-imposed rules, spiritual disciplines, and accountability partners, I tried to control the actions and desires of my flesh. Somehow I never noticed, or perhaps could not under-stand, Paul's clear admonition to the Colossians.

> *Therefore, if you died with Christ from the basic principles of the world, why, as though living in the world, do you subject yourselves to regulations—"Do not touch, do not taste, do not handle," which all concern things which perish with the using—according to the commandments and doctrines of men? These things indeed have an appearance of wisdom in self-imposed religion, false humility, and neglect of the body, but are of no value against the indulgence of the flesh.[7]*

As time passed and frustration mounted, I began to recognize that the problem was worse than what I had imagined. I came to understand that sin was a nature that governed from within, and that my actions and desires were simply its visible fruits. I wanted a way out, but I was born of Adam's seed and had only ever known his kind. How could I find freedom from myself? It was then, in my confusion and desperation, that I humbled my heart and allowed the Lord to enlarge my view of the cross of Christ. For the very first time, I saw a solution in the cross that was much larger than forgiveness of sin. I had come into Adam through birth, and the cross offered me a way out through death.

Our Death in the Cross

It still amazes me that after years of studying and teaching the Bible, I had somehow managed to overlook so

---

[7] Colossians 2:20-24

many New Testament verses that clearly describe *our* death with Christ at the cross.   No doubt, much of my blindness was due to the fact that my flesh wanted nothing to do with a cross that required the end of what I called life. If given a choice, the natural man will always prefer a more Adam-friendly gospel.   But along with this, I also came to realize that the church rarely presents the cross as the crucifixion of the believer.   It seems that this is espe-cially true when we evangelize or teach new Christians.

When I was nine years old, I remember spending a week at a Christian camp during my summer vacation from school.   One night, just before bedtime, all of the young campers gathered outside around a large bonfire while one of the leaders began to explain the gospel to us using the following story.   He said, "Imagine that you are kneeling down in the middle of the road, busily tying your shoe, and completely unaware that there is an enormous bus barreling toward you at high speed.   At the same moment, Jesus is off on the side of the road watching with horror as the inevitable is about to take place – you are about to be crushed.   The bus driver clearly does not see you, and with the speed the bus is moving, you have about ten seconds before it's all over.   Then suddenly, moved with compassion, Jesus forsakes His own safety, and with tears streaming down his face, rushes to the center of the road, pushes you out of harm's way, and is crushed by the bus in your place.   This is what Christ did for you at the cross!"

This is a moving little anecdote that certainly invokes feelings of gratitude for Christ's sacrifice and indebtedness for his love.   Nevertheless, the picture painted by this story is entirely wrong. The truth is actually far greater than what this story relates, but it doesn't make quite as nice of a campfire story for kids. If we were to change the story to reflect the truth of the gospel, it would need to be told like this: "Imagine that Jesus is the one in the middle of the street about to be crushed by an oncoming bus. You, however, are standing on the side of the road, hiding from the danger, and watching things unfold from a safe distance. All of the sudden, with compassion in His eyes, Jesus runs over to you, picks you up, carries you back with Him into the middle of the street, and holds you tightly as the bus strikes and crushes you both. Then, Jesus miraculously rises from the dead, stands up next to your lifeless body, and says, 'Now, if you want to live, I will be your resurrection and your life.'"

I realize that this version of the story is not quite as emotionally appealing, but it illustrates what the New Testament declares to be the starting point of all spiritual understanding: unless you die with Him, you cannot live with Him. Unless you know the death of Christ as the end of all you have been and known in Adam, you will never truly experience Christ as the true life that makes all things new.

Once this reality begins to come alive in our hearts, we realize that the Bible is literally filled with descriptions of our inclusion in Christ's death. In the Old Testament, even the most familiar stories suddenly point to this very thing. In the story of the Exodus, for example, Israel did not simply stand by while God killed a lamb and then struck the firstborn of Egypt. God told Israel to kill the lamb, paint the blood over their doors, *enter in* to the bloody door, and *eat the dead lamb* in its totality. In several clear pictures, God demonstrated that the death of the lamb was an experience for all of His people. For years I thought that the destroyer passed over their homes because God was allowing Israel to live. But having seen a bit more of the cross, I recognized that the destroyer passed over the houses in Goshen because, in God's eyes, they had *already* died in the lamb. When judgment came to Egypt that night, the blood over their doors was like a sign that said, "In this house, all have participated in the death of the lamb. There is nothing left here to judge."

In the New Testament, we find the truth of our death with Christ clearly stated in all of the gospels and repeatedly affirmed in the epistles. On numerous occasions Jesus made statements like, "For whoever desires to save his life will lose it, but whoever loses his life for My sake will find it."[8] And when He was just days from being crucified, Jesus said, "Now is the judgment of this world; now the ruler of this world will be cast out. And I, if I am lifted up from the earth, will draw all men to Myself."[9] What is Jesus referring to when he speaks of being lifted up and drawing all men to Himself? John answers the question for us in the following verse: "This He said, signifying by what death He would die."[10] Although Jesus would be lifted up on the cross alone, He knew very well that far more than His natural body was about to be crucified and buried. This incredible sacrifice provided by God would be the judgment of the entire adamic world. In

---

[8] Matthew 16:25, See also Matthew 10:39, Mark 8:35, Luke 9:24, 14:26, 17:33, John 12:25

[9] John 12.31-32

[10] John 12:33

the words of Paul, "If one died for all, then all died."[11]

As we read through the letters of the apostles, we find the truth of our death with Christ to be the only foundation upon which we can expect to experience spiritual life and true freedom from sin and death. Paul asks the Roman believers:

> *Or do you not know that as many of us as were baptized into Christ were baptized into His death? Therefore we were buried with Him through baptism into death, that just as Christ was raised from the dead by the glory of the Father, even so we also should walk in newness of life. For if we have been united together in the likeness of His death, certainly we also shall be in the likeness of His resurrection.*[12]

Before the cross is anything else, it is first the judgment and death of the adamic man. It is an end before it can be a beginning. Walking in the newness of His life is the *result* of baptism into His death. Notice Paul's clear language in the following verses: "You have died with Christ to the elements of the world;"[13] "For you died, and your life is hidden with Christ in God;"[14] "For he who has died has been freed from sin;"[15] "But now we have been delivered from the law, having died to what we were held by, so that we should serve in the newness of the Spirit and

---

[11] 2 Corinthians 5:14
[12] Romans 6:3-5
[13] Colossians 2:20
[14] Colossians 3:3
[15] Romans 6:7

not in the oldness of the letter;"[16] "For if we died with Him, we shall also live with Him;"[17] and perhaps the clearest statement of them all, "I have been crucified with Christ, nevertheless I live, yet not I but Christ lives in me."[18]

These are not obscure verses taken out of context. These are common and foundational Scriptures that we somehow ignore. And though Christians can claim wrong teaching as the primary reason for our ignorance, there is a greater and deeper reason why we have not turned our attention to these verses. The reason is simple: the adamic nature despises the truth of the cross because it demands his death. In many different ways, often without realizing, we hide from the cross because it rejects what we are and what we think we have to offer. It doesn't differentiate between the worst and the best of the adamic man. It simply calls for his death. Like the sword of King David in the kingdom of Israel, the cross lets nothing that breathes remain alive.

In the church, we appreciate sermons and theologies that deal with the cross, so long as these remain concepts and doctrines that don't actually touch the things that we call life. We decorate our churches and homes with crosses, but in our hearts the meaning of this symbol is often the idea that Jesus died so that we don't have to. We don't remove the cross from the Bible, but we readily misinterpret its meaning and minimize its accomplishment. The true gospel of the cross – our death with Christ followed by His resurrected Life in us – is a gospel that Adam avoids with all of his strength and cunning.

---

[16]   Romans 7:6
[17]   2 Timothy 2:11
[18]   Galatians 2:20

The Greatest Misunderstanding in the Church

Though it is extremely common and largely accepted, perhaps the greatest misunderstanding in the church today is the idea that Christ died *instead of* us. Though there is truth to this statement when properly understood, most believers hear words like these and imagine that Christ faced the judgment and death of the cross so that we would not have to do so. Nothing could be further from the truth. Christ did not die so that Adam could continue living. He did not suffer the judgment of God in order to save flesh from wrath. The truth is exactly the opposite. Christ's death on the cross was the judgment of the world, God's perfect reckoning with all things that fell short of His glory. Our salvation *begins* with baptism into Christ's death, where we face the end of the old man together with his deeds. All that we are by nature bears the judgment of God in the body of Jesus Christ. This is the doorway of salvation. The greatness of God's gift to us is that one man is put away in Christ's death and another Man is offered in Christ's resurrection. *First* we are granted a death that we could not die. *Then* we are offered a life that we could not live. This is the grace of God and the great triumph of the cross.

What we often fail to realize is that if Christ died instead of us, then we are left to live *our* lives for God. What's wrong with this? What's wrong is that this is exactly the helpless condition that Christ came to address! If we are living our lives for God, then we are still in the flesh, still under the law, and still slaves to sin and death.

With this misunderstanding, Christians waste their lives trying to copy Christ's behavior, desperately striving to achieve a better version of themselves. We write books and teach in pulpits how to behave like good Christians. We teach methods of prayer that supposedly empower us to change and obey. Believing Adam must live for God, we devote ourselves to the impossible, we wait for that which has already come, and we condemn ourselves for what God has already put away from His sight.

When Jesus promised believers eternal life, He was not talking about *our* life made longer. Eternal life is not an endless extension of Adam's days. Eternal life is Christ's life given to the human soul. Of course this life never ends, but we need to understand that eternal life is a different *kind* of life, and we receive it at the cost of our own. We cannot receive eternal life without forfeiting the life we have known. These are strong words, but they are not mine. These are Jesus' words, and the words of the apostles throughout the New Testament.

Whether we understand it or not, every man and woman born of the Spirit has been baptized into Christ's death on the cross. Receiving Christ's life means participation in His death. This is God's perspective regardless of our comprehension. Once again in the language of types and shadows, our salvation involved killing the Lamb, painting His blood over our homes, entering in through the blood, and eating His flesh. Israel was not first joined to the Lord at Mt. Sinai. Israel was joined to the Lord when they walked through a blood-covered door and ate the dead lamb. In like manner, we were not first joined to Christ in His resurrection. We first join Him in His death, and in Him and with Him we experience God's judgment of the adamic man. We were not raised with Him until we were crucified with Him. He was not our life before He was our death and burial. God put us away by the sacrifice of His Son, and when Christ came out from the tomb He gave Himself as the resurrection and the life to His body, the church. The adamic race is forever left in the grave, but every redeemed soul comes forth in newness of life and can say with the apostle Paul, "I have been crucified with Christ, nevertheless I live, yet not I but Christ who lives in me."[19]

---

[19] Galatians 2:20

Chapter IX

The Cross as a Beginning

Ever since the day that he took and ate from the tree of the knowledge of good and evil, Adam had an appointment with death. God had warned him saying, "Of the fruit of the tree which is in the midst of the garden you shall not eat it, nor shall you touch it, lest you die."[1] Adam chose to eat, and was immediately separated from the tree of life in the Garden of Eden. This is certainly a picture of the death that God had promised, but I believe the true fulfillment of God's word was yet to come. Some years later, death visited the entire inhabited earth and wiped out Adam's descendants in a devastating flood, but this too was not the consummation of what God had foretold. Finally, in the fullness of time, God sent His Son into the world as the "Last Adam"[2] and Son of Man, to keep Adam's appointment with death. The cross dealt with the entire adamic race in the body of Jesus Christ. In one awesome death, all came to judgment, and God fulfilled the promise He made in the Garden of Eden.

---

[1]   Genesis 2:17, 3:3
[2]   1 Corinthians 15:45

Judgment

We see the judgment of Adam pictured in Old Testament types and shadows, announced by Jesus Himself, and then proclaimed as a finished work in the writings of the apostles. But what does all of this mean? What does it mean for us to be crucified with Christ, baptized into death, dead to sin? We've discussed the nature of Adam and recognized that God's righteous law demanded his death. But what actually happened at the cross? What changed? The world appears to continue on as it always has. Jesus called the cross the "judgment of the world,"[3] but humanity still believes the lie and continues to manifest the nature of sin.

These are important questions, and to answer them we need to begin with an understanding of the word judgment. When the Bible speaks of Adam's judgment at the cross, it is not describing a physical end of adamic humanity or the destruction of the natural world. Although we often use these two words synonymously, there is a difference between judgment and punishment. When someone is on trial for a crime, they first must meet with a judgment. The judgment is a decision that separates truth from lies, distinguishes right and wrong, legal and illegal, and then pronounces guilt or innocence. In other words, judgment has to do with a dividing or ruling between two things. The person is first judged, and only then are they sentenced or punished. Punishment is what is allotted to those who are judged to be guilty of a crime. So judgment is the division; punishment is the penalty for wrongdoing. The distinction is significant.

---

[3] John 12:31

At the cross, God established a great *division*. For centuries, He had maintained a covenant relationship with the physical seed of Abraham in the natural land of Israel, all as a picture of spiritual things that were coming. He required sacrifices and offerings that pointed to Christ; He set up a High Priest that represented Christ; He demanded a righteousness in the law that testified of Christ's nature. For centuries God involved Himself with sinful people and figurative ceremonies that involved temporal things and natural places. But at the cross, all of this came to a screeching halt. With one perfect sacrifice, God simultaneously "revealed His wrath on all ungodliness and unrighteousness of men,"[4] and put away from Himself all that fell short of the glory of God. With the cross, God concluded the covenant of shadows with the adamic man, and began a new covenant with a new man. He ended the age of natural types and figures, promises and prophecies, and began a new day where He could be known and worshipped in spirit and truth. Jesus said to the woman at the well,

> *Woman, believe Me, the hour is coming when you will neither on this mountain, nor in Jerusalem, worship the Father.... But the hour is coming, and now is, when the true worshipers will worship the Father in spirit and truth; for the Father is seeking such to worship Him. God is Spirit, and those who worship Him must worship in spirit and truth.*[5]

---

[4] Romans 1:18
[5] John 4:21-24

The cross ended and judged the old and then began the new; it fulfilled the shadows and ushered in the eternal age of spiritual substance. The first was divided from the second, flesh was divided from spirit, and Adam was forever divided from God. After Christ's work on the cross, God had but one thing to say to the entire adamic race: "If you want to see the kingdom of God, you must be born again."[6]

God did not have to destroy the planet or kill human bodies in order to judge the world. Far more devastating and conclusive than fire and brimstone that destroyed Sodom and Gomorrah, or another universal flood, was a cross that forever divided the living from the dead. The work of the cross declared only one Man alive to God, and all others "dead in trespasses and sin."[7] From that moment on, any human soul desiring to live had to be made alive together and raised up in the resurrected Son of God. This is the greatness of our salvation! God gave His Son as both an end and a beginning, as our death and as our resurrection out from among the dead.

It is true that after the cross, the adamic man continues to live and to fill the earth with the increase of his kind, but God now has no relationship with this man. The cross stands forever as a fixed boundary between the first and the second, the old and the new, and God no longer relates to natural men in natural covenants. He no longer involves Himself with the physical symbols, ceremonies, and places that merely represented aspects of Christ and His work. Now God relates exclusively to the

---

[6] Paraphrase of John 3:3
[7] Ephesians 2:1

risen Son of God Himself, and to all who have "been made alive with Christ, raised up together, and made to sit together in the heavens in Christ Jesus."[8] He has rejected Adam and accepted another Man, and we become "accepted in the Beloved."[9]   The reality of this new relationship is the focus of coming chapters. But now we must understand just how much changed at the cross from God's point of view.   Adam did *not* change.   But God's relationship to Adam ended abruptly when Jesus cried out, "It is finished."[10] Adam was not repaired. He was incorporated into the death of Jesus Christ and put away from God.   In one perfect judgment, God executed His wrath, vindicated His righteousness, and divided from Himself[11] all things that were not born of His Spirit.

One Plan from the Beginning

If the Spirit of God has His way in our hearts, we begin to see the cross of Christ as an enormous chasm that separates Christ from everything that is other-than Christ. The cross is a sword that cuts between two men. Watchman Nee writes, "We died in Him as the last Adam, we live in Him as the second Man. The cross is thus the

---

[8]   Ephesians 2:5-6

[9]   Ephesians 1:6

[10]   John 19:30

[11]   In saying this, I am not denying the reality of God's Spirit still present in the world, always drawing and inviting natural men and women to find life in Christ. Nor am I suggesting that God never touches the world with miracles or intervenes in natural things. I am, however, saying that God has no covenant *relationship* with Adam or with his natural world. The difference should become clear in following chapters.

mighty act of God which translates us from Adam to Christ."[12]   The cross also divides between two creations. The first creation was made for the habitation and increase of the first man, Adam.   As we have seen, this man and creation testified of another to come.   The new creation of which the Bible speaks is not another physical planet, but rather a people newly created through the resurrection of Jesus Christ for the habitation and increase of the second Man. Having been joined to Christ by faith and raised with Him from among the dead, we are now "being built together for a dwelling place of God in the Spirit."[13] We are the new temple for His glory, a body for His expression, a kingdom for His increase. And as partakers of Him, we are dead with Him to all things of the first, and alive in Him to all things of the second.   In his second letter to the Corinthians, Paul explains, "So if anyone is in Christ, he is a new creation; old things have passed away; behold, all things have become new."[14]

Part of God's eternal plan was the reality that the natural realm would foreshadow and anticipate the spiritual fulfillment. First God established the natural pattern or testimony, then he fulfilled the pattern in His Son. Speaking of the corporate body of Adam and the corporate body of Christ, Paul writes to the Corinthians:

> *And so it is written, "The first man Adam became a living soul." The last Adam became a life-giving spirit. However, the spiritual is not*

---

[12] Watchman Nee, *The Normal Christian Life,* (Tyndale House Publishers, Inc.; Reprinted edition August 1, 2008)

[13] Ephesians 2:22

[14] 2 Corinthians 5:17

first, but the natural, and afterward the spiritual. The first man was of the earth, earthy; the second Man is the Lord from heaven. As is the earthy, so also are those who are earthy; and as is the heavenly Man, so also are those who are heavenly. And as we have borne the image of the earthy, we shall also bear the image of the heavenly Man.[15]

In the heart of God, the cross has always been much more than a solution to the problems created by sin. Even before Adam and Eve believed Satan's lie and ate the forbidden fruit, the eternal plan of God involved taking away the first and establishing the second. Sin is certainly dealt with by the cross, and that is a wonderful thing. But God has always wanted something far greater than a sinless natural creation. A world without sin would still be a physical, temporal, and external testimony of His true spiritual purpose. We need to understand that the natural man and creation came up short of God's ultimate intention even before sin entered the picture.

The following analogy may help to illustrate. If you were a soldier in World War I and had been separated from your new bride for over a year, you would no doubt

---

[15] 1 Corinthians 15:45-49. Despite some common interpretations, this chapter is not dealing with individual resurrected bodies. The word body is singular throughout the chapter, and Paul's topic is consistently the two corporate men, Adam and Christ. The corporate body of Adam was sown into death through the crucifixion and burial of Jesus Christ. The corporate body of Christ was raised up with far greater glory. Even as we, being in Adam, have borne the image of the first corporate head, we must now, having been made alive in Christ, bear the image of the Second.

be thrilled if a picture of her unexpectedly arrived in the mail. You would probably carry it with you wherever you went, stare at it as often as you could, and long for the time when her actual presence would replace the photograph. In the absence of your wife, the picture would be a great blessing. But no matter how perfect the picture, your heart would no doubt still yearn for the actual person. Now imagine that one night, while you were sleeping, an insensitive prankster in your platoon thought it would be funny to take your wife's picture and draw a mustache, beard, and bushy eyebrows on her face. When you awake, you reach for the photograph as always but this time find that it has been ruined. Sadness and anger fill your heart because the image of your beloved wife has been permanently disfigured. The picture no longer accurately represents the one your heart longs to see.

In some ways, this story demonstrates what we have been trying to describe. Both the natural creation and God's dealings with the natural descendants of Abraham were multifaceted pictures of His eternal purpose in Christ. We have already discussed a variety of ways that the first man, creation, and covenant functioned as a copy and testimony of the second, and the New Testament is filled with clear affirmations of this reality.[16] We understand that sin soon entered the world through Adam, but we must also realize that sin did not change God's purpose or desire. It did not alter God's plan to one day replace the shadow with the substance, to exchange the picture for the person. The presence of sin in the world was like drawing

---

[16] See, for example, John 5:39, Luke 24:27, Galatians 4:21-31, Colossians 2:16-17, Hebrews 8:5, 9:23, 10:1

a mustache and beard on a beautiful photograph of God's eternal purpose in Christ. It certainly ruined the image of what it was meant to reflect, but it didn't change what God ultimately wanted or what He was going to do. And even if the created picture had remained perfect, it was still only a picture or testimony. In our analogy, with or without the mustache and beard, the soldier's heart longed to one day put away the picture and embrace his wife.

It is the same with God's purpose in Christ. Speaking as though Adam and Eve could have avoided sin is a hypo-thetical idea and was probably never a possibility. Never-theless, the point remains: with or without sin, God's eternal plan involved taking away the first and establishing the second. At no point was God satisfied with the blood of bulls and goats. He was *never* pleased by works of the flesh, physical temples, or earthly kingdoms. These were all pictures, and ones that mankind was continually disfig-uring. But disfigured or not, God wanted more than the blueprint; He desired to move into the house. The Bible speaks of Christ as the "Lamb having been slain before the foundation of the world"[17] because the cross has always been the means by which God would bring about His eternal purpose. The cross was not plan B. It was not God's reaction to man's rebellion. In the heart of the Lord, the cross has forever represented the end of the natural shadows, the dawning of the spiritual fulfillment, and the eternal partition that stands between the two.

Once we begin to see this reality, we realize that from the very beginning God has been telling and re-telling the story of the first and the second. As we have seen in the

---

[17] Revelation 13:8

story of Cain and Abel, the first was rejected and the second accepted. Later in Genesis we see that Ishmael, the first son of Abraham, was cut off from his father's house, and Isaac was established as the true and only son of promise. Shortly thereafter Esau, the first, squandered his birthright and thereby lost his inheritance. Jacob, the second, becomes the recipient of both. With Jacob's two wives, Leah was the firstborn daughter of Laban, but Jacob's heart was always set on Rachel, the second born. Jacob accepted the first in order to gain the second, but Rachel was always the wife that he loved. Joseph had two sons, Manasseh the firstborn, and Ephraim the second. When the two were brought to Jacob to receive his blessing, the elderly patriarch crossed his arms and laid them on the boys' heads. Joseph saw that Jacob was about to give the greater blessing to the younger of the two and objected saying, "Not so, my father! For this one is the first-born; put your right hand on his head!"[18] But Jacob insisted, explaining that the second would be far greater than the first. When Israel was in the Promised Land, the establishing of their kingdom was the story of two kings. Saul, the first, became a picture of all that God rejected. David, the second, was a man after God's own heart. There are many more examples like these, and together they make one thing unmistakably clear — God has always understood the cross of Christ as a judgment, a great division between two things. The cross is how God put away all that pointed to, but fell short of, His one eternal purpose. The cross is also how He made alive and established all that is pleasing in His sight.

---

[18] Genesis 48:18

A Nation Born in a Day

In all of the Old Testament stories we just mentioned, the first and the second are represented by two individual characters.   One man is rejected, the other is accepted. However, in the fulfillment of these pictures, Christ plays the role of both men.   By nature He was not the sinful adamic man, yet He took upon Himself Adam's nature and transgressions and brought them into the grave. Paul says, "For He made the One who knew no sin to be sin on our behalf, that we might become the righteousness of God in Him."[19]   And to the Galatians he writes, "Christ has redeemed us from the curse of the law, having become a curse for us, for it is written, 'Cursed is everyone who hangs on a tree.'"[20]   But then, having drunk the cup of God's wrath towards all unrighteousness, and having removed it from His sight, Jesus rose up from among the dead. With His work now finished, it was as though He was projected out from death, vomited up from the belly of the earth like Jonah from the whale. He needed to die there, but He was too righteous to remain there.   The Psalmist had written, "For You will not leave my soul in Sheol, nor will You allow Your Holy One to see corruption."[21] With judgment accomplished, Christ had no more business with sin and death, with Adam and his fallen seed. If death could have spoken the morning of the resurrection, it would have repeated Pharaoh's words to Moses: "Rise up, go out from among my people, both you

---

[19] 2 Corinthians 5:21
[20] Galatians 3:13
[21] Psalm 16:10

and the children of Israel."[22]

Like a seed that leaves its husk in the ground and then bursts out of the soil, Jesus left Adam in the grave and came out from the tomb alive from the dead. We often speak of the resurrection of Christ as merely an event that took place 2000 years ago. On Easter Sunday we remember and celebrate the story of Christ's return from the grave, but there is so much more involved here than the reappearance of the crucified Son of God. The resurrection of Jesus Christ is the dawning of a new day, the birth of a new corporate man, and the beginning of the harvest of God's precious Seed. Just prior to the cross, Jesus had said, "Truly, truly, I say to you, unless a grain of wheat falls into the ground and dies, it remains alone. But if it dies, it bears much fruit."[23] What is this fruit that Jesus spoke of? It is the increase of His Seed in the souls of those who are made alive with Him! Jesus Christ was planted in the earth as a lone, dying seed. But just as a farmer's seed is sown into the earth with great expectation for a harvest, so God's Seed was planted in death only to appear again with an increase of His kind. This increase does not consist of many other seeds attempting to copy the original. The harvest of God is the increase of the One in and through the many branches that are joined to Him.

The Bible also compares the resurrection of Christ to the birth of a child. In a normal birth, the head appears first, but the head is always attached to a body. In fulfillment of this natural picture, Christ came out of the grave as the head of a new corporate spiritual body, the church.

---

[22] Exodus 12:31
[23] John 12:24

Jesus was the first to leave behind the world of sin and death, but every member of His body makes this same exodus when they are joined by faith to Him. Paul explains, "He is the head of the body, the church, who is the Beginning, the firstborn from among the dead."[24] Elsewhere he calls Christ, "the firstborn among many brethren,"[25] and says, "For if we have been planted together in the likeness of His death, certainly we also shall be of His resurrection."[26] Jesus spent three days in the womb of death, and the earth shook with labor pains. But on the morning of the third day, the Head appeared and opened the way for the rest of His body to follow. When Jesus rose from the dead, "one new man"[27] was born – Christ the head, the church His body, and all sharing one life, one faith, one Spirit, and one Father.

The Law and Prophets had spoken of this day. In several Old Testament stories, we see the birth of the first followed by the long awaited birth of the second. Hagar gave birth to Ishmael when Sarah's womb was closed. But after years of waiting for the promise of God, Sarah's dead womb miraculously brought forth Abraham's true heir. This same story replays with Jacob's two wives Leah and Rachel, and with the two wives of Elkanah.[28] Paul tells us plainly in Galatians that these things represent two

---

[24] Colossians 1:18

[25] Romans 8:29

[26] Romans 6:5 (Literal Translation)

[27] Ephesians 2:15

[28] After years of watching Leah bear children, Rachel finally gave birth to Joseph. Elkanah's wife Peninnah was not the wife he loved the most, but she conceived several times before Hannah at last gave birth to Samuel.

covenant people, two Jerusalems, two corporate sons.[29] Natural Jerusalem was the first to bear children. First was the natural covenant people with their earthly increase in the land of Israel. Then suddenly God's beloved Zion (spiritual Jerusalem,[30] the second wife) travailed and brought forth a new nation in a day. Seeing this from afar, Isaiah the prophet cried out,

> *Who has heard such a thing? Who has seen such things? Shall a land be born in one day? Shall a nation be brought forth in one moment? For as soon as Zion was in labor she brought forth her children.*[31]

This new nation is obviously not a natural people, but rather the "sons of resurrection"[32] that are made alive and raised with Christ. Paul describes this corporate new man in his letter to the Ephesians. He explains that Jew and Gentile were put to death in the body of Christ, and out from the grave came one corporate new man who was neither Jew nor Gentile, but Christ all and in all.

> *For He Himself is our peace, who has made both one, and has broken down the middle wall of separation, having abolished in His flesh the enmity... so as to create in Himself one new man from the two, thus making peace, and that He might reconcile them both to God in one*

---

[29] Galatians 4:21-31

[30] Hebrews 12:22

[31] Isaiah 66:8

[32] Luke 20:36

body through the cross, thereby putting to death the enmity... For through Him we both have access by one Spirit to the Father.[33]

Resurrection is therefore not only Christ's journey from death to life, but the journey and experience of His entire body as well. Jesus said, "I am the resurrection."[34] He did not say, "I *do* resurrections." Resurrection is not a thing, it is a Person, and when we are baptized into Him, Christ's journey from death to life becomes our own. In fact, resurrection life is what Christianity is all about. Pastor and author James Fowler writes,

Christianity IS resurrection. At Easter time we do not just celebrate another event in history even if it be regarded as the greatest event in history. Resurrection is not just a historical event; it is an on-going dynamic of the life of God in Jesus Christ. We do not just assent to the historicity or theological accuracy of the resurrection of Jesus Christ; we encounter resurrection. We encounter and have personal relationship with the One who is "the resurrection and the life." One cannot count themselves a "Christian" unless they have encountered, received, and are participating in the resurrection life of Jesus Christ.[35]

---

[33] Ephesians 2:14-18
[34] John 11:25
[35] Jim Fowler, *Christianity Is Resurrection,* www.christinyou.com, pg. 1

True Circumcision

Jesus entered the grave having been made sin on our behalf, but He appeared again without a trace of the adamic man. Adam and his deeds were removed from Christ and left in the tomb like His burial clothes. Christians generally understand these things, and believe that Christ arose from the dead entirely free from the sin that He bore on the cross. Our struggle is in understanding that the same is true of every individual member of the Lord's body. Whether or not we've seen and experienced this incredible truth, the New Testament insists that we are equally "dead to sin and alive to God in Christ Jesus."[36]

In the old covenant, circumcision was a sign given by God that pointed to this very reality. With circumcision, blood was shed and flesh was removed as a prerequisite for experiencing relationship with God. No male in Israel could know the benefits of God's covenant, or even approach His dwelling place, unless they bore in their body this foreshadow of the cross. The Israelites who left Egypt were a stubborn generation. They grumbled and rebelled against God, and neglected to circumcise their sons for 40 years in the wilderness. God allowed the first generation to grow old and die, and then commanded Joshua to bring the second generation into the Promised Land. However, before God permitted Israel to possess *anything* in the land of their inheritance, He first required that all males be circumcised, leaving their foreskins at the banks of the Jordan River. Though certainly an awkward and uncomfortable requirement for hundreds of thousands of grown

---

[36] Romans 6:11

men, God wanted all to see that crossing the Jordan meant leaving flesh behind. The doorway to their inheritance was also the end of Israel's bondage to the fleshly adamic man.

Like everything else in the Old Testament, physical circumcision was only a testimony of greater things to come. When a male was circumcised he lost only a small piece of the flesh, and there was no real internal change. But when we in the new covenant experience the fulfillment of this picture in Christ, the entire adamic man is cut from our soul by the cross of Jesus Christ. Paul describes this in his letter to the Colossians, saying, "and in Him, you were also circumcised with the circumcision made without hands, in the removal of the body of the flesh by the circumcision of Christ."[37] And to the Philippians he writes, "We are the circumcision, who worship God in the Spirit, rejoice in Christ Jesus, and have no confidence in the flesh."[38] Paul understood that coming to live in Christ was like crossing a great divide and leaving all things of the first behind. In an often misunderstood Scripture, Paul describes his experience of the cross saying,

> But when it pleased God, who separated me from my mother's womb and called me through His grace, to reveal His Son in me, that I might preach Him among the Gentiles, I did not immediately confer with flesh and blood.[39]

This phrase, "who separated me from my mother's womb" is seen by many as a reference to Paul's sovereign

---

[37] Colossians 2:11
[38] Philippians 3:3
[39] Galatians 1:15-16

call to ministry, and it is often translated "God set me apart before I was born."[40]   But the Greek word translated "separated" means divided, severed, excluded.   I doubt Paul was boasting in his unique appointment as apostle. Rather, he was describing an experience of the cross where God had cut him loose from one kind of life and revealed in him Another. The apostles understood that the cross had opened a blood-covered door, parted a sea before them, and invited them out of Adam's world and into the universe of Christ.   This became so real to Paul that he could say, "But God forbid that I should boast except in the cross of our Lord Jesus Christ, by whom the world has been crucified to me, and I to the world."[41]

The Way Out

The gospel of Christ is often proclaimed as man's way out, but we often fail to see just how much is left behind. Christ is not merely our way out of hell, or an escape from bad habits and bad company. The cross of Christ is the way God provided for us to die to one man and world and be made alive in Another. Of course we don't comprehend the fullness of this change when we are newly born again. In fact, both natural and spiritual babies begin their life in perfect ignorance of who and where they are. But babies are meant to grow up. Growing up in both realms means learning an entirely new reality that has been suddenly thrust upon you.   For Christians, this should be the

---

[40] See for example the NIV, NLT, ISV, God's Word Translation.
[41] Galatians 6:14

progressive discovery of a new life, a new creation, and a new covenant, all made real through the resurrection of Jesus Christ.

The Old Testament is filled with pictures of a spiritual exodus out of Adam and into Christ. In each case, the story involves leaving one life behind and learning another that is revealed by the Lord. God's very first words to Abraham were, "Get out of your country, your family, and your father's house, and go to a land that I will show you."[42] Abraham's journey began when all that he knew to be life was cleanly cut away. He then was brought into a new land with a new inheritance, and told, "Lift your eyes now and look from the place where you are—northward, southward, eastward, and westward; for all the land which you see I give to you and your seed forever."[43] Similarly, Lot and his family were called out of a city that God had dedicated to destruction. They were instructed by angels to head to the mountains and warned to never look back. Years later, the nation of Israel entered a blood-covered door and found themselves separated forever from the kingdom of Pharaoh. Though the Egyptians attempted to thwart their exodus, God said to His people, "Stand still, and see the salvation of the LORD... For the Egyptians whom you see today, you shall see again no more forever."[44]

All of these stories illustrate for us the incredible reality of the cross. Jesus Christ bore in Himself the judgment of the adamic man, rose out from the world of sin and death, and invited us to leave with Him. Though our

---

[42] Genesis 12:1
[43] Genesis 13:14-15
[44] Exodus 14:13

bodies continue on the earth for a time, our souls are now alive from the dead, set free from sin, and hidden with Christ in God. Not one of these Old Testament stories portrays the Lord fixing man's prior condition. God did not give Abraham an inheritance in his native land of Ur of the Chaldeans. He did not raise up activists to fight for a more conservative Sodom and Gomorrah. And when the children of Israel groaned under slavery and oppression, God did not send Moses to change the living conditions in Egypt. Contrary to some of our best-selling books, God's goal is not the improvement of the natural world. He has no expectation for the progress of the adamic race. Like the Israelites of long ago, our hearts often long for nothing more than a modified version of Egypt. But what God offers the world is a blood-covered door that leads out of one man and into Another. God's salvation is an exodus from Adam, an entrance into Christ, and an exhortation to never look back.

Chapter X
A New Relationship

As Christians we often speak of having a personal relationship with God, but how well do we understand the nature of this relationship? In my case, after finally begin-ning to see the reality of the cross, I realized that I knew almost nothing at all. I clearly remember the day when it suddenly dawned on me that, despite having been raised in the church and having given years to full-time ministry, I had virtually no real understanding of what it meant to be *in Christ*.

If you were to ask twenty people in the body of Christ to describe their relationship with God, you would likely get twenty very different responses. Most believers would try to answer this question by describing what God means to them, and perhaps recounting the things they do throughout the day or week to interact with Him. They might say something like: "I love Him and trust Him to take care of me and my family;" or "I read His Word in the morning and talk to him on and off throughout my day;" or "He's there for me whenever I have a problem or need some direction." These are all very fine things to say, but they are not at all descriptions of the relationship that God has given us in His Son. Statements like these describe how we feel about God or how we try to communicate with Him, but God has established a very specific *kind* of relationship with believers, and it is essential that we understand it.

Even in the natural realm there are different kinds of relationships and we intuitively understand that not all of them are the same. The relationship between a grandfather and grandson is a very different relationship than the one that exists between a husband and wife. Though we may not formally define these relationships with words, we realize that there are all sorts of unspoken rules, expectations, agreements, and assumptions that govern how we interact with each other. It would be very strange, for example, if I offered to push my grandfather on a swing, tickle him, and then braid his hair. These are perfectly normal activities for a parent with a small child, but it would be ridiculous for a grown man to relate this way with an elderly grandfather.

An even clearer illustration can be seen within the context of marriage. A husband and wife share a very specific kind of relationship, one that is unique and exclusive between just the two of them. In this relationship there is a common understanding that governs behavior, activities, and roles. There are emotions and interactions that only the two of them share together. There are other actions and ways of relating that are entirely inappropriate and damaging to marriages. Marriages work well only when both parties agree about the nature and purpose of the relationship.

The New Covenant

Through the work of the cross, God established an entirely new relationship with us that the Bible calls the new covenant. The word covenant should not be an intimidating or complicated theological term for Christians. A covenant is nothing other than a specific kind of relationship, very much like the examples that were just given. Throughout the Old Testament we read of covenants made between God and man, and others established between individual people. In each case, the covenant is simply a *defined relationship*. It is an understanding or agreement that specifies how two parties will interact.

The new covenant that was established through the death, burial, and resurrection of Jesus Christ was an entirely new kind of relationship that God made with His creation. It was a new way for man and God to live and relate together, one that had never existed prior to the resurrection. What is the nature of this relationship? How is it defined and understood? How does God see and relate to us now? What are the agreements and boundaries involved? Very often, we don't know the answers to these questions. Sometimes we don't even realize that these are vital questions, and that discovering their answers is what it means to experience relationship with God. It is one thing for Christians to know that we have a relationship with God. It is another thing to genuinely know, understand, and experience the reality of that relationship.

Unless we share God's perspective of the covenant He has made with us, we will walk in the vanity and imagination of the natural mind. There is only one relationship with God that exists. It is ours to experience but not ours to define. And whether we realize this or not, it is incredibly easy to invent our own personal version of what it means to relate to God. We can walk through our lives thinking our thoughts about God, praying the prayers that are relevant to our experiences, and learning the Scriptures that seem to support our ideas. We collect ideas that we have read in books or heard from pastors, parents, and friends, and from all of these things we assemble an idea of what it means to have a relationship with the Lord. Doing this is so common and accepted that we rarely ever think to question it. But *our* ideas about God's covenant with man are never correct, simply by virtue of being ours. In fact, man's ideas about God are at the root of every idol, whether or not we carve these ideas into physical statues or images.

Christ as Our Covenant

Understanding and experiencing the new covenant begins with the realization that this new relationship with God is not a what, it is a Who. As strange as it may sound, Jesus Christ IS our relationship with God. He *is* the covenant that God has made with man. I am not merely saying that Jesus is the cause or the means of our relationship with God. I am saying more than that. God's relationship with every believer *is* His resurrected Son.

Long ago, God spoke of the coming Messiah through the prophet Isaiah in the following way:

> *I, the LORD, have called You in righteousness,*
> *and will hold Your hand; I will keep You and*

give You as a covenant to the people, as a light to the Gentiles.[1]

Thus says the LORD... "I will preserve You and give You as a covenant to the people, to restore the land, to cause them to inherit the desolate heritages."[2]

What does it mean that Jesus Christ is given to us as a covenant? In a few words, it means that the new covenant is not just *a way* that God has decided to relate to you. Rather, the new covenant is the Person, the Son, *in whom* God relates to you. Every aspect of our relationship with God is an aspect of Christ Himself. Christ is how God sees you, where God sees you, and how God knows you. He is the substance, the nature, and the boundaries of God's relationship with human souls. We relate to God in Christ, by Christ, and as the body of Christ. Our relationship with God is the incredible reality that our souls have come to live in and by His resurrected Son.

The short phrase "in Christ" or "in Him" appears hundreds of times in the New Testament because everything that God has given us, every aspect of our salvation and inheritance, is a participation[3] in the resurrected life of Jesus Christ. Paul says, "But of Him you are in Christ

---

[1] Isaiah 42:6

[2] Isaiah 49:8

[3] This statement could be misinterpreted in at least two ways. By participation in Christ I do not mean that we possess divinity (or even spirituality) *in ourselves*. Nor do I use this word to suggest that we contribute something inherently *of ourselves* to the relationship. I simply mean that we are made recipients, partakers, vessels, and ultimately living expressions of all that God has given us in and as Christ.

Jesus, who became for us wisdom from God—and right-eousness and sanctification and redemption."[4] Throughout the letters of the apostles, we are said to be made alive in Him, newly created in Him, reconciled in Him, and accepted in Him. Grace is said to be a reality for us only *in* Christ, along with life, love, freedom, redemption and forgiveness. In Him all of God's promises are yes and amen. In Him we find our true inheritance and our true relationship with God. In fact, it is Christ's Spirit within us that cries out Abba Father! The Spirit teaches us to remain in Him. The apostles admonish us to walk in Him. And as His body we grow up to know the truth as it is in Christ Jesus, because in Him are hidden all of the treasures of wisdom and knowledge. "We are His workmanship, created in Christ Jesus,"[5] and our purpose is to be rooted, grounded, and built up together in Him as a dwelling place of God in the Spirit.

This reality of our placement into Christ is the very heart of the gospel. It is the way by which God has loved the world and given Himself to all who believe. When the Scriptures declare all of these realities to be "in Christ," this is not the same as saying that they are "part of Christianity." Being in Christ means much more than adherence to a belief system or regular church attendance. When the Bible declares us to be in Christ, it is declaring the person, location, and substance of everything that God offers the human soul. Again, Christ is not simply the reason that God relates with us; He is the very relationship itself.

The following analogy may be helpful. Some years

---

[4] 1 Corinthians 1:30
[5] Ephesians 2:10

ago, my wife Jessie and I brought our families together, made public vows to one another, and entered into the covenant relationship called marriage. In a figurative way, Jessie became bone of my bone, flesh of my flesh, and the two of us became one. From that moment on, and for as long as we live, I vowed to relate to my wife in a very specific way. Bound up in our new marriage relationship were natural responsibilities, financial commitments, physical and emotional expectations, and much more. I promised to love her, to provide for her, to protect her, and be faithful to her. It was an exclusive relationship, just between the two of us.

After a short time, Jessie conceived and our first son Ezra began to grow in her womb. My wife and I continued to share the same relationship, but suddenly there was another person involved with us. Inside of her was the life of another, one that was miraculously joined to her and alive because of her. And now, because of the covenant that Jessie and I already shared, this new child began to benefit from a relationship that existed before he was even conceived. As I continued to provide for my wife, I naturally provided for the child within her as well. When Jessie was safe and secure, Ezra too was protected from harm. Whenever I hugged my wife, I also embraced the little one inside of her womb. In a sense, Ezra found himself participating in a relationship that he did not initiate or understand. He was actually experiencing some aspects of *my* relationship with *my* wife! Clearly this was not a relationship that he could define or change, but in many ways it was a relationship that he could benefit from and enjoy. You could even say that, for nine months, Jessie *was* Ezra's relationship with me. She was the location and person in whom I related to my son. Ezra did not have a relationship with me apart from her, and yet he became a partaker and participant in all that I shared with my wife.

In a similar way, Christ is our relationship with God the Father. Those who are born of His Spirit are immediately made partakers of His life. Christ is in us, and we are in Him, and so like Ezra, we have been granted access to a relationship that existed long before we did. Though we experience and benefit greatly from it, we did not initiate or define this relationship, and we do not naturally understand it. It is something that God the Father planned and foreknew, God the Son accomplished through the cross, and God the Spirit must make known to each believing soul. Similar to Ezra's relationship with me in Jessie, our relationship to God in Christ is already established regardless of our understanding. The measure of our comprehension has no effect on how God sees us and relates to us. Like all covenants, the new covenant is a defined relationship, and it is therefore both foolish and dangerous to give room to our ideas and imaginations.

The Danger of Spiritual Imaginations

When it comes to spiritual reality, imagination is worse than ignorance because, whereas ignorance lacks understanding, imagination *replaces it* with something that isn't real. This was a far greater problem in my heart than I ever realized, and I've found it to be extremely prevalent in the church at large. When I use the word imaginations, I am not simply referring to outlandish, silly, or unorthodox ideas about God. Imaginations are *any and every* idea about God that do not originate from His mind and work in us by His light. To whatever extent we have not seen and understood God's perspective of this relationship, to that extent our minds are filled with imaginations.

If you were sitting at night by a campfire in the middle of the woods, there would be a small circle of light emanating from the fire. Within that circle of light you would be able to clearly see all that was going on. But if you heard a strange sound that came from the woods, beyond the reach of the light, you would naturally begin to imagine what caused the sound. If five friends were camping with you, each person could have a very different idea about the source of the noise. One believed he heard a bear. Another is certain it was a falling tree. Whether you are in agreement or not, the point is that imagination automatically prevails wherever there is no light.

For this very reason we are all naturally bound to wrong ideas about spiritual reality. We have all imagined far more than we have actually seen of the incredible relationship that God has given us in His Son. Reading Scripture is important, but even committing the entire Bible to memory will not necessarily alleviate this problem or heal our blindness. Spiritual ignorance is not a lack of information; it is a lack of light. Familiarity with God's words does not mean that we are seeing the realities that His words describe.

With regard to the new covenant, we frequently expose our misunderstandings when we say things like, "I'm working on my relationship with God," or "I used to have a good relationship with God, but now I don't." The truth is that our relationship with God never changes. It cannot get better, nor can it get any worse. You don't need to work on this relationship because you could neither fix it nor ruin it. Once again, if you are born of the Spirit, then your relationship with God is a person, the Lord Jesus Christ. God doesn't give you a small piece of Jesus and then make you work for the rest. There are not different versions of Jesus for different people. There is only one Son of God, and one relationship that God offers the world in Him. The only thing that changes in this relationship is our awareness, understanding, and experience of it. The problem is never that we need a better relationship. The problem, as we have said, is that we have very little understanding of what it means to be in Christ.

Where we have not seen the truth, we naturally seek to know and relate to God in a way that makes sense to our mind, meets our personal needs, and aligns with our individual desires and emotions. Without realizing what we're doing, we come up with our own answers to important questions like: How does God feel about me? What does He want from me? What is He doing? How do I please Him? Trying to answer these questions without His light, we end up striving to do what God has already done and seeking to produce what God has freely given. In our confusion, we pray for what we already have and wait to go somewhere that we already are. We blindly pride ourselves in works of the flesh while condemning ourselves for things that God does not recognize, all the while trying to believe what we do not understand, and love and serve a God we do not know. And when time, effort, prayers, and tears are added to all of our wrong ideas, they become firmly entrenched strongholds of the mind that are very difficult to tear down.

The Round-Trip Journey of God's Word

Throughout the remainder of this chapter, I will be referring to the diagram on the following page.

To really understand our relationship with God we need to go back to the beginning. I don't mean the beginning of our lives, or even the beginning of the natural creation. Long before anything was created, there was a perfect relationship that existed within the Godhead. The Father, Son, and Spirit enjoyed a relationship of union, where all things were shared between them. They shared one life and love and glory. They saw with the same light, and rejoiced together in truth and righteousness. Describing this relationship Jesus said, "The Father loves the Son and has given all things into His hand."[6] The author of Hebrews explains that the Son is "the radiance of His glory, the express image of God's person."[7] John tells us, "In the beginning was the Word, and the Word was with God, and the Word was God. He was in the beginning with God."[8] Speaking of Christ, the eternal Word and Wisdom of God, Proverbs says,

> *The LORD possessed me at the beginning of His*
> *way, before His works of old. I have been*

---

[6] John 3:35
[7] Hebrews 1:3
[8] John 1:1-2

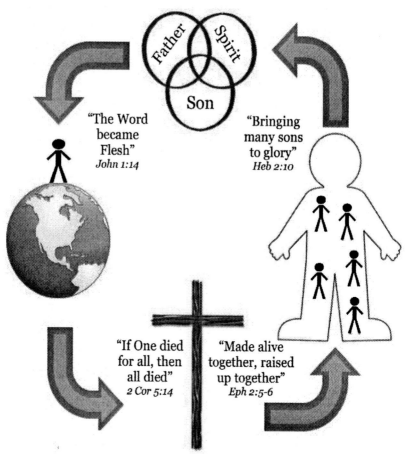

established from everlasting, from the beginning, before there was ever an earth... Then I
was beside Him as a master craftsman; and I
was daily His delight, rejoicing always before
Him, rejoicing in His inhabited world, and my
delight was with the sons of men.[9]

---

[9] Proverbs 8:22-23, 30-31

These may well be familiar Scriptures for many Christians, but we need to stop for a moment and realize that before these were descriptions in the Bible or doctrines in our minds, they were aspects of a perfect and eternal relationship between God the Father and His only Son.

This same Son, the eternal Word of God, humbled Himself, took on the form of a human bondservant and entered into the world to die. God the Son became a man, not primarily to teach or to heal, but to bear in Himself the judgment of all that had fallen short of the glory of God. As we have mentioned, Jesus died the death of "the first," the death of Adam and his fallen creation. We were baptized into His death, buried with Him, and thus made partakers of God's absolute judgment and rejection of the adamic man. But having finished His business with the fallen adamic world, and having paid the full price of redemption with His own blood, death could no longer hold Christ and He rose out from among the dead. From God's perspective, Adam was left in the grave forever, but Christ arose to offer Himself as the door, the life, and the eternal dwelling place for every soul who desires to follow Him. Immediately upon new birth, believers come out of the realm of slavery and death with Christ, in Christ, and having no life but Christ. With this diagram, my intention is to illustrate that what Christians call "getting saved," God might call "being made alive in My Son" or "participation in My Son's resurrection." What Christians call "*their* relationship with God" is actually something far greater – it is an inclusion in Christ's eternal relationship with His own Father.

Just prior to going to the cross, Jesus prayed to His

Father saying, "And now, O Father, glorify Me together with Yourself, with the glory which I had with You before the world was."[10] Christ desired to return to glory, to leave Adam's world and finish His round-trip journey. But just as Isaiah foretold centuries earlier, the Word of God would not return to His Father empty-handed.

> *For as the rain comes down, and the snow from heaven, and do not return there, but water the earth, and make it bring forth and bud, that it may give seed to the sower and bread to the eater, so shall My word be that goes forth from My mouth. It shall not return to Me void, but it shall accomplish what I please, and it shall prosper in the thing for which I sent it.*[11]

God's plan involved more than retrieving Christ from the grave and restoring Him to heavenly glory. It was the will of God that Christ "bring many sons to glory"[12] in Himself. This was "the joy set before Him"[13] as He walked to Jerusalem to die. Christ's great expectation was that "they all may be one, as You Father, are in Me, and I in You; that they also may be one in Us."[14] He prayed, "Father, I desire that they also whom You gave Me may be with Me where I am, that they may behold My glory which You have given Me; for You loved Me before the foundation of the world."[15] Constrained by God's eternal purpose,

---

[10] John 17:5
[11] Isaiah 55:10-11
[12] Hebrews 2:10
[13] Hebrews 12:2
[14] John 17:21
[15] John 17:24

Christ left his disciples for three days (death, burial, resurrection) in order to prepare the way for their return with Him, in Him, to His Father. He promised His disciples, "If I go and prepare a place for you, I will come again and receive you to Myself, that where I am, you may be also."[16]

Contrary to so many unfortunate misunderstandings of these verses, Christ's final words to his disciples had nothing to do with distant future events or geographical locations. Jesus had walked and ministered for over three years with these men. His mission and His desire involved bringing all believing souls into a living union with the Father, Son, and Spirit, but first He had to make that relationship accessible through the mighty work of the cross. For three days the disciples were overcome with sadness, confusion, and fear. During the same three days Christ put away one world, made all things new in Himself, and then appeared again to His disciples just as He had promised. At last, having judged the adamic man and satisfied the righteousness of God, Christ could appear again and receive His people unto Himself. In perfect fulfillment of the Old Testament pictures, the death of the true Passover Lamb was both the judgment of God's enemies and the opening of an impassible sea. Now all who believed could make their great exodus as "one new man,"[17] "Israel My Son, even my Firstborn."[18] Every type and shadow, every promise and prophecy, had looked forward to this new day and anticipated this incredible new relationship. Jesus had also spoken longingly of this day, saying,

---

[16] John 14:3, emphasis mine
[17] Ephesians 2:15
[18] Exodus 4:22

A little while longer and the world will see Me no more, but you will see Me. Because I live, you will live also. In that day you will know that I am in My Father, and you in Me, and I in you.[19]

Some years later, having understood and experienced this very thing, Paul the apostle proclaimed the finished work of the cross to believers in Colossae, saying, "You have died, and your life is hidden with Christ in God."[20]

Allow me to reiterate that not one of these verses has to do with physical locations or future events. The preparation of our eternal dwelling place, the great exodus from the adamic world, and this incredible relationship of union with God in Christ, all of these things were accomplished through Christ's work on the cross and are present realities *in Him*. Christ is not *still* working to prepare a place for us in His Father. We are not *still* waiting for Him to bring us where He is. We are told over two hundred times in the New Testament that we are *now* in Christ. These are present, spiritual realities that have nothing to do with the death of our physical bodies. Paul was not writing letters to corpses when he told the church that they had died and their life was hidden with Christ in God. He was writing to believers whose bodies continued to live in the earth, but whose souls had been baptized into Jesus' death and were made alive with Him, raised, and seated in heavenly places in Christ. For every Christian then and now, with or without a natural body, Christ is made unto us "all things

---

[19] John 14:19-20
[20] Colossians 3:3

that pertain to life and godliness."[21] He is our justification through His blood, our liberation from sin, and our resurrection out from death. He is the righteousness, the truth, and the love that now works in us. But perhaps even more foundational than any of these, and absolutely vital for spiritual understanding and growth, is the reality that Jesus Christ is *the life* of His body, the church.

Christ as Life

Having judged sin through His death, Christ was able to offer the world salvation through His life. Paul explains, "For if when we were enemies we were reconciled to God through the death of His Son, much more, having been reconciled, we shall be saved by His life."[22] What does it mean to be saved by His life? It means, quite simply, that His life is our salvation. Salvation is not some thing that Jesus gives to us. Salvation is the life of Jesus Christ being given to us. It is crucial that we understand this. Christ does not give you salvation. Jesus Christ is made unto you salvation, and wisdom and righteousness and sanctification and redemption.[23] These things become ours because they are aspects of Christ, and because Christ is our life.

The reality of Christ being the life of the believer is something that I overlooked for years. I had heard Christians refer to Christ as their life but I always assumed this simply meant that Jesus was the most important thing to

---

[21] 2 Peter 1:3
[22] Romans 5:10
[23] 1 Corinthians 1:30

them, or that without Him they could not imagine living. I had also read verses in the New Testament where Christ is clearly called the life of the Christian soul. For instance, Paul says, "When Christ, who is our life, is revealed, then we are revealed together with Him in glory."[24] Somehow, I read over these verses without being struck by the implications of these words. At the time, the idea of knowing Christ as my life just didn't make sense to me. I had spent years trying to know Him as my Lord, to thank Him for being my Savior, to adore Him as my heavenly Bridegroom, and to fear Him as my King. The Bible spoke of Jesus by many names and I wanted to know Him in these ways and relate to Him in each of these roles. But only when the reality of the new covenant began to dawn in my heart did I realize my profound misunderstanding. I could never know what it meant for Christ to be Savior, Bridegroom, and King until I understood these titles in relationship to Christ being the life of my soul.

In other words, Jesus is my Savior because He is the eternal life that forever dwells within me. He saved me by filling my soul with Himself. Jesus is my Bridegroom because, "He who has been joined to the Lord has become one spirit with Him."[25] Bride and Bridegroom are words used to describe an inward union where my soul is joined in covenant to God's eternal Spirit. Paul explains, "Therefore, my brethren, you also have become dead to the law through the body of Christ, that you may be married to another—to Him who was raised from the dead, that we should bear fruit to God."[26] Christ is my King because His

---

[24] Colossians 3:4

[25] 1 Corinthians 6:17

[26] Romans 7:4

life establishes its reign in my soul, taking captive all things contrary to Himself, putting away flesh, and conforming my soul to His righteous rule.

Jesus is many things to us as believers, but only because He is first our life. All of His many names and roles become real to us only as internal realities and experiences of Christ's indwelling life. They are not external ideas or concepts for us to study and try to appreciate. They are not physical relationships or future experiences. So much of our confusion and failure to genuinely know the Lord comes from an underlying misunderstanding of the nature of our relationship with Christ. The foundational reality upon which all spiritual understanding must rest is the fact that we were crucified with Christ, and He is now the risen life of every believing soul.

The Only Relationship

In the diagram on page 154, on the right side of the cross, you can see that there is just one new man, and all are made partakers of Him. Through the cross, we were both put to death in Christ and then made alive *in Him*. When a person is born of the Spirit, God does not establish a new or separate relationship with that individual believer. The truth is actually far better than that. New birth means that we are all granted access into God's exclusive and eternal relationship with His one and only Son. To be sure, we never *become* Christ, but we are transferred out of Adam, accepted in the Beloved, and made "heirs of God and joint heirs with Christ"[27] in all that He is and has.

Christians often talk about their personal relationship with God, and from one perspective it is correct to speak that way. Our relationship with God is extremely personal in the sense that He is the life of each individual soul. He is guiding us into the truth, working in each of us "both to will and to do for His good pleasure."[28] However, there is a sense in which this language can be misleading. Our relationship with God is not private, independent, or in any way separate from Christ. In fact, it is not even *our own* relationship; it is Christ's relationship with His Father. From a heavenly perspective, your relationship with God is not any different than my relationship with God. Though Christians may differ very much in spiritual understanding, God has only one relationship with all believers. This one relationship is a Person, and we must come to know and relate to Him as His body. Paul says, "By one Spirit we were all baptized into one body... and have all been made to drink of one Spirit."[29] This is the nature of the New Covenant.

Returning to the analogy of my wife's pregnancy, I mentioned that my son Ezra was brought into a relationship that existed before he did. In a sense, Jessie *was* Ezra's relationship with me during the nine months that he grew in her womb. However, if Jessie had conceived octuplets, and eight babies were growing together inside of her, every one of them would have the exact same relationship with me through my wife. Though each one of these

[27] Romans 8:17
[28] Philippians 2:13
[29] 1 Corinthians 12:13

babies is an individual human being, there would still be only one way, one place, one person, in whom they could experience a covenant relationship with their father. Every aspect of their life and growth and relationship would be confined within the boundaries of one person, and at least for a time, separation from that person would mean certain death.

In the words of T. Austin-Sparks, "God has shut up everything of Himself within His Son, and it is not possible now to know or have anything of God outside of the Lord Jesus, His Son. God has made this a settled thing; it is final, it is conclusive."[30] This is so true. All things of God are bound up in one place, in one Man, in the Lord Jesus Christ. Nevertheless, through the work of the cross, God has made a way to offer the world everything that He is and has by inviting us into that Son. Christ is more than the agent through whom God has saved us. He is the salvation itself. More than that, Christ is the place where our soul comes to dwell, the life itself by which we live, and the very relationship by which we commune forever with God.

---

[30] T. Austin-Sparks, *The School of Christ,* Chapter 3

Chapter XI

The Fulfillment

The New Testament frequently speaks of the finished work of the cross as the fulfillment of the law, the prophets, and the eternal purpose of God. On multiple occasions Jesus described His own coming and redemptive work as the fulfillment of the Old Testament Scriptures. And after the resurrection, when the Spirit of God was poured out upon the new covenant church, the apostles repeatedly insisted that this was nothing other than what "all the prophets, from Samuel onwards... had foretold."[1]

What does it mean for Christ to fulfill the law and the prophets? How should we understand the word *fulfill*? In the mind of most people, the concept of fulfillment has to do with the realization of something that has been foretold. We say things like, "He told us months ago that the Yankees would win the World Series and now his prediction has been fulfilled." Or, "She promised she would arrive before 7:00pm and she fulfilled her word." This is certainly a valid use of this word, but the way that the Bible

---

[1] Acts 3:24

uses the term fulfillment carries much more meaning. Although it still involves the realization of a promise or prediction, the fulfillment of the law and prophets by Jesus Christ was more than just the arrival of the promised Messiah or the fact that He accomplished certain things that were spoken beforehand. Christ fulfilled every prophecy and promise not simply by *doing* things that were predicted by the prophets, but by *becoming* in His resurrection the eternal reality of all that God had promised. The distinction is essential. The fulfillment of the law and prophets involved a change from shadow to substance. In other words, Christ fulfilled the things written in the Scriptures by ushering in a change from natural types and figures to spiritual realities. When Christ came, He filled up God's Old Testament descriptions with their spiritual and eternal substance; He made all things[2] new in Himself.

Imagine that you had a large, empty paper bag sitting in the center of your dining room table, and that this particular paper bag had the shape and color of a pineapple. Not only did the bag look like a pineapple, but all around it, on the bottom and on every side, somebody had taken a pen and written descriptions of the taste, size, color, texture, etc., of this fruit. Imagine now that this paper bag sat on your table day after day, week after week, year after year, doing nothing more than describing a delicious fruit, until one day a man walked into your house and

---

[2] The "all things" that Christ made new are the "all things" of the Old Testament types, shadows, promises, and prophecies. For example, through the work of the cross, the Lord raised up a new temple, a new priesthood, a new kingdom, a new covenant, etc., all of which have Christ as their substance and location.

filled the empty bag with real pineapples. At that moment, it would be correct to say that the testimony of the pineapple had been *fulfilled.*

This simple analogy illustrates something of how the Bible uses the term fulfillment. It would be true to say that the arrival of the real pineapples fulfilled a series of predictions that were seen in, or written upon, the paper bag. But something much more significant has happened as well. By filling the paper bag with real pineapples, the substance has now replaced the shadow; the actual fruit has literally taken the place of a multitude of testimonies and descriptions. This is more than a realized prediction. The presence of real pineapples represents a total change in substance and form. For years there was just an empty bag on your dining room table. Now, however, you can sit down at the table and enjoy the actual fruit.

It is in this sense that Jesus Christ has fulfilled the law and the prophets. He not only accomplished the things that were spoken about Him; He also replaced the shadow with the substance and became the reality of every testimony. Through the cross, an unspeakable and permanent change took place. It's not that God changed His mind or altered His plan. In fact, just the opposite is true. Through the cross, God fulfilled His plan and accomplished His eternal desire by filling up every shadow, prophecy, and promise with the actual Person of Jesus Christ. In one way or another, Jesus Christ is the living reality that has replaced every Old Testament shadow. All fulfillment is both in Christ and it is Christ. He is the essential substance, place, and experience of everything God has promised.

From the Old to the New

In order to know and live in the reality of the new covenant, we need to comprehend the incredible change in man's relationship with God that resulted from the cross. We discussed the new covenant in the previous chapter and saw that it is a new relationship where redeemed humanity comes to live in and by the resurrected Son of God. By faith we are made partakers of Christ's death and burial, and consequently we receive Christ as our resurrection and our life. Paul's statement in Galatians 2:20 is a perfect description of the nature of this new relationship with God – "I have been crucified with Christ, nevertheless I live, yet not I, but Christ lives in me." But if this is the new covenant, what was the old covenant? The answer is surprisingly simple: the old covenant was actually the exact same relationship in the form of natural types, shadows, descriptions, and pictures. It was an empty paper bag that in every way pointed to and anticipated the coming spiritual substance.

Every covenant that God made with mankind prior to the coming of His Son was a natural picture of the coming spiritual reality. In other words, every Old Testament covenant painted a picture of what it would mean for a people to live in Jesus Christ. Christians are generally more familiar with the covenant that God made with Israel through Moses because this covenant receives the most attention in the Old Testament. The Mosaic Covenant is by far the clearest and most detailed picture of humanity finding death and then life *in* Jesus Christ. But all of the covenants between God and man, from Noah to David, served this same purpose. They are not isolated covenants with distinct purposes for different dispensations. They are various perspectives of the *one eternal covenant*, a collective picture of the true spiritual relationship that was to come.

We have to remember that God saw the end from the beginning.[3] Before the creation of the natural world or the existence of any earthly covenant, God's heart was set on a single thing. He had one aim from the beginning. Every aspect of natural creation, and every detail of God's inter-actions with humanity, flowed out from His eternal perspective. In other words, all natural things, including the covenants we read about in the Old Testament, were made with a view to His ultimate intention for man in Christ. These covenants were not experiments or trials, or unrelated, temporary institutions. They came out from God's view of His purpose just like a shadow is projected from a solid object, or a portrait emerges from what an artist is seeing. In a very real sense, God's perfect end was in view even before He created natural things to bear its image. He foreknew a people living in His Son before any of the Old Testament covenants created physical pictures of this reality. This is how we need to understand the old covenant. It is as though God were staring intently at the coming union between Christ and the church, and with that reality in view, He formed an earthly replica, a natural

---

[3] The truth is that the end and the beginning are the same; they are both Christ. He is the Alpha and Omega, the Beginning and End. The only difference between the end and the beginning is that in the end, we are brought back to the beginning in Christ. We return with Him, in Him, to the glory that He had with His Father before creation.

representation, portrait, or shadow of that anticipated spiritual relationship.

Therefore, there is a sense in which the old covenant is exactly the same as the new covenant. And yet, there is a sense in which they are completely different. They are the same in that they both have everything to do with Christ and with the reality of a people living in Him and relating to God the Father through Him. They are entirely different in that one is but a shadow or testimony; the other is the spiritual substance. They never contradict each other because a shadow aligns perfectly with its corresponding object. Yet, at the same time, the two are entirely distinct from each other because a shadow contains nothing of the actual object that is casting the shadow. You cannot hug the shadow of a loved one, or eat the shadow of a meal.

Therefore, the arrival and presence of Jesus Christ in His body the church *is* the newness of the new covenant. This is not a newness that is primarily related to time, that is to say, the new covenant is not simply *newer* or more recent. It is not like how someone might say, "Over there is my old soccer ball, but here is my new one." In this example, both soccer balls are the same kind of object and serve the exact same purpose. The only difference is that one was made some years before the other. The difference between the old and new covenants would be more like someone saying, "That horse is my old means of transportation, but this jet airplane is my new way of getting around." The jet is not simply newer with respect to time. Compared with the horse, the jet is entirely new in nature and kind. One is a muscular animal that eats grass. The other is a flying metal machine that burns fuel. In a similar way, the new covenant is not simply the most current relationship between God and man. Once again, the newness of the new covenant is the presence and experience of Christ Himself.

The Old Covenant Shadow

When we begin to understand these things, the books of Old Testament become a comprehensive portrait of Jesus Christ and our relationship to God in Him. In fact, in many Scriptures it is clear that the Holy Spirit carefully designed it this way. For instance, when God instructed Moses to build the tabernacle and its furniture, He solemnly warned him three times saying, "See to it that you make them according to the pattern which was shown you on the mountain."[4] The obvious implication in these Scriptures is that the tabernacle was to be carefully built to represent something else. What was the pattern that God showed Moses? The book of Hebrews tells us it was a "copy and shadow of the heavenly things"[5] that have now been realized in Christ. Not just the tabernacle and its furnishings, but "every jot and tittle"[6] of the law was an intentional brushstroke that depicted something of God's eternal purpose in His Son. Jesus did not come to destroy these pictures, patterns, and descriptions, but to fulfill them, to make them spiritually and eternally real in Himself.

---

[4] Exodus 25:9, 25:40, 26:30
[5] Hebrews 8:5
[6] Matthew 5:18

Therefore, we must understand the old covenant as a relationship with God in Christ through types and shadows, and the new covenant as the spiritual realization of every detail. The diagram on the following page attempts to illustrate this reality.

With the diagram on the following page I am attempting to illustrate how both old and new covenants are relationships with God in Christ. With the arrival of the new, "He has made the first obsolete."[7] But for centuries the old covenant functioned as a God-given pattern of a people abiding in Christ. As we have mentioned, God's perspective of this corporate people is given to us in Exodus – "Israel is my Son, even My First-born."[8] When Israel walked in covenant, within the boundaries of the law, they experienced a relationship with God that included life, blessings, forgiveness, increase, victory, etc. All of these were natural pictures of what have now become spiritual blessings in Christ.[9] But whenever Israel transgressed the covenant by walking outside the boundaries of the law, they encountered death on every side.

Under the old covenant, God had His people build a tabernacle that represented Christ dwelling in their midst. He carefully designed the priesthood to depict every aspect of the relationship. He gave them laws that reflected the nature of Christ. He required sacrifices and offerings that spoke of both the finished work of the cross and its ongoing effects in the midst of God's people. Every year Israel had to celebrate the seven annual feasts which

[7] Hebrews 8:13
[8] Exodus 4:22
[9] See Ephesians 1:3

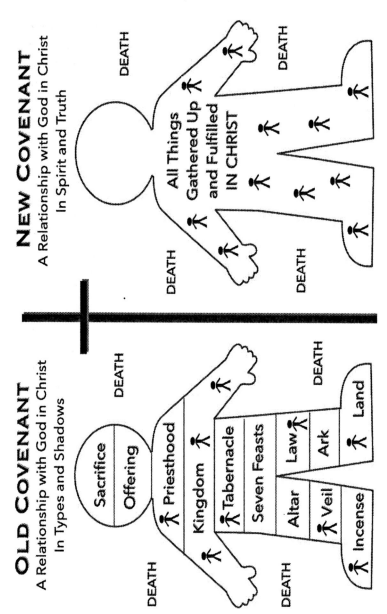

testified of Christ's journey from a single dying seed to a multi-membered resurrected harvest.[10] Their tribes, their garments, incense, crops, purification rites, relationships, rituals – *every* aspect of Judaism[11] – was an old covenant representation of a new covenant reality. But when God had filled up time with a complete testimony, Christ came and fulfilled the pattern with Himself. In the words of Paul, "But when the fullness of time had come, God sent forth His Son."[12]

This is precisely what Jesus explained to the Samaritan woman at the well. Like so many of us, the mind of this woman was full of religious questions and controversies. Perceiving Jesus to be a prophet, she asked him to settle what were then popular theological debates: Which race was the true people of God? Where was the correct place to worship Him? Jesus assured her that the true pattern was with the Jews, and that the Messiah arose from among them. But then, with just a few sentences, He dismissed the entire world of natural shadows and physical testimonies because the spiritual Substance had come. He said to her,

> *Woman, believe Me, the hour is coming when*
> *you will neither on this mountain, nor in Jerus-*

---

[10] For more on the feasts, see Jason Henderson, *The Feasts of Israel*, MSF Printing, 2012

[11] With the word Judaism, I am referring exclusively to that which had its origin in God, and am not including the man-made traditions that were added to and mixed with God's revelation. Of these traditions Jesus said, "You make the word of God of no effect through your tradition which you have handed down." (Mark 7:13)

[12] Galatians 4:4

*alem, worship the Father. You worship what
you do not know; we know what we worship,
for salvation is of the Jews. But the hour is
coming, and now is, when the true worshipers
will worship the Father in spirit and truth; for
the Father is seeking such to worship Him. God
is Spirit, and those who worship Him must
worship in spirit and truth.*[13]

The hour had come where worshipping God was no
longer about natural bloodlines, physical places, or cere-
monial representations of spiritual things.   God is Spirit!
And the physical pattern was never what His heart desired.
Standing before this Samaritan woman was the living
fulfillment of every promise and purpose of God.   The
pattern had a limited and passing glory, and with the
coming of Christ a far greater glory, and thus a far greater
kind of worship, had arrived.

The Greater Glory

What is glory? Glory has to do with the self-revelation
of God. God glorifies Himself by making Himself known,
causing Himself to be seen, experienced, and understood.
In the Old Testament, things or people glorified God when
they were used by Him to display or express something of
His nature, truth, or purpose. Through every aspect of His
involvement with man, be it the flood of Noah, the exodus
from Egypt, or just the furniture in the tabernacle, God was

---

[13] John 14:21-24

putting Himself on display. These things glorified God because in a specific and deliberate way, they caused Him to be seen and known among men.[14]

The natural and temporal revelations of God through events, objects, words, miracles, and people are what the Bible refers to as the lesser or passing glory. These things could never make God fully known or give true expression to His greatness. Rather, they offered God's people a temporary testimony, a fleeting demonstration or description of something that was in fact spiritual and eternal. For example, God is obviously not a burning bush, but he used a burning bush to reveal Himself to Moses. God is not a golden ark, but the Ark of the Covenant represented His presence in the midst of Israel. To a certain degree these things glorified God, but from before the creation of the world God had a plan to glorify Himself in a far greater way, to fully disclose Himself in and through His Son. Only through Jesus Christ could God perfectly make Himself known. Christ is the true Word of God, the way that God communicates Himself. He is "the radiance of His glory, the express image of His Person."[15] Though many Old Testament saints saw miracles and visions that testified of the Lord, John tells us that "No one has seen

---

[14] It is in this sense also that man comes to glorify God in Christ. Man does not possess something called glory that we can give to God. Humans do glorify God, but this is not by offering something of ourselves to Him, but rather by becoming in ourselves something that is from Him and expressive of Him. Believers give glory to God when our souls and our lives become a showcase for something that God is and something He has done. Like a diamond receiving and reflecting the sun, we glorify God when we become an increased expression of something that He is. God is always the source and the recipient of glory.

[15] Hebrews 1:3

God at any time. The only begotten Son, who is in the bosom of the Father, He has declared Him."[16] For this reason Jesus tells His disciples, "He who has seen Me has seen the Father."[17]

Notice how Paul compares the glory of God under the old covenant to the greater glory that has come in the new.

> *But if the ministry of death, written and engraved on stones, was glorious, so that the children of Israel could not look steadily at the face of Moses because of the glory of his countenance, which glory was passing away, how will the ministry of the Spirit not be more glorious? For if the ministry of condemnation had glory, the ministry of righteousness exceeds much more in glory. For even what was made glorious had no glory in this respect, because of the glory that excels. For if what is passing away was glorious, what remains is much more glorious.*[18]

Although things like the law, the tabernacle, and the miracles under the old covenant held a measure of glory, Paul's point is that the true self-revelation of God awaited the finished work of Jesus Christ in the cross. Only by being joined to Christ in His death, burial, and resurrection can a soul come to see and know the greater glory of

---

[16] John 1:18 The word "declared" here is the Greek word *exēgeomai* which means to unfold or uncover the true meaning of something. The English word exegesis is derived from this Greek word.

[17] John 14:9

[18] 2 Corinthians 3:7-11

God. In fact, just prior to the cross Jesus said, "'Father, glorify Your name.' Then a voice came from heaven, saying, 'I have both glorified it and will glorify it again.'"[19] God had already made Himself known in types and shadows, but the time had come to glorify Himself again in spirit and truth. The cross of Christ not only glorified God by manifesting His love in a visible, external way, but even greater than that, it made a way to bring us into Christ where all things of God are fully given and revealed. Speaking of this reality, the author of Hebrews tells us that Jesus "brought many sons to glory."[20] Paul, in a letter to Timothy, explains how God "called you by our gospel, for the obtaining of the glory of our Lord Jesus Christ."[21] And Jesus, on the night before His crucifixion, prayed these words: "Father, I desire that they also whom You gave Me may be with Me where I am, that they may behold My glory which You have given Me."[22]

God's plan involved glory from the very beginning. In all that He created, and through His activity in the natural creation, God made Himself known to varying degrees. Yet every aspect of the natural creation, and every way that He involved Himself in it, was a testimony of a far greater kind of self-revelation. In order to truly glorify Himself in His people, God had to actually bring us into Himself where He could be known.

In the Old Covenant, Moses longed to see the glory of God. In response to the cry of his heart, God brought him up to the top of His mountain, hid him in the cleft of the

---

[19] John 12:28
[20] Hebrews 2:10
[21] 2 Thessalonians 2:14
[22] John 17:24

rock, and made His glory pass before him. In perfect fulfillment of this story, God now raises us up in heavenly places in Christ, hides us in His Son, and opens the eyes of our heart to see far more than Moses ever did. Moses saw the "back parts"[23] of God because that is all his covenant allowed. However, "We all, with unveiled face, beholding as in a mirror the glory of the Lord, are being transformed into the same image from glory to glory."[24] We have come to "the light of the knowledge of the glory of God in the face of Jesus Christ."[25]

Our union with Christ is the fulfillment of every old covenant promise to know and abide in the glory of God. Now in Christ, we have both come to glory, and glory has come to dwell in us. This is the great "mystery which has been hidden from ages and from generations, but now has been revealed to His saints... Christ in you, the hope of glory."[26] The primary point in all of this is that an incredible change has taken place at the cross. God fulfilled the old covenant expectation for glory by replacing the natural shadows with the eternal and spiritual substance, and He has done this *in* Christ's body, the church.

A Change in Form and Place

Whether we're talking about the fulfillment of glory or the law or whichever types and shadows from the Old Testament, the word fulfillment always implies a change in

---

[23] Exodus 33:23
[24] 2 Corinthians 3:18
[25] 2 Corinthians 4:6
[26] Colossians 1:26-27

form and in place. The change in form is from the natural[27] to the spiritual. The change in place is from external to internal. This is universally difficult for Christians to understand at first. As human beings, the world that we naturally understand is external to us and knowable through our five senses. It is hard to believe and comprehend how or why God would seek to accomplish His eternal purpose *within* the human soul. The world outside of us seems so much more real, impressive, and important. Wouldn't God prefer to dwell and reign and establish His righteousness in the majestic natural creation? Wouldn't it be more of an accomplishment to fill planet Earth with the glory of God? The Scriptures answer with an emphatic no, but still we stumble over clear Bible verses and try to squirm our way out of obvious implications. Isaiah, for example, tells us that although heaven is God's throne and earth is His footstool, His home and eternal resting place is the soul of "him who is humble, contrite of spirit, and trembles at My word."[28] Jesus confused and offended the Pharisees insisting that the Kingdom of God "would not come with outward observation [Lit. ocular evidence]; nor will they say, 'See here!' or 'See there!' For indeed, the kingdom of God is within

---

[27] The old covenant obviously involved a good deal of supernatural events as well, but we must keep in mind that even God's *supernatural* activity in the earth made use of the natural realm. God worked miracles in Egypt, supernaturally parted the Red Sea, manifested Himself in a pillar of cloud and fire over the tabernacle, etc., but although these things had God as their source, they were still physical, external manifestations that men experienced with natural senses.

[28] Isaiah 66:2

[Lit. inside of] you."²⁹ Paul tells the church in Rome that the "the "the sufferings of this present time are not worthy to be compared with the glory which shall be revealed *in us*."³⁰ Though all of this certainly has outward and visible manifestation through our physical bodies in the earth, the consistent witness of Scripture describes the transition from promise to fulfillment as a change from external and natural to internal and spiritual.

Righteousness Fulfilled In Us

Nowhere is the concept of fulfillment more misunderstood, both in the apostles' day and in ours, than when it comes to the subject of righteousness. This is the topic of much of Paul's letter to the Romans. What is righteousness? How is it fulfilled? Biblically speaking, the word righteousness has to do with rightness, with a perfect alignment or conformity to God's nature and command. There really is only one thing that fits this description – Jesus Christ Himself. Christ, as the eternal Son of God, the "express image of His nature,"³¹ is the substance and definition of righteousness. He is the only One who rightly aligns with all that God is and desires.

For centuries leading up to the cross, God required that Israel relate to Him according to the written description of Christ's nature and work found in the Mosaic Law. However, as we have mentioned in a previous chapter, the

---

²⁹ Luke 17:20-21 "Outward observation" is Strong's G3906; *inspection, that is, ocular evidence.* "Within" is Strong's G1722; *inside.*

³⁰ Romans 8:18, emphasis mine

³¹ Hebrews 1:3

law described Christ and it required Christ, but it did not give Christ. In other words it demanded a righteousness that they did not possess. Though at times they could conform to the law in outward actions, they were always inwardly contrary to it. There was another nature working within them – the law of sin and death – warring against the law of God. Consequently, the law, which was good in itself, became a "ministry of condemnation"[32] and a "ministry of death"[33] to the unrighteous adamic man. This is exactly the predicament that Paul describes in Romans chapter seven.

> *Or do you not know, brethren (for I am speaking to those who know the law), that the law has jurisdiction over a person as long as he lives? For the married woman is bound by law to her husband while he is living; but if her husband dies, she is released from the law concerning the husband. So then, if while her husband is living she is joined to another man, she shall be called an adulteress; but if her husband dies, she is free from the law, so that she is not an adulteress though she is joined to another man.*[34]

With this analogy, Paul is saying that the relationship between the law and the natural man is comparable to the relationship between a husband and a wife. Just as a wife is bound to her husband until death (even though she may

---

[32] 2 Corinthians 3:9
[33] 2 Corinthians 3:7
[34] Romans 7: 1-3

long to be joined to another), so too the adamic man is bound to the law of God. Watchman Nee uses the following anecdote to expound upon these verses.[35]

Imagine there is a wife who is married to a man named Law. Mr. Law is a very good and righteous man. He is honest, faithful, and consistent, always living according to his standards. And even though Mr. Law is a perfectionist who insists that everything be done in just the right way, he cannot really be blamed or criticized for this because his expectations are entirely legitimate. He asks for nothing that is unreasonable or inappropriate. There is really nothing wrong with the man, and nothing wrong with what he expects from his wife.

The problem in the relationship lies with her. She is inconsistent, careless, and weak. She wants to please her husband but she finds their marriage incredibly frustrating and discouraging because she constantly falls short of his expectations. She is aware of her mistakes and knows that he has every right to demand what he does, but realizing this does not make the relationship any easier. The two are a horrible match, and the woman has all but given up hope.

Secretly this woman longs to be married to another man. There is a man she knows that is just as good and honest and consistent as Mr. Law. And even though this other man has the exact same standards and demands as her husband, everything he expects of her he also gives her the ability to do. Every weakness of hers he makes up for by his strength. Every one of her failures becomes an

---

[35] The following is an adaptation of an analogy found in: Watchman Nee, *The Normal Christian Life,* chapter 9 *The Meaning and Value of Romans Seven*

opportunity for him to succeed on her behalf. If only she could marry this other man and be free from a life of perpetual failure and condemnation! But alas, she is bound to Mr. Law until one of them dies. In the words of Paul the apostle, "The law has jurisdiction over a person as long as he lives."[36]

It is with regard to this very situation that Paul presents the miraculous solution in the following verses of Romans 7.

> *Therefore, my brethren, <u>you also were made to die</u> to the Law through the body of Christ, so that you might be <u>joined to another</u>, to Him who was raised from the dead, in order that we might bear fruit for God.*[37]

Can you see what Paul is saying? You are the woman. The first husband is the written Law consisting of right-eous commandments. Christ is the second husband. And the fruit that Paul mentions is the increase of Christ, the harvest of God's perfect Seed. The law does not die because the righteous standard of God never changes. But w h e n *we die* with Christ we are freed from this condemning relationship and are joined to the very One that the law describes! This freedom from the law is not the liberty to live our own lives without fear of judgment, as some wrongly suggest. Far from it! Our liberty in Christ is the freedom *from* our lives and all of the condemnation that rightly goes with it. We are crucified to the flesh and made alive by the Spirit, receiving in our soul the life of the

---

[36] Romans 7:1
[37] Romans 7:4, emphasis mine

One who produces the fruit of His Spirit.

Christ, the second husband, requires of us just what the law has always demanded, but now that we are joined to Him, we discover that He gives to us, and works *in us*, all that He also requires of us. This is called grace. Grace is a relationship with God where Jesus Christ is made unto us all that God has ever desired and required. John says, "For the law was given through Moses, but grace and truth came through Jesus Christ."[38] Grace is where the Person of righteousness fulfills the law *in us* by His own indwelling Spirit. Christ in us is the fulfillment of the law. In the very next chapter of Romans, Paul says exactly that.

> *For the law of the Spirit of life in Christ Jesus has set you free from the law of sin and of death. For what the Law could not do, weak as it was through the flesh, God did by sending His own Son in the likeness of sinful flesh, on account of sin: He condemned sin in the flesh, so that the righteous requirement of the Law might be fulfilled in us, who do not walk according to the flesh but according to the Spirit.*[39]

We should pay careful attention to how Paul uses the word fulfillment in these verses. He deliberately does not say that righteousness is fulfilled *by us*. Jesus once told the Jews, "Unless your righteousness exceeds the righteousness of the scribes and Pharisees, you will by no

---

[38] John 1:17
[39] Romans 8:2-4, emphasis mine

means enter the kingdom of heaven."[40] This statement no doubt shocked His listeners, but Jesus knew that true righteousness is not produced by any natural man. He said, "With men this is impossible, but with God all things are possible."[41] Through the finished work of the cross, the righteous requirements of the law can now be fulfilled *in us* because the Person of righteousness Himself lives and governs within His body, the church. True righteousness does not consist in actions done by man, but rather in the obedient Son who lives in man, the righteous King who establishes His kingdom in the land of our soul. The multitude of written old covenant commands are fulfilled by the "implanted Word"[42] who imparts His nature and forms Himself in our soul. In this way the shadow is replaced by the substance. The law of the letter has become "the law of the Spirit of Life in Christ Jesus."[43] The natural and the external are now perfectly realized in the spiritual and internal. Christ Himself fulfills all that God desires, and He does so in the soul of everyone who is born from above.

---

[40] Matthew 5:20
[41] Matthew 19:26
[42] James 1:21
[43] Romans 8:2

Chapter XII

Spiritual Blindness

Both the Old and New Testament are literally filled with descriptions of what God has accomplished through the cross. Among other things, we've mentioned how the cross brought the judgment of the adamic world in the death of Christ and the birth of a new creation in His resurrection. It established a new covenant with God, changing the shadow to the substance, and thereby fulfilling every promise and prophecy in the person of Jesus Christ. However, the question remains for many, "Why do these things seem so foreign to me? If all of this is true, then why isn't it my experience?" This is an important question and one that receives a great deal of attention in the apostles' letters to the churches.

Born Into a New World

I think we can begin to answer this question by reflecting upon the birth of a child. When babies are born they suddenly find themselves in a world that they do not understand. To them, everything about this world is entirely new and different. Their little bodies shiver with cold having never before felt the air. Their eyes squint when they see light for the very first time. The sounds and touches, the breathing, the eating, the people, *everything* is so foreign and strange. There is virtually nothing in this new world that feels familiar or that makes any sense to a baby.

As adults, we understand that the reason for their ignorance and confusion has nothing to do with a lack of life. In other words, we understand that growing up to adulthood will not involve acquiring more human life, but rather coming to know, understand, and use the life that is already there. Even newborn babies have all the life they need, and all that they will ever possess. And as we try to help our babies become accustomed to their new environment, we know that the goal is not to make the world feel more like the womb. We may do this in the beginning to comfort a newborn by swaddling them and holding them tight, but we realize that learning to be at home in the world will eventually involve leaving womb-life far behind.

As always, the natural was designed to parallel the spiritual. The experience of a newborn baby is in many ways a perfect picture of what happens when a person is born of the Spirit. With spiritual birth, the human soul suddenly finds itself in a life and world that is foreign to us in every way. Though our bodies continue to experience the natural realm, our souls are immediately "delivered from the dominion of darkness and transferred into the kingdom of the Son of His love."[1] Right away we are "made

---

[1] Colossians 1:13

alive together with Christ...raised up together, and made to sit together in the heavenly places in Christ Jesus."[2] But just like natural babies, spiritual babies are perfectly ignorant of the life we have received and the realm that is now our true home. In Christ everything is different and new, and our understanding of natural things is of no use to us here. In fact, the most foolish thing we can do is attempt to utilize the wisdom and knowledge of the adamic man to understand spiritual reality. Scripture is replete with warnings against this very thing. Even to Job, a good and God-fearing man, the Lord spoke from a whirlwind saying, "Who is this who darkens counsel by words without knowledge?"[3] To Isaiah He says, "For My thoughts are not your thoughts, nor are your ways My ways... for as the heavens are higher than the earth, so are My ways higher than your ways, and My thoughts than your thoughts."[4] In Paul's first letter to the Corinthians, he says plainly, "But the natural man does not receive the things of the Spirit of God, for they are foolishness to him; nor can he know them, because they are spiritually discerned."[5] In speaking of the natural man, Paul is not merely referring to non-believers. This term certainly includes unsaved people, but the natural man is simply the man that we are by nature, including whatever measure of his thoughts, ways, and desires still operate in the hearts of Christians. The natural man cannot understand spiritual things because he lives in a world of shadows and sees with an entirely different

---

[2] Ephesians 2:5-6
[3] Job 38:2
[4] Isaiah 55:8-9
[5] 1 Corinthians 2:14

light, a light that Jesus called darkness.[6]

Just like natural babies born into a brand new world, our failure as Christians to experience the fullness of the world that is Christ is not due to a lack of spiritual life. Christ's life is not given out in measures or degrees. Once we are born of the Spirit, we have all of Christ that there is to have. Our failure to abide in and experience the greatness of Christ has only to do with the fact that like an infant, we have no spiritual understanding of who or where we are. And again, far worse than spiritual ignorance is the presumption that natural understanding will be useful in this new World.[7] That would be like a baby attempting to employ the knowledge accumulated during nine months in the womb to understand things like birds, oceans, sunlight, and rain. Womb-knowledge simply isn't helpful once you're on the other side. In the same way, natural knowledge and human intellect are simply not the way to know the truth as it is in Christ. To know spiritual reality you must have spiritual understanding. And spiritual understanding is not *our* understanding of spiritual things. Spiritual understanding is the understanding of the Spirit Himself working in the human heart.

---

[6] Matthew 6:23 – "If therefore the light that is in you is darkness, how great is that darkness!"

[7] With the word "World" here I am simply referring to Christ. Jesus Christ is obviously a Person, the second Person of the Trinity, the eternal Son and Word of God. But He is more than just a divine being. As those who come to live in Him, we experience Him as so much more than an external God. He is, for our soul, a new realm of life and truth and light and love. He is the temple of God, the mountain of God's inheritance where God and His redeemed creation live together as one. He is the Head to His body, the church, the Light to the heavenly Jerusalem, the Vine in which many branches abide, and so much more.

What I am suggesting to you is that as believers, we are immediately born of the Spirit and "our life is hidden with Christ in God."[8] And yet, we are in Him as those who cannot naturally see. We have received Christ as our life, but unless He is also the light that shines in our hearts to show us all that is spiritually real, then we walk in total darkness. Without question, spiritual sight is the greatest need in the heart of every born-again man or woman. Again, T. Austin-Sparks' comments are helpful.

> *As we contemplate the state of things in the world today, we are very deeply impressed and oppressed with the prevailing malady of spiritual blindness. It is the root malady of the time. We should not be far wrong if we said that most, if not all, of the troubles from which the world is suffering, are traceable to that root, namely, blindness. The masses are blind; there is no doubt about that. In a day which is supposed to be a day of unequalled enlightenment, the masses are blind. The leaders are blind, blind leaders of the blind. But in a very large measure, the same is true of the Lord's people. Speaking quite generally, Christians are today very blind.*[9]

We Are the Darkness

Accepting our total ignorance of all spiritual things is an incredibly important step towards spiritual growth. It

---

[8] Colossians 3:3

[9] T. Austin-Sparks, *Spiritual Sight*, Chapter 1 - The Man Whose Eye Is Opened

may feel like a step backwards for those who have been Christians for years, but it is an essential step that few are willing to take. The truth of the situation, if we are willing to face it, is actually uglier than mere ignorance. Paul describes the natural condition of the human heart and mind as "darkness"[10] and "enmity towards God."[11] Our minds are not only lacking truth, they are naturally quite hostile to it.

If you think back to the creation account, the very first thing that God spoke into existence was the light. He said, "Let there be light! And there was light."[12] Then we read that God divided the light from the darkness. But where did this darkness come from? God never said, "Let there be darkness!" The obvious answer to this question is that darkness does not need to be created. It is simply the absence of light. Darkness is nothingness; it exists wherever light does not. So in the beginning God began His work of creation calling attention to these two things. He gave them names and then divided them from each other. By doing so, the Lord painted a vivid picture of something that all believers need to understand: darkness is a reality and an experience wherever light is not shining.

What is light? Simply put, light is what shows us what is real. Only in light can you see what is around you. Only in light are you aware of what is true. In darkness nothing can be seen or known for certain. And the darkness that we read about in the Genesis creation story was only a type and shadow of a much more serious condition. True darkness is the condition of the human soul that lives and

---

[10] Ephesians 5:8
[11] Romans 8:7
[12] Genesis 1:3

thinks in the perfect absence of spiritual light. In fact, because of the lie and the subsequent fall of man, the condition of humanity became the enemy's kingdom of darkness.[13] It is a kingdom where Satan can influence and deceive in any way he wishes because there is no light for us to discern what is real. This is the darkness of the fallen adamic soul, the darkness that resides in us until the light of Christ shines within.

Though most have a far more elevated view of themselves, the truth remains that the darkness of the human heart is a far blacker place than any external or natural darkness. Of it Jeremiah writes, "The heart is deceitful above all things, and desperately wicked; who can know it?"[14] Jesus warned the Jews saying, "If the light that is in you is darkness, how great is that darkness!"[15] Elsewhere He said to them, "This is the judgment, that the light has come into the world, and men loved darkness rather than light, because their deeds were evil."[16]

In Ephesians 5, Paul tells the church, "Formerly you were darkness, but now you are light in the Lord. Walk therefore as children of light."[17] Notice how he says "you *were* darkness." He does not say "formerly you were influenced by darkness," or "formerly you had lots of dark ideas

---

[13] See Luke 4:5-7 "Then the devil, taking Him up on a high mountain, showed Him all the kingdoms of the world in a moment of time. And the devil said to Him, "All this authority I will give You, and their glory; <u>for this has been delivered to me</u>, and I give it to whomever I wish. Therefore, if You will worship before me, all will be Yours."

[14] Jeremiah 17:9

[15] Matthew 6:23

[16] John 3:19

[17] Ephesians 5:8

and desires." According to Paul, darkness is not something we believed; darkness is what we were. It was our nature and constitution. It was how we saw and related to the world. So Christ came into a world of darkness as the only existing light. He was not just the brightest light; He was the only true light in a world of pitch black humanity. For this reason He said, "I am the light of the world. He who follows me shall not walk in darkness, but have the light of life."[18]   And seeing Him from far off, Isaiah the prophet wrote:

> *Arise, shine; For your light has come! And the glory of the LORD is risen upon you. For behold, the darkness shall cover the earth, and deep darkness the people; But the LORD will arise over you, and His glory will be seen upon you. The Gentiles shall come to your light, and kings to the brightness of your rising.*[19]

Jesus Christ offers the world a light, and the light that He offers is the *light of life*. We must understand that the light is part of the life; it is not separate. Therefore, in order to know Christ's light, mankind has to receive and walk in Christ's life, leaving their own behind, crucified and buried. Just like natural light and darkness, Adam and Christ can never mix together. The presence of the one dispels the other, and in every way knowing the one costs us the other. In God's view, the two have been divided from the very beginning.

Therefore, in order for us to know anything other than darkness and fallen adamic imaginations, we need the light

---

[18]   John 8:12
[19]   Isaiah 60:1-3

that is Christ to shine in our souls, displacing everything that was formerly there. When this happens, there is a terrible and wonderful realization that takes place. From deep within us, from a place we have never before been able to see, our soul cries out, "I see it now! I am not a good man who struggles with darkness. I am the darkness pretending to be a good man!" Suddenly we understand why man hides from God's light: men love darkness because we are evil, and the light proves it beyond any shadow of doubt. And men love religion because it is a fictitious place where we can sit in darkness and pretend to have light. With religion we teach about light, but we keep a safe distance. We sing about light, but we dare not approach it. Because the moment that God's light actually touches our soul, the world we have known comes to an end and we start over in Christ with absolutely nothing but Him.

Jesus Christ is not a light that merely shines *upon* us, guiding us, helping us, and filling in the blanks. He is a far greater light than that. When we experience the light of His life it is as though God shouts, "Let there be light!" in our hearts, dividing it from the darkness, filling our soul with His eternal perspective, and removing everything else. With this very reality in view, and using Genesis 1 as the pattern, Paul writes to the Corinthians:

> *For it is the God who commanded light to shine out of darkness, who has shone in our hearts to give the light of the knowledge of the glory of God in the face of Jesus Christ.*[20]

---

[20] 2 Corinthians 4:6

The spiritual light that shines in our heart is that of which natural light is only a type and shadow. Christ is the greatest of all lights, the one who "makes the moon disgraced and the sun ashamed."[21] With natural light we can see the earth and we become aware of what is physically real. But when the light of life dawns in our hearts we awake from the dead and the eyes of our heart behold the face of Jesus Christ.

The Carnal Mind

What is our primary problem as Christians? Why don't we experience all that the Bible presents to us as a finished work in Christ? The answer is almost too simple to satisfy us. Our primary problem is that we do not know the truth. Often we don't even understand *how* to know the truth. We have received salvation, but we do not know the salvation that we have received. We know that Jesus is the truth, but we know very little of the truth that is Jesus. Just because we are Christians does not mean that we know what it means to relate to God in His Son. Just because we know certain things to be true, does not mean that they feel true or seem real to us in any way.

The natural man thinks that acquiring information is learning, and that can certainly be true when it comes to natural things. But spiritual realities are not learned by gathering information, even if that information consists of Bible verses and correct theology. As a matter of fact, the natural mind is not even the correct faculty for knowing spiritual reality. Nobody tries to hear a sunset or attempts

---
[21] Isaiah 24:23

to see a Mozart piano solo. We know that the ear is not the faculty for seeing, nor the eye the correct faculty for hearing. In a very similar way, the things of God are simply not accessible to the natural mind. Notice Paul's strong words on this subject to the Ephesians:

> *This I say, therefore, and testify in the Lord, that you should no longer walk as the rest of the nations walk, in the futility of their mind, having their understanding darkened, being alienated from the life of God, because of the ignorance that is in them, because of the blindness of their heart.*[22]

And to the Romans he writes:

> *For the mind of the flesh is death, but the mind of the Spirit is life and peace; because the mind of the flesh is enmity towards God; for it is not being subjected to the Law of God, for neither can it be. And those being in the flesh are not able to please God.*[23]

Paul does not say that the mind of the flesh is *at* enmity with God. He says that it *is* enmity with God. The famous preacher Charles Spurgeon has this to say about Paul's statement:

> *The carnal mind, Paul says, is enmity against God. He uses a noun, and not an adjective... It*

---

[22] Ephesians 4:17-18, emphasis mine

[23] Romans 8:6-8; LitV Translation, Jay P. Green

is not black, but blackness; it is not at enmity,
but enmity itself; it is not corrupt, but corrup-
tion; it is not rebellious, it is rebellion; it is not
wicked, it is wickedness itself.[24]

When Scripture speaks of the carnal mind, or the mind of the flesh, it is not just referring to what we consider immoral or improper thinking. The carnal mind is simply the earthly, natural, unrenewed mind. It is the mind of the adamic man no matter what he is thinking or desiring. This mind does not apprehend spiritual reality because of both natural limitations and inherent corruption. We have already discussed how the nature of sin reigns in the natural man. Man sees all things through the lens of the lie, interacting with the world from a purely self-centered and self-motivated perspective. But even if sin did not govern the natural mind, it was still created by God to understand and relate to a natural, physical environment. The mind is great for driving cars and doing crossword puzzles, but when it trespasses into the realm of spiritual understanding it only causes problems.

True spiritual knowledge takes place in the soul.[25] It is an inward experience of resurrected life, not a mental accumulation of true concepts. I'm not suggesting that we need to be un-intelligent people in order to know Christ, but the truth is that knowing the Lord has nothing to do with being smart. God's goal is not to educate human minds about the person and work of Jesus Christ. God's desire is to form the life of His Son in our souls, and until

[24] Charles Spurgeon; Sermon entitled "*The Carnal Mind Enmity Against God*" April 22, 1855
[25] I use the terms heart and soul synonymously.

that begins to happen, all of our Christian knowledge is superficial and powerless. Natural intelligence and education can certainly be helpful in the earth, but they are not a true advantage in spiritual growth. At times such things can even become a distraction, being yet another occasion for human pride.

Oftentimes, we grow frustrated in our relationship with the Lord because we expect God to make Himself known to our natural mind. We want Him to explain Himself, to make sense of things before we will believe Him. But God's goal has nothing to do with gratifying our natural minds or satisfying our curiosity. His interaction with human hearts is not with the hope that we will mentally understand and agree with His words. Rather, His dealings with us are always directed towards a greater experience of the living, implanted Word of God. This can be easily demonstrated in the gospels, especially the gospel of John. There were so many occasions where Jesus could have answered questions, explained Himself in plain language, or removed all doubt as to who He was. But His teachings were never aimed at the natural mind of man.

At one point there was a crowd of thousands swarming around Him, astounded by the miraculous multiplication of bread and fish, and ready to proclaim Him king of Israel. But rather than offer them a three-point sermon clarifying His messianic mission, He said, "Most assuredly, I say to you, unless you eat the flesh of the Son of Man and drink His blood, you have no life in you."[26] How strange this must have sounded, especially to an audience who had been forbidden by God to drink blood since

---

[26] John 6:53

the time of Noah! Nearly all of them were confused and offended. They grumbled to each other, "This is a hard saying; who can understand it?... and many of His disciples went back and walked with Him no more."[27] Then Jesus, without explaining Himself or saying a single word to console the crowd, turned to His disciples and said, "Do you also want to go away?"[28]

On another occasion, the Jews were arguing with Jesus about His Father. Not understanding His words, and growing increasingly offended as the conversation wore on, the Jews resorted to insults saying, "Do we not say rightly that You are a Samaritan and have a demon?"[29] But Jesus knew they could not understand, and He knew the reason why. He said, "Why do you not understand My speech? It is because you are not able to hear My word... I know that you are Abraham's descendants, but you seek to kill Me, because My word has no place in you."[30] Their failure to understand was not due to mental weakness or a misinterpretation of words. They could not understand Jesus' teaching because there was no room for His Word in their heart.

There is a difference between asking questions and seeking the truth. People ask questions for a lot of different reasons. Sometimes we are just curious and desire more information. Sometimes we are motivated by pride and seeking to amass knowledge. Much of the time our questions about spiritual things are not even really questions; they are simply attempts to confirm what we

---

[27] John 6:60, 66
[28] John 6:67
[29] John 8:48
[30] John 8:43, 37

already think we know. We ask questions hoping to fit the answers into our preconceived ideas, theologies, and concepts. All of this can have the outward appearance of seeking truth, but to people with these motivations Jesus would still say, "You cannot understand My words because there is no room in your heart for My Word."

Even as Christians who faithfully read the Bible we can be "ever learning and never coming to the knowledge of the truth,"[31] because the truth is a Person who desires to make Himself known in the heart. In saying this, I am in no way questioning the greatness and importance of Scripture. From my abundant citations you can see how much I value God's written words. The Bible is true, reliable, and infallible, but even so, knowing God is much more than learning and believing true words with the natural mind. History is filled with shameful acts that are the direct result of fallen natural minds attempting to interpret and fight for spiritual reality. God's words without God's light can be a very dangerous thing.

Tablets of the Heart

The old covenant was a specific relationship with God, carved on tablets of stone, and placed inside the Ark of the Covenant. It was written for eyes to read, minds to learn, and hands to obey, and therein lay its weakness. The weakness of the old covenant was not with the words themselves but with the man who tried to understand and obey it. The adamic man was contrary in nature and spiritually blind. Even when he diligently studied and taught

---

[31] 2 Timothy 3:7

God's words, he never truly knew the Lord or walked in His ways.[32] But God's eternal purpose involved a far greater covenant, and one that was written in an entirely different place. Nearly 600 years before Christ, the prophet Jeremiah foretold a great change in God's relationship with man.

> *"Behold, days are coming," declares the LORD, "when I will make a new covenant with the house of Israel and with the house of Judah, not like the covenant which I made with their fathers in the day I took them by the hand to bring them out of the land of Egypt, My covenant which they broke, although I was a husband to them," declares the LORD. "But this is the covenant which I will make with the house of Israel after those days," declares the LORD, "I will put My law within them and on their heart I will write it; and I will be their God, and they shall be My people. They will not teach again, each man his neighbor and each man his brother, saying, Know the LORD, for they will all know Me, from the least of them to the greatest of them," declares the LORD, for I will forgive their iniquity, and their sin I will remember no more."[33]*

---

[32] After 1500 years of possessing, studying, and teaching the Law of Moses, Jesus could still categorically say to the Jews, "No one knows the Son except the Father. Nor does anyone know the Father except the Son, and the one to whom the Son wills to reveal Him." (Matthew 11:27)

[33] Jeremiah 31:31-34, emphasis mine

At about the same point in history, the prophet Ezekiel foresaw the same coming reality.

> *Then I will sprinkle clean water on you, and you will be clean; I will cleanse you from all your filthiness and from all your idols. Moreover, I will give you a new heart and put a new spirit within you; and I will remove the heart of stone from your flesh and give you a heart of flesh. I will put My Spirit within you and cause you to walk in My statutes, and you will be careful to observe My ordinances.[34]*

One could argue that Christians begin life in the Spirit at a considerable disadvantage. We are born into a world that is perfectly foreign, and the natural faculties that we are accustomed to using are of no help to us in Christ. This may be true, but God has provided all that we need to walk in the light because the new covenant is "not written with ink but with the Spirit of the living God, not on tablets of stone but on tablets of human hearts."[35]

---

[34] Ezekiel 36:25-27
[35] 2 Corinthians 3:3

Chapter XIII
Old Covenant Mentality

Although we sometimes use these terms synonym-ously, there is actually a great difference between the New Testament and the new covenant. The New Testament is a book, a collection of Spirit-inspired letters and narratives that make up the latter part of the Bible. The new covenant, however, is not a book; it is a relationship between God and the human soul in Jesus Christ. The New Testament *describes* the new covenant, but the two are not the same. This distinction is important because even though someone could read you the New Testament over and over, they could never teach you the new covenant. This is what the old covenant prophet Jeremiah described when he wrote about the greater covenant to come. He said, "No more shall every man teach his neighbor, and every man his brother, saying, 'Know the Lord.'"[1] Knowing the Lord is not a matter of familiarity with His words. Knowing the Lord has to do with God

---

[1] Jeremiah 31:34

placing you into His Son and then teaching you by His Spirit a life and relationship that are entirely new. Jesus said to the Jews, "It is written in your prophets, 'And they shall all be taught by God.'"[2]   Indeed, this is what our experience as Christians should be.   By His own Spirit of Truth, God desires to make real in our hearts everything that is real to Him.   However, to whatever extent Christians continue in their own ideas and understanding, they will inevitably hold onto natural shadows even after the spiritual substance has come.   In other words, where we have not been taught by God, we unknowingly attempt to relate to God in a man and a relationship that He has left behind.

The Painting and the Person

Imagine that there was a young artist who all her life had dreamed of getting married.   In her mind she had already envisioned the perfect man, the one who would fulfill all of her expectations. Somehow she knew that they would one day meet and fall deeply in love.   But in the meantime, while she patiently waited for him to appear, she sat down at her easel and began to paint the man of her dreams.   She began by sketching his outline, and then slowly and painstakingly added every detail that she longed to see become a reality.   She made him tall and athletic, with dark, wavy hair. She painted kindness in his eyes, a witty smirk on his lips, and a face that somehow projected both wisdom and humility.   On and on she

---

[2]   John 6:45

painted, for hours, weeks, and eventually months, perfecting the image of the man she longed to marry. When it was finally finished, and every detail of the painting expressed something of her expectation and desire, she sat down in front of her masterpiece with longing and excitement filling her heart.

One night, after some years had gone by, she went out to enjoy an evening with some friends. While they sat at a restaurant together, talking and laughing, a young man sitting alone on the other side of the room suddenly caught her eye. Her jaw dropped open and her eyes grew wide; she could hardly believe what she was seeing. It was him! It was the man in her painting, the exact same man! He was the same height with the same wavy hair. He had kindness in his eyes and the exact same expression on his face. He was the living, breathing reality of everything she had depicted in her painting. And he was looking at her the same way that she was looking at him.

After spending the evening together it was clear to both of them that they had met the person with whom they would spend the rest of their lives. When she returned home later that night, the first thing the artist did was walk to her room and take down the painting that had hung on the wall all of these years. She wrapped it in newspaper, and with a great smile of satisfaction, placed it in the attic where it would now be out of sight. She no longer needed the painting now that the person himself had finally come.

As we read this story I think it is obvious to us why the young artist put her painting away. It was not because she was tired of waiting, or because she eventually changed her mind about what she wanted. Quite the opposite was true.

She put the painting away because the perfect fulfillment had come. Now that she had met him, every detail of his portrait, no matter how perfectly it was painted, fell far short of experiencing his presence. But what if this story had taken an unexpected and tragic turn? What if, rather than beginning a life-long relationship with the man she met in the restaurant, the young woman decided to go home and continue her relationship with the painting? What if he called her on the phone the following evening and she refused the call, preferring rather to sit in her bedroom and stare at the painting? That would be absurd! Hollywood would never dream of making a movie like that.

As absurd as it is, this is precisely what we do with the presence of Christ in the new covenant and the relationship that has been given to us in Him. Though it may not be our intention, we invariably hold onto the pictures and shadows of Christ from the old covenant even after the Person and fulfillment of those pictures has come. God has put away the painting of Christ consisting of ceremonies and sacrifices and works of the law. He has folded it up like an old garment and put it away, because in Christ "all things have become new!"[3] But in more ways than we realize, our blindness to what has been made new keeps us enslaved to a man and a covenant that were crucified and buried with Christ. Paul was constantly dealing with the churches about this very thing. To the Galatians he writes:

> *But now after you have known God, or rather are known by God, how is it that you turn*

---

[3]   2 Corinthians 5:17

again to the weak and worthless elements[4], to which you desire again to be in bondage? You observe days and months and seasons and years. I am afraid for you, lest I have labored for you in vain.[5]

The days, months, seasons, and years mentioned here were parts of the old covenant system to which these Christians were still adhering. They were aspects of the God-given testimony of Christ, parts of the painting that had all come to their fulfillment as spiritual realities in Christ. Paul feared that, failing to see the present Substance, the Galatians were returning again to the elementary and powerless pictures. In their blindness they were actually enslaving themselves again to a testimony of something that had already come. To the church in Colossae, Paul writes something similar:

So let no one judge you in food or in drink, or regarding a festival or a new moon or sabbaths, which are a shadow of things to come, but the substance is of Christ... Therefore, if you died with Christ from the basic

---

[4] This word "elements" is the Greek word *stoicheion*, Strong's G4747. This is an important word used in the New Testament to describe the basic elements, first principles, or the ABC's of God's revelation to man in the old covenant shadows. When Paul refers to "the weak and beggarly *stoicheion*," he is referring to things like the laws, sacrifices, offerings, feasts, etc., that were shadows of the substance which is Christ. This word appears seven times in the New Testament, always with the same meaning. See Galatians 4:3, 4:9, Colossians 2:8, 2:20, Hebrews 5:12, 2 Peter 3:10, 3:12

[5] Galatians 4:9-11

> *principles of the world, why, as though living
> in the world, do you subject yourselves to regu-
> lations—'Do not touch, do not taste, do not
> handle,' which all concern things which perish
> with the using—according to the command-
> ments and doctrines of men? These things
> indeed have an appearance of wisdom in self-
> imposed religion, false humility, and neglect of
> the body, but are of no value against the indul-
> gence of the flesh.*[6]

Again, the issues of food and drink, feasts and
sabbaths, were aspects of the old covenant. There were
very specific laws regulating clean and unclean foods. The
seven annual feasts were mandatory convocations for every
Jewish family. These things Paul calls "shadows of things
to come," but the substance of each of them was the person
of Jesus Christ. Paul understood that these believers had
died with Christ to the world of Adam and to his covenant
of types and shadows. Why then, he asks, having been
raised up with Christ into a new life and covenant, were
they seeking to find righteousness in rules for behavior and
works of the flesh? Why were they holding onto the
painting when the Person had come?

This old covenant mentality is something that every
Christian struggles with. Regardless of whether we are
familiar with the Old Testament and its ceremonies and
laws, we all naturally try to relate to God in the flesh in a
way that makes sense to our natural minds. Obviously
Christians do not usually build altars of stone and sacrifice

---

[6] Colossians 2:16-17, 20-23

goats during Sunday morning service, but when we fail to see what God has accomplished at the cross, we seek to please Him according to our own understanding of regulations, commandments, and doctrines of men.

An old covenant mentality is when we fail to see what it means to relate to God in Christ and so we hold to a fictitious relationship that involves things that God has made obsolete, things He does not even recognize. When we haven't seen our death with Christ or His indwelling life in us, we go right on trying to satisfy Him with the very man that the cross has rejected. We ask the Lord, "Can I touch this? Can I go here? Can I say that? Do you want me to sing this? Build that? Pray this? Do that? Should I wear this and not that? How much should I tithe? How much should I fast? Somebody please tell me how I'm supposed to act!" But the truth is that you're dead. The cross is the end of your act. And all of these questions demonstrate a great misunderstanding of the relationship you have with God. Our confusion is like a son or daughter thinking they were a cat, and doing everything in their power to relate to their parents and please them as a pet. "Do you want me to purr louder? Use the litter box? Catch mice? Do I shed too much? Meow too loudly?" If a child were to ask these questions, it would be difficult to know how to answer. The very questions themselves are senseless because they arise from a series of profound misunderstandings. Obviously the child does not know the first thing about who they really are or the relationships that they have. And unless they can be convinced of the greatness of their confusion, little, if any, progress will be made.

The Hand Analogy

The authors of the New Testament frequently refer to Jesus as the Head of His corporate body, the church.[7] This is more than a simple metaphor. We are literally joined to Christ like a body is to a head and as such we are meant to function as members that give expression to His mind, nature, and will. The natural body was no doubt designed by God to testify of this far greater Head-body relationship.

To illustrate just how little we comprehend this incredible reality, let's consider our natural bodies for a moment. Take, for example, the relationship that exists between the hand and the head. Obviously the human head and hand are bound together in a living union. Though there is distinction between them, there is no separation. They share the exact same life and purpose. But imagine, for the sake of illustration, that one day my hand suddenly grew lips, coughed a few times, and began to speak. Then turning to me it says, "Oh Jason, how I long to be closer to you. My heart's desire is that you would come and visit with me, that our relationship would be far more intimate."

After recovering from the initial shock of watching one of my body parts speak, I look at my hand and say, "Hand, there has obviously been some sort of misunderstanding. That is a very nice thing for you to say, but you see, you are already joined to me, and I am joined to you. In fact my very life is flowing through you at this very moment. There is no way that we could ever be any closer."

---

[7] See for example, Romans 12:4-5; 1 Corinthians 12:12-27; Ephesians 1:23, 3:16, 4:12-16, 5:23; Colossians 1:18, 1:24, 2:19

The hand seems puzzled, pauses for a moment, and then replies, "Wow, that is deep! I'll keep that in mind. Now would you please tell me what I can do to be more like you? I'll do anything you ask. I will pray, fast, do good deeds. You name it."

Feeling a bit confused and not exactly sure how to respond, I eventually answer, "But Hand, you don't have to be like me. That's not even what I want. I don't want you to try to copy my life. I simply want you to contain and manifest my life."

At this point the hand is becoming a bit frustrated. It replies, "That sounds interesting... I think I read about that in a book one time. But let's get *practical* here. Can you just give me a list of good things that I can do to please you? How about a seven-step plan to reach my appendage potential? Or how about a prophetic word that explains how to operate in my five-finger calling? Or maybe a book called 'What Would Jason Do?' I just want to be useful in the body!"

Feeling quite sorry for the hand, and nearly certain that I'll never give him the answer he's looking for, I reply, "Poor Hand, there is something very foundational that you don't seem to understand. You can go ahead and try to do all sorts of things to please me, but the only thing I really want is for you to let me live my life in and through you. Apart from me you can do no good thing because, when it comes to my body, goodness is bound up with my life and my will. Your misunderstandings are having a drastic effect on your experience of our relationship. Why do you want to serve me as one who is separate when you can live as one who is joined?"

The hand hangs his head in sorrow and for a while says nothing. Finally, after several minutes of silence, he says, "There must be somebody that can explain these riddles in a way that makes sense to me. I need to find another member of this body who can interpret Jason's words and tell me what I need to do."

This is a ridiculous little story but it illustrates something important. What was wrong with my hand? In a few words, my hand's problem was that it had a life and a relationship that it did not understand. It clearly had no idea where it was, or to whom it had been joined. And to make matters worse, instead of allowing me to enlighten and explain, the hand tried to define the relationship and then relate to me according to what felt familiar and logical. He tried to employ his own understanding in a body that did not belong to him. The sad result was that all of his assumptions and suggestions were absurd to me. They were not at all what I wanted from my hand. And even though I did everything in my power to help him understand, my true words did not mix with the hand's firmly established ideas. The frustrating outcome was that two separate and opposing minds were trying to operate in the same body.

Like the hand in this story, one of our most funda-mental problems in the body of Christ is the failure to comprehend our union with Christ. Paul wrote, "He who is joined to the Lord has become one spirit with Him."[8] This is something that old covenant believers never experi-enced. At times God dwelt as a cloud in the midst of their camp, but He did not dwell in their souls. His people

---

[8] 1 Corinthians 6:17

served an external copy and shadow of this living union with their specific rules, sacrifices, ceremonies, and works of the law. But even though the cross has now fulfilled these shadows, removed the veil, and grafted us into Christ as branches joined to a vine, we continue striving to please the Lord with "the weak and worthless elemental things."[9]

If truth be told, this is more than a simple misunderstanding. Though our desires to serve God in the flesh may seem to be expressions of humility and simple confusion, lying beneath our confusion is often a contentious adamic mind filled with religious pride. We don't like to admit it, and perhaps we are often unaware of it, but we actually *prefer* a relationship with God that is external and separate. Not only does this make more sense to our natural minds and give us something practical that we can do, but it also allows us to hold onto our natural lives and strive to make them acceptable to God. Holding onto an old covenant mentality is just one more way that we try to save ourselves from the cross.

The point I'm trying to make is that to whatever extent we perpetuate our external, man-centered ideas about relating to God, we will fail to experience the life of Christ to which we have been joined. When there are multiple minds operating in the one body of Christ, the result is always confusion, division, and continual disappointment. There is no end to the list of ways we attempt to drag our own adamic goals and old covenant mindsets into the Lord's body. We need to face this. It is not a question of *if* we are doing this; it is always a question of *how*, or *in what way*. Nobody makes a smooth and seamless trans-

---

[9] Galatians 4:9 NASB

ition from the old covenant to the new, or from the mind of Adam to the mind of Christ. Learning Christ involves an incredible collision of minds, natures, and realms. Darkness meets light for the first time, and the human soul must be progressively conquered by a foreign and righteous King.

When our hearts refuse to let go of the old man with his external covenant of types and shadows, Christianity can become a confusing tangle of contradictory ideas where we are easily "tossed to and fro and carried about with every wind of doctrine."[10] Like the hand in the aforementioned story, we end up praying for things we already have and longing for things that have already come. In our songs we beseech the Lord to come down and visit like the days of old when, in fact, He has already made us members of His own body. Though we no longer use the Jewish temple or animal sacrifices, we still imagine there to be spiritual places, holy priests, and sacred garments, rituals, and words. We actually think the house of God is a building that we visit on Sundays rather than the Spirit-born soul of man. In our blindness, we try to know the Lord with the wrong mind, serve Him with the wrong man, and relate to Him through aspects of a covenant that has been obsolete for over 2000 years.

Knowing God's Gift

The next few chapters will deal with God's great solution to all of these problems, and how His truth becomes what is most real to us. But now we are still seeking to

---

[10] Ephesians 4:14

pinpoint the nature of our problem, to understand why the finished work of the cross often feels more like a doctrine than a present reality. The deficiency is not at all in what God has accomplished or given to us. The deficiency is always in what we have come to see, and the degree to which we are still holding on to religious ideas that God does not recognize.

The journey of spiritual growth is not like a staircase where we slowly progress from point A to B and onward to point Z. When it comes to spiritual life, we actually begin at Z, but with an A comprehension. In other words, we start at the end, having received the fullness of Christ the moment we are born of the Spirit. Z isn't where we are going; Z is where we already are. What then do we need? We need God's view of where we are and what we have to be the governing reality of our soul. So moving from A to B to C, etc. is really the process of our spiritual (not natural) comprehension catching up with spiritual reality. It is not about gaining new ground or reaching new levels of devotion, discipline, and service. Our journey of faith is a progressive, Spirit-given discovery and experience of all that we already have in Christ.

Imagine you had a close friend and you wanted to give them something really special for their birthday. You begin to save up your money and by the time their birthday arrives you are able to buy them an outstanding new computer. This computer is state-of-the-art, head and shoulders above the current competition. It is incredibly fast and has a virtually inexhaustible amount of memory. It has incredible graphic capabilities, high quality speakers and camera, and it comes loaded with an expensive software package, along with a full three year warranty. The birthday finally comes and you excitedly give your friend his gift. He opens it with a smile, sets it up on his desk, plugs everything in, and then immediately locates and begins to play the free version of solitaire that comes with every new computer. Wanting him to experience the full capacity of this incredible machine, you begin to describe all of its traits, abilities, programs, etc. But without looking up from his game, your friend calmly replies, "No thanks. Solitaire is really all that I'm interested in." And for the next several years, throughout the entire life of this amazing computer, it is never once used for anything other than a simple card game. Sadly, your friend never realized what an incredible gift you had given.

In some ways this is what we do with God's gift of salvation. We receive so much from God in one single package, but our comprehension of what we have becomes the limitation of what we experience. When we are born again, we know virtually nothing about this vast and bottomless ocean of divine grace, brilliance, love, and purpose that has been accomplished by Christ and "has been poured out in our hearts by the Holy Spirit who was given to us."[11] Were someone to ask us what we just received in Christ, our answers would be very much like the friend who imagined solitaire to be the fullness of his present. We might say, "I just received a free ticket to heaven!" Or, "God just gave me forgiveness of sins!" There is truth in these statements, but what else is involved in salvation? Have we seen the width and length and depth and height of the life that now resides in our soul?

---

[11] Romans 5:5

Have we seen in Christ the crucifixion of the world, the removal of the adamic man? Have we seen the resurrection and the life, the greatness of the new creation, the peace that exists in this one new man, the glory of the church? Or are we content with spiritual solitaire? All that God is and has, has been given to us in the Person of Jesus Christ, but the question that confronts us is whether we are satisfied with a small and blurry view of God's great gift. Are we content with old covenant shadows, trying to serve as one who is separate rather than live as one who has been joined? If we are, then that is all that we will know. The experience of Christ's indwelling life corresponds to the measure of His light that we allow to shine in our soul.

Chapter XIV
The School of Christ

Everyone who genuinely longs to know the truth will be confronted by the Spirit of God with an important question. It is a question that arises at almost every step of our walk with the Lord and our response to it plays an important part in our spiritual growth. The question is simply this: how wrong are you willing to be? Most Christians are willing to have their behavior corrected and their beliefs adjusted, but far fewer are willing to accept the incredible depth of our spiritual ignorance.

Imagine there was a patient in a psychiatric hospital who made an appointment with a doctor to seek help for depression. When he sat down with the doctor he began to explain his predicament. He said, "Doctor, I have been a government spy for nearly 20 years now. For the most part, I've been very content with my job. I've always found it exciting and rewarding, but ever since Sally and I decided to have children and the twins were born, I've found my job to be increasingly difficult. I still enjoy the work, but the time away from the family is becoming a burden. There is growing tension between my wife and I and a sense of distance between me and the kids. The mounting stress is starting to take its toll on me. For the first time in my life, I've really been struggling with depression. Can you help me?" The doctor thinks for a moment and then replies, "Well, that depends. How wrong are you willing to be?" The patient gives the doctor a confused look and says, "What do you mean?" The doctor responds, "I mean exactly what I said – how wrong are you willing to be? What if I told you that you are not a government spy and that you never have been one? What if I told you that you are not married, and that you don't have any children? What if I told you that you have been living in a psychiatric hospital for the past several years refusing medication to treat your schizophrenia? I most certainly can help you, but how wrong are you willing to be?"

With this story I am not at all implying that our spiritual ignorance has anything to do with mental illness. I'm simply trying to illustrate how our attempts to grow in Christ can be severely hindered by refusing to let the Lord take us all the way back to our most fundamental misunderstandings. It's easy for believers to read Christian books and involve themselves in various types of Christian education. It is another thing altogether to enroll in the Holy Spirit's school of Christ[1] where the true knowledge of God is "hidden from the wise and learned but revealed unto babes."[2] The work of the Spirit in the heart of every believer is never towards an objective learning about

---

[1] I borrow the term *School of Christ* from T. Austin-Sparks' incredibly valuable book by the same name. All of his books and articles are available for free on www.austin-sparks.net.

[2] Luke 10:21

Christ, but rather the inward learning of Christ, and there is all the difference in the world between these two things. The one results in an accumulation of ideas and information in the mind. The other results in the formation of Christ in the soul. T. Austin-Sparks says this:

> *We have been led to think in these meditations about being in the School of Christ, where all the learning, all the instruction, all the discipline, is toward knowing Christ, learning Christ; not learning about Christ, but learning Christ... We could take up everything there is about Christ as doctrine, as teaching, but that is not what we are after. That is not what the Lord is after at all. It is Christ Himself. He Himself is the living, personal embodiment, the personification of all truth, of all life, and the Lord's purpose and will for us is not to come to know truth in its manifold aspects, but to know the Person, the living Person in a living way, and that the Person being imparted to us, and we being incorporated into the Person, all the truth becomes living truth rather than merely theoretical or technical truth.[3]*

I believe everyone is invited by God into His school of Christ. Everyone is offered a front row seat and is granted the most competent Teacher that a soul could desire. In this school there are neither honor students nor those who are unfairly disadvantaged. ADD is not an issue, and high

---

[3] T. Austin-Sparks, *The School of Christ*, chapter 6, An Open Heaven

test scores will not help you. The cross has perfectly leveled the playing field so that natural giftings, intelligence, and personal connections are not at all decisive factors. The only relevant issue that confronts you every day in the Spirit's school of Christ is simply this: do you truly want to know the Lord? Don't fool yourself; words cannot answer this question. The question is answered by your heart every single day of your life.

A Different Kind of Knowing

One would think that our spiritual education starts when the Holy Spirit shows us something we don't know about Jesus. But even before this can really begin, He must show us something we don't understand about knowing. Failure to know Christ is not first a lack of information; it is first a misunderstanding about what knowing God even means. There are many ways to learn about Christ, but there is only one way to learn Christ. And just like all spiritual things, we soon realize that true spiritual knowledge is entirely foreign to the adamic man.

When it comes to natural knowledge, we are used to learning things through our senses. We see things with our eyes, hear with our ears, touch with our hands, and so on. This kind of knowing works well for most natural things, but we need to realize that there are some fairly serious limitations involved. First of all, natural learning generally involves observing and experiencing things that are external. We touch and see and hear things that are outside of us. And even after perceiving with our senses, we are still two steps away from saying we have learned something. First we must try to understand what we have perceived, and then we make some sort of application. I don't mean to get technical about the human learning process, I just want to make a simple point: natural knowing is not only external, but it also leaves *u s* as the ones who supply the comprehension and make the applications. And my point is that we are all so familiar with this kind of learning that we instinctively try to employ it in our relationship with God. We make a great mistake when we do this, however, because although God can be experienced by our five senses and our natural mind, He cannot be known that way.

The reason this is so important is because trying to know God the way we know other natural things is not only futile, it is dangerous as well. To illustrate why, imagine that a woman goes to church and sees a miracle right before her eyes. An old friend with a long history of illness is suddenly and completely healed by the Lord. Having witnessed something truly amazing, the woman says to herself, "That was incredible! I just saw the power of God heal my friend! This obviously means that He loves people, and therefore He must also love me!" For the next several months she is thrilled to be a Christian and never misses an opportunity to share with others about the love of God that she has come to know. But let's stop and ask an important question – how did she come to know God's love? The answer is that she witnessed something external to her, supplied her own understanding, and drew her own conclusions. In this particular case her conclusions happened to be true; God does indeed love people. But this kind of knowledge reveals its shortcomings another

Sunday morning when the same woman brings her daughter to church who has just been diagnosed with cancer. Following the service she leads the child to the front of the sanctuary where the leaders of the church gather to pray for her, just as they did with the friend who was healed. This time, however, the child is not miraculously healed. The leaders pray for hours but there is no noticeable change. And the mother, having witnessed something very different today, walks away heartbroken with new conclusions about the power and love of God.

Though for a time the woman in this story had drawn accurate conclusions about God based upon natural experiences, she had never truly known the Lord. I don't mean to say she was not saved. But receiving Christ and knowing Christ are not the same thing. The apostle Peter learned this lesson in a very unmistakable way. He had walked and talked with Jesus for months, perhaps years. He had seen the Lord with natural eyes and witnessed countless signs and miracles in the natural realm. There is no doubt that Peter had long believed Jesus to be the promised Messiah. However, one particular day as Jesus and the disciples came to Caesarea Philippi, Peter experienced a different kind of knowing, a deeper and brighter seeing that took place in the heart. When asked by Jesus, "Who do men say that I, the Son of Man, am?" Peter exclaimed, "You are the Christ, the Son of the living God!" Knowing very well what was taking place in Peter's heart, Jesus called attention to it, saying, "Flesh and blood has not revealed this to you, but My Father who is in heaven."[4] In other words, Jesus said, "Peter, seeing Me in flesh and

---

[4] Matthew 16:13-17

blood has not caused you to know me this way. Seeing this natural vessel, even when performing supernatural signs, is not the reason you can see what you see. What you now recognize and have come to understand is the work of My Father revealing His Son."

We see a similar thing in the story of the apostle Paul. Paul was no doubt shaken to the core when the Lord appeared to Him on the road to Damascus. In an instant he knew he had been wrong; he knew that Jesus was the Son of God, and that by persecuting the church Paul had been persecuting Christ Himself. This outward appearing of the Lord was clearly the turning point in Paul's life. But even though he saw a bright light with his natural eyes and heard the audible voice of God with his natural ears, this is not the kind of knowing that transformed Paul's soul, nor the knowing that he wrote about in his letters to the churches. In fact, Paul never mentioned this experience in any of his letters to the churches. Luke, the author of Acts, mentions it three times in retelling the story of Paul's conversion and his defense before Jewish and Roman authorities. But Paul never once encourages the body of Christ to seek similar external experiences of God, or to long for audible voices, bright lights, or miracles in the natural realm.[5] On the contrary, Paul wrote consistently

---

[5] By saying this, I am not at all intending to downplay the significance of this event in Paul's life. I am only suggesting that it was a different kind of seeing and knowing that Paul desired the churches to know. And contrary to how some understand Paul's statement to the Corinthians that they desire the gift of prophecy (1 Cor 14:1), I do not believe he is encouraging them to yearn for visions, dreams, and external supernatural experiences. Rather, his desire is that they would know the mind and speak the heart of God to the church for their edification.

and exclusively about a greater kind of beholding, an inner knowing, seeing, awakening, and comprehending that causes the heart to be transformed into the image of Christ.

Spiritual Learning

Learning Christ does not take place when natural senses are shown something about Christ in the natural realm. Nor is Christ truly known through dreams, visions, or other such supernatural experiences.[6] The soul begins to genuinely know Christ when the light of His life shines in the heart and causes us to progressively see with His perspective, walk in His truth, and be conformed to His nature. In other words, knowing Christ takes place when God, by the work of His Spirit, reveals His Son in us. This should in no way be considered an unusual or mystical experience that only occurs in the lives of unusually gifted individuals or in those with certain callings to ministry. This should be the common experience and continual expectation of every born again believer. The Spirit of God

---

[6] Many Christians believe that dreams and visions are the seeing of true spiritual reality. That simply isn't so. Dreams and visions, when they are in fact from God, are still, in a sense, natural experiences. I don't mean that they are material, earthly, or physical. Obviously they are not. I mean that they are a means by which God tries to make spiritual reality known through natural images, thoughts, stories, pictures, and impressions. And though God may be their author, they still require man's understanding and application. Dreams and visions are "dark sayings" (Numbers 12:8), and very much like parables, stories, or other types and shadows, they are arrows that are meant to point us to the true seeing and knowing of Christ in the inner man.

desires to reveal and form Jesus Christ in every single member of His body.

We need to understand something as Christians: Jesus Christ lives in us. I know that this is a very fundamental Christian belief, and that the concept is universally familiar in the church. I know that Christians often talk about feeling His presence within them and being guided by His voice in their heart. In some sense we all know that Christ is there within us. But when we think about what is involved in knowing Him, our mind almost always defaults to the various external ways that we know things and people in the natural realm. For example, we pray to Him as though He were off somewhere in the sky. We look for hidden clues in our daily lives about what God is trying to communicate. "Lord, what are You trying to tell me with this flat tire? God, what are You attempting to teach me through this sudden success in my business?" We talk about Him coming and going in prayer meetings and worship services, and we imagine Him to still be the bearded Nazarene with sandals and a robe. At times we say He is positionally[7] within us, but that our true encounter with Christ awaits a future day when we stand before a heavenly throne. We search for a prophet or

---

[7] There are a variety of Christian teachings that suggest that certain aspects of salvation are positionally, technically, or legally ours, but that the true experience of them awaits the death of the body or some sort of future consummation. In most cases, I believe this sort of teaching is an attempt to explain away our failure to experience all that Scripture declares to be "now in Christ" by asserting that what God has given is still, in some way, out of reach. When we are not experiencing what the Bible describes, it comforts our flesh to say these things must be "positionally" ours, but experientially still future. The statements of Jesus and the writings of the apostles do not support this idea.

leader in the church that can tell us what God's will is for our lives. My point is that knowing that Christ is within us is not the same as knowing Christ. He should not reside within us for 75 years like a foreigner in a strange hotel. He is in us in order to be revealed and formed in our soul. And as the Lord opens the eyes of our heart we begin to see Him in a new and awesome kind of light. It is in this light that we learn Christ and we come to bear the image of the Life that has been given to us by God.

The pages of the New Testament are literally filled with descriptions of this very thing. In the gospels, both Jesus' words and miracles clearly spoke of a new kind of seeing with a different kind of light. He called Himself "the Light of the world"[8] and spoke to his disciples about becoming "sons of the light."[9] He talked about a light and a darkness that fill the inner man.[10] He healed a man who was born blind and then used the occasion to speak of true blindness and true sight saying, "For judgment I have come into this world, that those who do not see may see, and that those who see may be made blind."[11] Over and over again Jesus spoke of those who had ears but could not hear and eyes but could not see, clearly lamenting the fact that the majority of His listeners could not see or hear beyond the natural realm.

Not only Jesus, but all of the apostles experienced and wrote about this greater seeing and knowing that takes place when Christ is revealed in the individual members of His body. Paul, in his letter to the Galatians, says, "God...

[8]   John 8:12
[9]   John 12:36
[10] Luke 11:34-36
[11] John 9:39

called me through His grace, to reveal His Son in me."[12] Notice he did not write, "to reveal His Son *to* me." There is a significant difference between these two statements. The Son was revealed to Paul on the road to Damascus. But throughout the next 35 years of Paul's life, the One who had been revealed to Him was increasingly revealed in Him. There are a variety of ways that Paul describes this same experience. In one letter he speaks of the "mind of Christ" working in the Lord's body to discern spiritual things.[13] In another place he explains how God is the One "shining in our hearts to give the light of the knowledge of the glory of God in the face of Jesus Christ."[14] It is in this new light that we can "look not at the things which are seen, but at the things which are not seen,"[15] and "mind the things above, not the things on the earth."[16] To the Corinthians he speaks of "beholding with unveiled face, as in a mirror, the glory of the Lord."[17] To the Romans he shares his desire to see them established "according to the revelation of the mystery kept secret since the world began."[18] To the Ephesians he expresses his earnest hope that they have not learned Christ with the "futility of the mind" but have indeed "heard Him and have been taught by Him, as the truth is in Jesus."[19] There are multitudes of similar examples in Paul's letters.

---

[12] Galatians 1:15-16
[13] 1 Corinthians 2:14-16
[14] 2 Corinthians 4:6
[15] 2 Corinthians 4:18
[16] Colossians 3:2
[17] 2 Corinthians 3:18
[18] Romans 16:25
[19] Ephesians 4:20-21

The other authors of the New Testament described this same reality in their own words. The apostle John, for example, says, "The anointing which you have received from Him abides in you, and you do not need that anyone teach you; but the same anointing teaches you concerning all things."[20] In another place John explains that "the Son of God has come and has given us an understanding, that we may know Him who is true; and we are in Him who is true, in His Son Jesus Christ."[21] Knowing Christ this way we can "walk in the light as He is in the light, and have fellowship with one another."[22] Peter tells the church that they have a "salvation ready to be revealed,"[23] and later speaks of the "day dawning and the morning star rising in your hearts."[24] Again, similar examples abound throughout the epistles.

When you look specifically at the prayers of the apostles recorded in the New Testament, it is clear that their foremost desire was for each member of the Lord's body to grow up in Christ by way of Spirit-given sight and understanding. For example, Paul prays for the Ephesians that God would give them "the spirit of wisdom and revelation in the knowing of Him, the eyes of your understanding being enlightened..."[25] Later in the same letter he writes:

For this reason I bow my knees to the Father of our Lord Jesus Christ... that He would grant

---

[20] 1 John 2:27
[21] 1 John 5:20
[22] 1 John 1:7
[23] 1 Peter 1:5
[24] 2 Peter 1:19
[25] Ephesians 1:17-18

you, according to the riches of His glory, to be strengthened with might through His Spirit in the inner man, that Christ may dwell in your hearts through faith; that you, being rooted and grounded in love, may be able to comprehend with all the saints what is the width and length and depth and height—to know the love of Christ which passes knowledge; that you may be filled with all the fullness of God.[26]

For the church in Philippi, Paul's prayer is that their "love may abound still more and more in true knowledge and all discernment."[27] To the Colossians he writes, "I do not cease to pray for you, and to ask that you may be filled with the knowledge of His will in all wisdom and spiritual understanding."[28] Later in the same letter he expresses his desire that they "attain to all riches of the full assurance of the understanding, to the full knowledge of the mystery of God, even Christ."[29] Even in his short letter to Philemon, Paul's prayer is that "the sharing of your faith may become effective by the acknowledgment of every good thing which is in you in Christ Jesus."[30]

Revelation

The idea of God revealing Himself to individuals in the body of Christ is sometimes met with skepticism and

---

[26] Ephesians 3:14-19
[27] Philippians 1:9
[28] Colossians 1:9
[29] Colossians 2:2
[30] Philemon 1:6

caution, much of which is well-deserved. There are plenty of people, both today and throughout church history, that have done and taught appalling things under the pretext of having received revelation from the Lord. There are also a large number of cults and false religions that have arisen as a result of people claiming to have been taught by God. For this reason, some Christians choose to avoid the topic of individual revelation altogether, saying that they prefer to stick with the security and authority of the Bible. God's revelation to man is complete, they say, and the Bible contains all that God has to say.

In a sense, this is very true. The Bible certainly does represent God's perfect and complete revelation to man, and no experience of personal revelation could ever add to it or contradict it. However, people who speak out against individual revelation fail to realize two important things. First, when reading the Bible, Christians from every denomination and background read with an expectation for God to deal with their hearts in a very personal way. In other words, whether they realize it or not, nearly every Christian believes that the Spirit of God teaches them individually. And second, while it is true that Scripture is authoritative and essential for every Christian, interpreting and applying God's written words with the carnal mind is just as dangerous as using our minds to imagine or interpret other kinds of communication from God. In fact, there are probably more atrocities committed in the name of the Bible than those done in the name of personal revelation. History has proven well that possessing and studying the Bible does not prevent the heart of man from misunderstanding, perverting, and misusing God's written revelation.   In both cases, the adamic mind is what is dangerous, and the nature of sin that governs this man is what twists and abuses God's communications with man. But just as misuse of the Bible does not, by any means, invalidate God's Word, neither does imaginary personal revelation invalidate genuine experiences of learning from the Lord or remove this reality from the pages of Scripture.

Much of the uneasiness that surrounds the idea of individuals learning directly from the Lord has to do with simple misunderstanding. Upon hearing the word revelation, many people immediately think of dreams, visions, audible voices, mystical experiences, or supernatural encounters with angels and demons. Although there are certainly stories of these things in the Bible, this is not at all the kind of revelation that the apostles describe in the many verses we just quoted.   In these and many similar verses, we can see that revelation is simply an experience of the Spirit of God teaching the soul all that it means to be in Christ. We received the fullness of Christ when we were born again, and yet like the man in John 9, we are born blind. We have no idea where we are, what God has given us, or what it all means. As we have mentioned previously, having received Christ does not mean that we know Him. And this would be a huge and insurmountable problem were it not for the fact that the Spirit of Truth is given to us with this exact job description. The Holy Spirit works in each of our hearts to teach us the new life that we have received.

This is precisely how Jesus described the ministry of the Holy Spirit to the church. Just prior to the cross, Jesus was speaking about his imminent death, burial, and resurrection. The disciples were troubled and confused, but Jesus comforted them explaining that His departure to the cross would result in the outpouring of the promised Spirit of God. It was better that He die, He explained, because not only would He come to them in resurrection and bring them with Himself to the Father, but He would also give them "another Helper, that He may abide with you forever."[31] This Helper, the Spirit of Truth who proceeds from the Father, He explained, "will teach you all things, and bring to your remembrance all things that I said to you."[32] He will "testify of Me"[33] and "guide you into all truth."[34] He will "glorify Me, for He will take of what is Mine and declare it to you."[35] And this is exactly what was taking place after the resurrection, not only with the twelve disciples, but with the entire New Testament church. The Holy Spirit guided them into all truth not by establishing new doctrines, theologies, and models of worship, but by shining the light of life in the heart of every born again believer.

Again, this should in no way be considered an abnormal or controversial occurrence. Quite the contrary, this is the ministry of the Holy Spirit that God Himself purposed for the growth of the body of Christ. The brilliant Puritan pastor Jonathan Edwards had this to say on the subject:

---

[31] John 14:16
[32] John 14:26
[33] John 15:26
[34] John 16:13
[35] John 16:14

There is such a thing as a spiritual and divine light immediately imparted to the soul by God, that is of a different nature from any that is obtained by natural means. This spiritual and divine light does not consist in any impression made upon the imagination. It is no impression upon the mind, as though one saw anything with the bodily eyes: it is no imagination or idea of an outward light or glory, or any beauty of form or countenance, or a visible luster or brightness of any object. It may be thus described: a true sense of the divine excellency of the things revealed in the word of God, and a conviction of the truth and reality of them thence arising from such a sight of their divine excellency and glory; so that this conviction of their truth is an effect and natural consequence of this sight of their divine glory.

He goes on to say:

It is rational to suppose, that it should be beyond a man's power to obtain this knowledge and light by the mere strength of natural reason; for it is not a thing that belongs to reason, to see the beauty and loveliness of spiritual things; it is not a speculative thing, but depends on the sense of the heart. The perceiving of spiritual beauty and excellency no more belongs to reason, than it belongs to the sense of feeling to perceive colors, or to the power of seeing to perceive the sweetness of food.[36]

Perhaps the clearest description of this reality in the New Testament is found in Paul's first letter to the Corinthians. The first two chapters present a strong contrast between the wisdom of God and the blindness and foolishness of man. Then, in the latter part of chapter two, Paul explains that there is a way for the human soul to actually know and experience the mind of the Lord. He begins with a quotation from Isaiah.

> *But as it is written: "Eye has not seen, nor ear heard, nor have entered into the heart of man the things which God has prepared for those who love Him."*[37]

It is amazing how many Christians, when quoting from this chapter, stop reading right here at the end of verse 9. In funerals and other religious services it is extremely common for speakers to read this one verse aloud, close their Bibles, and comment about how nobody knows the mysteries of spiritual life and future rewards that God has prepared for believers. The implication, in almost every case, is that the knowledge of these mysteries awaits the death of the natural body. But the very reason Paul quoted this verse from the Old Testament was to immediately contrast it with the fact that these once hidden things are

---

[36] Jonathan Edwards, Sermon entitled: *"A Divine and Supernatural Light, Immediately Imparted to the Soul by the Spirit of God, Shown to be both a Scriptural, and Rational Doctrine"* (1734)

[37] 1 Corinthians 2:9

exactly what the Spirit of God is now revealing! He continues in the following verse saying:

> *But God has revealed them to us through His Spirit. For the Spirit searches all things, yes, the deep things of God. For what man knows the things of a man except the spirit of the man which is in him? Even so no one knows the things of God except the Spirit of God. Now we have received, not the spirit of the world, but the Spirit who is from God, that we might know the things that have been freely given to us by God.*[38]

Let's look carefully at what Paul is saying here. He starts by speaking on a purely human level. Nobody knows what is real in a person except for the spirit of that person within them. For example, I cannot truly know you because I cannot experience your heart or inner-man. I never really know what you are feeling, thinking, fearing, or longing for. I can watch your actions and hear your words, but I can only guess at what is behind these things precisely because I have no access to your spirit. I cannot see or truly know your heart. We all instinctively understand these limitations in human relationships and therefore often find ourselves saying things to one another like, "Don't judge me! You have no idea what is going on in my heart!"

If this limitation exists between two human beings, how much more must we be naturally limited in our ability to know Almighty God! Nothing external to Him could

---

[38] 1 Corinthians 2:10-12

ever truly know Him, much less a blind and fallen adamic man. Without a miracle of grace, trying to know God would be like an inchworm seeking to know the most intimate thoughts and desires of a human being. Our efforts to know Him would be futile because only the Spirit of God knows the deep things of God, that is, His most internal qualities, nature, character, purpose, and will.

But the good news of the gospel is that God has indeed accomplished such a miracle of grace. He has done the unthinkable in order to make Himself known. He didn't just drop off a book that describes Himself in inchworm language; He actually opened a door through the cross and invited us into Himself. He gave us the life of His Son and then put His own Spirit within us making us partakers of His understanding and perspective. This is what the Spirit of God seeks to do in each of us – bring us to God's perspective of the unsearchable riches of Christ who is our life. In the words of Paul, the Spirit was given that "we might know the things that have been freely given to us by God."[39]

Knowing God is a work of the Spirit through the revelation of Jesus Christ in the believer. God gives us Christ as our life, which is unspeakably wonderful in and of itself. But along with new life He also gives us His light which allows us to progressively see and experience all that He has given. Centuries before Christ came to us as "the true Light that enlightens every man,"[40] King David saw Him from afar and exclaimed, "For with You is the fountain of life; in Your light we see light!"[41]

---

[39] 1 Corinthians 2:12
[40] John 1:9
[41] Psalm 36:9

Chapter XV

The Necessity of Christ Revealed

Christians are often plagued with uncertainty about God's will for their lives. One of the most common questions to arise in a believer's heart is – *what does God want me to do?* The shelves of Christian bookstores are lined with books that attempt to answer this question, telling believers how to do the will of God. There are books that focus on Christian morality, suggesting that God's greatest desire for us is the development of moral character and victory over bad habits. There are others that focus on sharing the gospel, contending that God's will for every believer is to do their part in world evangelization. Other books insist that God's will for our lives is bound up with spiritual disciplines, intercessory prayer, eschatology, worship, serving the poor, prosperity, or Christian education. And for those who are overwhelmed by the options, there are books that combine all of these into a practical and attainable five simple steps. Hungry hearts are sometimes drawn to books like these because they are searching for a purpose that extends beyond this natural world of shadows. But God's will for our lives will never be found in a book.

The Will of God

The common thought in the church is that God has a specific and unique destiny in mind for each member of the body of Christ. Our job, we assume, is to figure out God's specific will and then accomplish in our lifetime the things He wants us to do. It is said that God is doing many different things, in many different ways, in countless different places all over the earth. God's will for our individual lives can depend upon a variety of different factors, things like where we live, what our giftings are, and what culture we were born into. We imagine that His purpose changes and adapts as we go through different seasons of our lives. We say things like, "I feel like God is calling me to something totally new now that I live in the city." Or "God's purpose for our church changed in 2003 with the arrival of the new pastor." The will of the Lord is seen to be very complicated and diverse, with multitudes of different plans, purposes, and callings.

We like to imagine the will of God in this way because it aligns well with our natural understanding of the world and of ourselves. We enjoy the idea of having a unique spiritual destiny, one that happens to involve a mixture of our own personal giftings and passions, and one that results in our eventual recognition and usefulness. In the mind of the adamic man our individuality is extremely important, and being special is one of our top priorities. In the church this drives us to create levels of ministry and hierarchies of callings. Not only that, but we have different kinds of churches with completely different vision statements, and within these churches exist smaller groups that focus on separate interests and callings. As a result, the concept of knowing and doing the will of God can feel like a tailor made to-do list that changes regularly and differs for each member of the Lord's body.

I am not at all suggesting that God is amassing an army of cookie-cutter Christians that all act and speak in exactly the same way. I am however saying that in the heart of man everything is diverse and individual, but in the heart of God there is one single purpose for all of creation. Man says, "God is doing this here and that over there. He has purpose A for this person, and purpose B for that person." But God says, "I desire the revelation, formation, and glorification of My Son in every single soul, at every time, in every place. That is My will for your life."

The body of Christ has many members, and of course not all of the members function in the same way. As Paul describes in his letter to the Corinthians, the eye and the foot play different roles in the body. But diversity in function does not mean diversity in purpose. I use the parts of my body in different ways, but my one purpose for all of them is to contain and express my life. I certainly don't make a list of chores for my body parts to accomplish on a daily basis. As long as my life is their source and motivation, I don't need to. Everything they do is an expression of my will. Sometimes my hand expresses my will by brushing my teeth. Other times, it lies still at my side for hours and does absolutely nothing while I sleep. The expression of my will changes, but the purpose for my members remains the same.

It is very much the same with the body of Christ. The life of Christ functions in different ways through the members of His body, but His purpose for every member is to live by the life of the Head. Experiencing Christ's life in this way will certainly have expression in outward ways through our natural vessels, but truly knowing the will of God will never consist in a fixed set of outward activities or a specific calling to ministry. God's will is a Person that He desires to live and be glorified in His body, the church. It is not a series of actions or accomplishments that humans do on God's behalf or a treasure map that we find and follow.

The Upward Call of God in Christ Jesus

Unfortunately, when Christians talk about their callings, they usually use this word to refer to their personal, individual roles in the earth or in the church. However, although roles and functions are certainly valid in the body of Christ, they do not constitute a person's calling. Paul, for example, was called an apostle by the Lord, but I doubt very much that Paul would have considered apostleship his calling. In other words, Paul's function in the Lord's body had a name, and that name was apostle (lit. sent one), and he functioned in that role. But if you were to ask Paul about his calling, he most certainly would have responded to you by saying something like this:

Not that I have already attained, or am already perfected; but I press on, that I may lay hold of that for which Christ Jesus has also laid hold of me. Brethren, I do not count myself to have apprehended; but one thing I do, forgetting those things which are behind and reaching forward to those things which are ahead, I press toward the goal for the prize of the <u>upward call of God in Christ Jesus</u>.[1]

Paul was used of the Lord in the church as an apostle and church planter, but his true calling had to do with God's invitation to dwell with Him above, to live in His Son, to bear in his soul the glory of the Lord. A simple word search in the New Testament will quickly reveal that every member of the Lord's body has the exact same calling. We are "called by the gospel for the obtaining of the glory of our Lord Jesus Christ."[2] We are called out of one country and into another,[3] called "out of darkness and into His marvelous light."[4] We are called unto liberty,[5] called to become children of God,[6] called to feast at the marriage supper of the Lamb.[7] Sadly, our individual roles in the earth are often more important to us than our eternal calling in Christ.

God calls every member of the body of Christ to abide

---

[1] Philippians 3:12-14, emphasis mine
[2] 2 Thessalonians 2:14
[3] Hebrews 11:13-16
[4] 1 Peter 2:9
[5] Galatians 5:13
[6] 1 John 3:1
[7] Revelation 19:9

in the Vine and to "bear much fruit."[8]   But what is fruit? Fruit isn't a busy branch. Fruit isn't a gifted branch. Fruit is always the increase of a seed!   God is not seeking the fruit of our individual labors, ideas, and abilities.   He desires the harvest of the Seed that has been planted in our soul. In John 15 Jesus explains:

> As the branch cannot bear fruit of itself, unless it abides in the vine, neither can you, unless you abide in Me.   I am the vine, you are the branches.   He who abides in Me, and I in him, bears much fruit; for apart from Me you can do nothing.[9]

Unless Christ is the substance and source, there is nothing in us that God considers true fruit. I believe Jesus could have said it this way: "For apart from me you can do many things, but from My Father's point of view they will all amount to nothing." Though we are often confused on this issue, the Vinedresser has no problem discerning between the plastic fruit of religion and the true increase of His perfect Seed.

In our search to know God's will for our lives, too often we have overlooked the fact that Christ alone is the object of God's true pleasure and satisfaction. It is true that the soul of man was uniquely created to be the vessel and dwelling place of the Lord. In all that God has made, only the human soul can receive His life and bear His increase and glory. However, we must never think that we

---

[8]   John 15:8
[9]   John 15:4-5

possess in ourselves what God is seeking. There is only One to whom God has ever said, "This is my beloved Son in Whom I am well pleased,"[10] and we need to understand that God's will for our individual lives is inextricably bound up with His one eternal purpose in Jesus Christ. To the Lord, all things are evaluated from the vantage point of His one purpose for creation. All things were created out from this purpose, and all things must be gathered up into this purpose, otherwise they exist without any purpose at all. Human beings may have many purposes for their lives, many purposes for their families, their jobs, their churches, or their ministries. But unless all of our individual, independent purposes are swallowed up and defined by the one purpose of God, we can still live purposeless lives.

The Mind of Christ

In order to know and do the will of the Lord, the members of His body must "grow up in all things into Him who is the Head, even Christ."[11] Paul tells us that every believer has the mind of Christ, but possessing His mind and being governed by it are two very different things. In an attempt to understand how to do God's will, Christians sometimes pray for daily instructions from God, or try to learn how to hear His voice. But this is yet another way that we unknowingly adhere to an old covenant mentality. Under the old covenant, God's people received external

---

[10] Matthew 3:17
[11] Ephesians 4:15

commands and instructions that described His will in types and shadows.[12]   But the greatness of the new covenant is the indwelling presence of God's Spirit who transforms our soul, writes the law on our hearts, and causes us to walk in His ways.   Learning to hear God's voice and following directions is not the way God wants to relate to you.   For centuries, man's relationship with the written law demonstrated beyond any doubt that doing the will of God required far more than possessing His instructions.   In fact, we have seen that one of the primary functions of the law was to demonstrate that such obedience was impossible!   In the new covenant, God doesn't want to tell you what to do; He wants to be the reason you do all that you do.   Rather than give you daily instructions, the Lord would much rather form His life in your soul so that all that you want and all that you do is naturally an expression of His will.

Right now all four of my children are still fairly young, and so my expectation for them is often simply that they obey the voice of their father.   At their age they need me to tell them what to do and what not to do, what is right and what is wrong.   But even in my relationship with my children, my desire as a father is not that they forever require my instructions in order to know what to do.   When they

---

[12] God's audible or written communications with man under the old covenant were always instructions or revelations that painted natural pictures of His eternal purpose in Jesus Christ. The command for Noah to build the ark, for Abraham to leave his country, kindred, and father's house, for Israel to paint blood on their doors or to take possession of the Promised Land, etc., none of these were random communications with humans for merely personal or natural benefit.   These interactions with individual people always looked beyond the present situation and testified of God's eternal and spiritual purpose in His Son.

are adults, I don't want them calling me on the phone dozens of times a day, still needing to ask me questions about right and wrong. Requiring constant external direction is not a sign of maturity, but rather a sign of immaturity. My desire for my children is to grow up to do by nature the things they have seen in their father. It is similar in our relationship with God. Rather than always seeking God's will in external instructions and commands, it is far greater for the body of Christ to do His will because His mind and nature are operating within us. Rather than trying to keep up with all of the best-selling Christian how-to books, the church should grow up in such a way as to be moved, motivated, governed, and constrained in all things by the indwelling life of God.

The simple truth is that nothing of the Lord's will is accomplished without the Lord's mind functioning in the Lord's body. This should not seem like a strange statement. All bodies work the same way. Can you imagine if your body was trying to do your will apart from your mind? Now *that* would be strange and extremely frustrating as well. In fact, if this were taking place in a human body we would consider the condition a disorder or a disease. There are actually conditions where the human body experiences this exact problem.

When I was in college, I had a friend named Chris who was born with cerebral palsy. His mind was perfectly normal; in fact he was an incredibly intelligent person. But Chris had very limited control over most parts of his body. His legs and feet were actually less affected by the cerebral palsy than the rest of his body. Amazingly, Chris did most things with his left foot, including steering his electric wheelchair, grabbing things that he needed, even typing papers for classes on a computer. His arms and hands, however, were a constant frustration for him. Not only was Chris unable to control his arms, but they virtually had a mind of their own. Entirely apart from Chris' will, they moved constantly, swinging, jerking, and flailing in every direction. They would often embarrass him, knocking something off a table, hitting a friend, or touching a stranger by accident. On more than one occasion, Chris told me that if his parents would have allowed it, he would have had both of his arms surgically removed years ago. He said that they did nothing beneficial for his body and only served to constantly annoy him.

Jesus once said, "If anyone does not abide in Me, he is cast out as a branch and is withered; and they gather them and throw them into the fire, and they are burned."[13] This is exactly what my friend Chris wanted to do with his arms. To him they were worse than paralyzed limbs. These arms had a will of their own, movement of their own, and they did all sorts of things on behalf of his body that did not proceed from his mind. It was Chris' body, but it wasn't what Chris wanted. And the heart of his problem is just what we have said: nothing of Chris' will could be accomplished without his mind operating in his body.

Practical Christianity

In saying these things, my desire is to call attention to the absolute necessity of Christ being revealed in His body,

---

[13] John 15:6

the church. Unless we grow to know Him as the life, nature, and mind that governs our souls, then we are exactly like Chris' arms. Worse than being unproductive Christians, we actually have a mind and will of our own working in the body of Another! Without even realizing the absurdity, we try to live our own lives for the Head. We have our own interpretations and ideas about the will of God. We have purposes of our own, ministries of our own, glory of our own, everything of our own, until Christ our life begins to be revealed in us.

Over the years, many people have asked me about the *practicality* of preaching the necessity of Christ being revealed. They say things like, "I can see that this is in the Bible, but it doesn't seem like a very practical message for Christians." But what is more practical than the mind of Christ actually living and reigning in His own body? What could be a more practical solution to Chris' cerebral palsy than somehow causing his arms to fully align with his will? I can tell you what Chris would *not* consider a true solution: using duct tape to attach his arms to the side of his wheelchair. This may temporarily prevent some embarrassment, but restricting his movement does nothing to address the real problem. This may be obvious to us in Chris' situation, but "practical" ideas just like this abound in the body of Christ. Having little idea what it means for a soul to be conformed to the indwelling Christ, our practical suggestions for spiritual living involve tips and tricks to prevent Adam from manifesting himself and embarrassing us. Effective Christianity, some say, means learning to control our carnal desires and holding on tightly to right beliefs and behavior. We love useful sermons that explain how to control our anger. We love a good action plan to deal with lust, or a workbook guaranteed to help control our fears. But this is duct tape Christianity, and it only serves to restrict the flesh. It does absolutely nothing to transform the soul. Putting a murderer in jail does not make him any less of a murderer. Steel bars do not change a man, they simply prevent him from committing more crimes. In the same way, our practical steps to controlling Adam's activity "indeed has an appearance of wisdom in self-imposed religion, false humility, and neglect of the body, but are of no value against the indulgence of the flesh."[14]

Other versions of practical Christianity focus less on controlling the flesh and more on trying to be like Jesus. We look for the right steps to follow, the effective prayers to pray, the key verses to memorize and claim for our lives. We gravitate towards teachings that have an immediate life application, ones that present us with a clear plan for imitating Jesus. But we somehow fail to realize that if Christ is not the life and source of all these things, then they are merely dead branches producing counterfeit fruit. Returning to the former example, I suppose that with today's advancements in medicine and technology, it might be possible to electrically stimulate Chris' right arm in such a way that by pressing a button he would reach out and shake a visitor's hand. This would certainly be an incredible feat of science, but it would not be an expression of life. In a sense, Chris would now be able to imitate the movement of a normal arm, but his actual condition would not have changed at all.

---

[14] Colossians 2:23

When people ask for something practical, what they usually mean is, "What can I do in the flesh to become more spiritual?" To that question there is no answer. God's salvation has to do with escaping the natural man, not training him. The gospel of the cross gives the soul a Who, not a how. And every bit of true spiritual progress is bound up with the revelation and formation of the One who is the will of God and the object of His eternal satisfaction.

What are we after as Christians? What is our expectation? If our goal is in any way related to God's eternal purpose then we must look outside the box of human discipline and fleshly imitation. When it comes to knowing and doing God's will, our most fundamental and vital need is that the body of Christ come to live by His mind. This is so much more than Jesus teaching us how to think, helping us make right choices, or pointing us in the right direction. This is the light, truth, and perspective of Christ Himself growing in us and defining our lives. As Christ is revealed in us, all that is real and true to Him progressively becomes the most real thing that we know. And consequently, all that the Lord does not see, recognize, or value, falls away from our hearts as when a snake sheds its dead skin. Walking in His light, our souls become branches that flow with His sap and produce the fruit of His Spirit. We are like arms with cerebral palsy that start to awaken from our disorder and move with the life of the Head. The will of Christ begins to have expression in His body, and it no longer matters what we do, only that He is the life behind it. We suddenly don't care whether we are seen or appreciated because it is "no longer I, but Christ who lives in me."[15] We understand what it means to "labor according to His power working mightily in me."[16] As His very own body, we know that we "can do all things through Christ who empowers me."[17] And apart from Him, we can do nothing at all.

The Spirit's Desire

When a person responds to the grace of God and acknowledges their need for Christ, the Lord works in the soul the miracle of new birth. Right away we are saved by faith through the grace of God, but as we have already discussed, we begin with virtually no understanding of the life we have received. The Spirit has presented Christ to our hearts and we have indeed seen and acknowledged Him in an inward way. But we generally begin life in the Spirit with the awareness of two simple things – the reality of our desperate need, and the fact that Christ is the only solution. In other words, in our first flash of spiritual perspective, we usually see little more than the incredible contrast between sin and righteousness, and we respond by crying out to God for forgiveness or salvation or eternal life. The truth is that it matters very little what our mouths say to the Lord at the time we are born again. God is not really responding to our words or judging the accuracy of our theology. He is giving His Spirit because of our need

---

[15] Galatians 2:20
[16] Colossians 1:29
[17] Philippians 4:13

and because our hearts have at last turned to Him and granted Him access.

Nobody begins their life in Christ thinking about abiding in the light or being conformed to the death of the cross. Nobody awakens from adamic death and immediately says with Paul, "for me to live is Christ and to die is gain,"[18] or comprehends that "we are the fragrance of Christ unto God."[19] These realities are far from entering our minds, though they are indeed realities of salvation. To the newly born child of God, the sum total of our spiritual intelligence is the simple awareness that we are the problem and Christ is the solution. This is the first thing that we see in His light. And although it is a very small view of a very great salvation, it is real, it is essential, and it is overwhelmingly wonderful. We have come to Him ignorant and in need, and we have found in Christ exactly what we needed.

At this stage of a Christian's life, there is usually great excitement and zeal. Why? Because we *know* what we have seen! Nobody has persuaded us through arguments or manipulated our emotions. We simply humbled our hearts, turned to Him, and saw something incredibly real. We saw it; we didn't just believe it. And often for weeks or months after new birth, Christians cannot stop talking about the reality of Christ and the gift of salvation in Him.

The Spirit-given awareness of Christ that becomes real at new birth is often what believers hold to as proof of God's existence or as evidence of their salvation, and most continue acknowledging Christ as Lord and Savior for the

---

[18] Philippians 1:21
[19] 2 Corinthians 2:15

remainder of their lives.   Tragically, however, this initial encounter with the Spirit of Truth often ends up being the believer's only true experience of spiritual sight, and everything else is done and built upon the memory of it. As time passes, what they have seen in His light turns into a memory, and the once unmistakable view of Christ falls to the earth and becomes a purely natural thing.   In other words, faith turns into belief, and living revelation turns into an often repeated testimony.   One true flash of light, and then religion, doctrines, and works of the flesh stack up higher and higher for decades to come.

This is not how things should be. New birth should be but the very beginning of the revelation of Jesus Christ. The way that we begin is also the way that we continue. After drawing us to Christ, the Spirit's work is not over. In a sense, His greatest work has just begun. Now that Christ lives in us by faith, the Spirit's job and desire is to transform the soul by teaching us the Christ that we received. Speaking to the Galatians of this very thing Paul says:

> *O foolish Galatians! Who has bewitched you that you should not obey the truth, before whose eyes Jesus Christ was clearly portrayed among you as crucified? This only I want to learn from you: Did you receive the Spirit by the works of the law, or by the hearing of faith? Are you so foolish? Having begun in the Spirit, are you now being made perfect by the flesh?* [20]

---

[20] Galatians 3:1-3

Paul was astonished and heartbroken that the very ones to whom he had proclaimed the gospel of the cross, and who had received the Spirit of God by faith, were now hindering the Spirit's work by pursuing spiritual growth in the flesh. Like so many today, the Galatian Christians believed that forgiveness of sin was the work of the Lord, but after receiving this gift, it was man's responsibility to take the baton from the Lord and continue the race towards spiritual maturity. Nothing could be further from the truth. Spiritual growth is the increase of Christ's government in the soul, the enlargement of His conquered territory, the formation of His nature and kingdom within. Though it has multitudes of external effects, the growth itself is internal and spiritual, and the only measure by which the Lord evaluates our progress is "the measure of the stature of the fullness of Christ."[21] We grow in our experience of the grace of Christ, the love of Christ, the truth as it is in Christ. We grow up in all things into Him who is the Head. But the only way that this growth takes place is when the soul is carried on by the Spirit of God to an ever greater view of the Lord Jesus Christ. Again, the way that we begin is also the way forward. We start in the Spirit by faith, and we must grow in exactly the same way. Sometimes believers wander for years in the wilderness of religion before finding their way back to the childlike heart that first saw the Lord in true spiritual light. That was certainly my experience. But five minutes or fifty years, it makes no difference to God. When our heart turns back again to Him, the veil is removed, and the Spirit continues revealing Christ our life exactly where He left off.

---

[21] Ephesians 4:13

Abiding in Christ

On the eve of His crucifixion, Jesus spoke plainly to His disciples about the necessity of abiding in Him.[22] The concept of abiding in Christ is usually a familiar one to Christians. It is something we hear in services and songs and we read on church signs and Sunday bulletins. But what does it actually mean for us to abide in Him? Is it simply a matter of remaining a Christian or continuing to be an active member of a local church? Does abiding in Christ speak of a daily devotional life, or a constant state of prayer? I submit to you that it is something far greater than any of these ideas. But to abide in Christ we must first be able to see Him.

In the natural realm we understand that the term abiding has to do with continuing in a certain place, or remaining in a fixed position or state. We don't usually speak of abiding in something that is foreign and unknown. In fact, just the opposite is true. We can abide in the love of our family, for example, precisely because this love is familiar and real to us. In much the same way, the reality of abiding in Christ requires a Spirit-given familiarity with the Person in whom we have been made to dwell. We cannot abide in a doctrine. We cannot live and walk in a theologically accurate idea. We can only abide in what we see and know to be real. Therefore, in order to remain in Christ, the light of His life must be showing us where we are and what it means. In our hearts, the light must cut between two realms, clearly separating two men— Adam and Christ. Only as the Spirit of Truth reveals Christ

---

[22] See John 15:4-7

in the soul do we learn to put off one man and abide in the Other. Only when His light shines do we see our true Home and understand what it means to remain there.

When Abraham left behind his country, kindred, and father's house, the Lord brought him into the land of his inheritance and told him that he and his seed would abide there forever. The Lord said:

> _Lift your eyes now and look from the place_
> _where you are_—northward, southward, east-
> ward, and westward; _for all the land which_
> _you see_ I give to you and your seed forever.[23]

In every way this promised land was a picture of Christ, our true inheritance, and the New Testament is clear that the seed who would inherit the land were the sons of Abraham by faith and not merely by blood.[24] But even in Abraham's journey of faith, which is the type and shadow of our own, he was instructed to lift up his eyes and see where he already was. As far as Abraham was able to see, that is how far he could know and experience his inheritance. In very similar language, Paul tells us that by spiritual sight[25] "we are able to comprehend with all the saints what is the width and length and depth and height – to know the love of Christ which passes knowledge."[26] As "the

---

[23] Genesis 13:14-15, emphasis mine

[24] See for example, Romans 2:28-29, 4:10-17, 9:6-8, Galatians chapter 3

[25] Paul uses the word faith in this Scripture, but faith is a kind of seeing and knowing given to us by the Spirit. See the following chapter for more.

[26] Ephesians 3:18-19

day dawns and the morning star rises in our hearts,"[27] we grow in our awareness of where God has placed us. His light shows us a new creation, and we come to know Christ as the true Promised Land that flows with milk and honey. In his letter to the Colossians Paul wrote:

> *If then you were raised with Christ, seek those things which are above, where Christ is, sitting at the right hand of God. Set your mind on things above, not on things on the earth. For you died, and your life is hidden with Christ in God. When* (literally – whenever, as often as[28]) *Christ who is our life is revealed, then you also will be revealed with Him* (literally – united to Him[29]) *in glory.*[30]

This Scripture does not describe a future event but declares the present and ongoing revelation of Christ our life and the glorious union that we have come to in Him. As we have seen in a previous chapter, glory is not a distant place or time. Rather, glory has to do with God making Himself known, causing Himself to be seen, understood, and experienced. Every Spirit-born believer has been brought to glory,[31] and has the Person of glory dwelling in their soul.[32] And inasmuch as He is revealed, we see ourselves already joined to Him, and already partakers of His eternal glory.

---

[27] 2 Peter 1:19
[28] Strong's # G3752 *hotan* – whenever, inasmuch as
[29] Strong's # G4862 *sun* – a primary preposition denoting union
[30] Colossians 3:1-4
[31] Hebrews 2:10
[32] Colossians 1:27

Again, the carnal mind objects and calls such ideas mystical or abstract. But nothing is more reasonable and practical than living fully aware of the truth. Nothing can change a soul more than seeing and walking in what is real to God, knowing His perspective as the anchor and compass of the soul. The alternative is to live in the vain imaginations of the carnal mind. From the apostles' perspective, there was nothing more foolish and fruitless than to "walk in the futility of the mind,"[33] "vainly puffed up by the fleshly mind,"[34] "behaving like mere men"[35] because our hearts refuse to see what God has done in Christ.

The natural mind says, "But how? How do I walk in His light and become an expression of His life?" Oh, how we hate to be left without our fleshly steps to spiritual success! We are so occupied with our search for religious methods and models that we fail to recognize the simple fact that humans naturally live whatever life is most real to them. How did we walk in sin for so many years? How were we so successful and consistent in manifesting the adamic man? Was it discipline? Was it effort? Were there steps to follow or classes to take? How did we do it? The answer is so simple: we lived the only life that we knew. Life always lives. The only question is what life do we know as our own?

When humans live in sin, our thoughts and actions correspond to our awareness of who we are and what is real to us. We don't need to work on sin because sin works in us. Sin defines our view, constrains our desires, and

---

[33] Ephesians 4:17
[34] Colossians 2:18
[35] 1 Corinthians 3:3

motivates our free decisions. This is true of all unbelievers. But even as Christians, we continue to think and act like Adam because in the darkness of the unrenewed mind he remains far more real to us than the life of Christ that we have received. We have accepted the One who is the truth, but the lie is still the lens through which we know ourselves and see the world. We have received eternal life in the Lord Jesus Christ, but in the absence of His light, the soul continues to live the only life that it has seen. What do we need? We need the nature, understanding, and perspective of Christ to become the operating reality of our redeemed soul. More than anything else, *we need Christ, who is our life, revealed in us.*

Chapter XVI
Living by Faith

All that we have been describing in the previous few chapters can actually be summed up in a very common New Testament word. That word is *faith*. Christians talk about faith perhaps more than any other biblical word, but familiarity with a word does not mean that we understand or experience the reality behind it. No matter how acquainted we are with words and concepts in the Bible, it is always a good idea to hold our ideas loosely and constantly look to the Lord for His understanding.[1]

Faith vs. Belief

Many people think of the words faith and belief as synonyms. If they acknowledge a difference between them, some might say that faith is simply a stronger belief, or that faith is a kind of belief that has to do with spiritual

---

[1] Learning natural things, like math or history, is a static kind of knowledge that involves acquiring, remembering, and holding tightly to facts and ideas with the mind. But spiritual knowledge always involves a *present* view of Christ in the light. We must be continually seeing and knowing Christ AS our understanding and experience of truth.

or religious things. In a discussion about baseball, it would be common to hear somebody say, "I believe that the White Sox are the best team in the Major League this year." However, in a conversation following a church service, someone might say, "I have faith that God is real and that He loves me more than I can understand." In these sentences, the words faith and belief are being used in very much the same way – to express a personal conviction, something that the speaker thinks is true. But even though these words may have become synonyms in today's vernacular, there is actually an enormous difference between them. In fact, when we begin to understand what faith meant to Jesus and the authors of the New Testament, we discover that human belief and biblical faith are contrary to each other in almost every way.

What are beliefs? Beliefs are simply conclusions that we have come to based upon experiences, observations, and information. They are our thoughts, ideas, opinions, interpretations, and deductions about things we cannot see. And perhaps the most important thing to understand about beliefs is that they are entirely *natural*, that is to say, they come from us, and they work in us as our own thoughts about what is real and true. Because of this, human beliefs are very personal and unstable things. God's truth never changes, but beliefs about the truth change all the time based upon subjective things like opinions, perspective, and desires. We have all experienced the weakness of human beliefs. We have all believed something with all of our heart only to suddenly reconsider when a more appealing belief came along. One minute we were perfectly convinced; the next minute an intelligent friend or an inspiring book transforms the way we see everything. When this happens we quickly and easily change our beliefs. Beliefs change as we pass through life experiences, as we discover new information, or as we encounter persuasive people. It's very easy to change a belief; all you have to do is change your mind. The mind is the author and finisher of human belief.

What is faith? Hebrews chapter 11 says, "Now faith is the substance of things hoped for, the evidence of things unseen."[2] What does it mean that faith is substance and evidence? Before anything else, it means that faith cannot be the same as belief![3] Nobody would say that their beliefs are substance and evidence. In fact, we know that just the opposite is true. Beliefs are what we hold to in the *absence* of something substantial and when we *cannot* demonstrate the reality or certainty of what we think is true. We rely on beliefs when we cannot see. But faith is just the opposite. Faith is a kind of seeing and apprehending that works in the soul by the Spirit of God. It is a view of spiritual reality that becomes real in us as a result of the revelation of Christ. Faith doesn't believe in spiritual ideas; it actually looks at and lays hold of spiritual reality. Though it does not see with natural eyes, faith sees with a light that comes from above and causes the soul to know

---

[2] Hebrews 11:1 There are a variety of English translations of this verse, but I believe this one best captures the meaning of the Greek. The word *substance* is the Greek word *hupostasis* and means essence, substance, reality. It is the same word used in Hebrews 1:3 when Christ is called "the express image of God's being/reality (*hupostasis*). The word *evidence* is the Greek word *elegchos* and means proof, evidence, demonstration.

[3] For this very reason I believe many modern translations replace substance and evidence with words like certainty and conviction.

and abide in what is real to God. Regardless of what men say, there is no such thing as blind faith. Belief is blind. But faith sees with a true and spiritual light, and it takes possession of all that God has made available in His Son.

The Author and Finisher of Faith

While belief involves our own ideas, thoughts, and conclusions about things we cannot see, biblical faith comes from another mind altogether. Faith is an experience of the mind of Christ working His own perspective and understanding in the human heart.[4] Scripture tells us that Christ is "the author and finisher of faith."[5] He begins His work of faith in our heart the moment we are born again. We are saved by faith. Then He who began this good work in us continues until the full day dawns and the shadows disappear from our hearts.

Contrary to so much that we hear in the church, faith is not something that man can produce or do. Closing your eyes and trying your best to believe something is not faith.

---

[4] As strange as it may sound, the coming of faith never confirms our prior beliefs, but rather destroys and replaces them. Because faith is the mind of the Lord working in us, it gives no place for even the most elevated ideas of man. God's thoughts are infinitely higher than ours. So the experience of faith replaces a human idea with divine perspective. It substitutes a man-made and man-centered belief with a spiritual view that is unspeakably more real. Somebody might ask, "What about a fundamental belief like the fact that Jesus is the Son of God – won't faith confirm that?" Yes and no. As a statement it is correct. But everything that we have thought and imagined about this statement, all of the ideas and concepts with regard to what it means for Christ to be God's Son, are going to be put away and replaced by faith's view.

[5] Hebrews 12:2

Memorizing Bible verses and claiming them out loud has nothing to do with faith. Going to church every day of your life and reciting long prayers will not produce a single mustard seed of faith. All true faith is a work of grace, a gift of the Lord, something that is entirely supernatural.

Christians frequently struggle with this idea because faith is sometimes presented in Scripture as man's responsibility. We know that Jesus often criticized the Jews for their lack of faith. He was saddened and seemed almost shocked by the faithlessness of His generation. If faith is a gift from God, a work of the Spirit in the human heart, why did Jesus clearly expect to find faith in Israel? How could He rebuke the Jews for lacking something that they needed to receive from God? The answer, I believe, is that Jesus' rebukes were not due to an expectation for man to *produce* faith, but rather because He knew very well that God desired to work the reality of faith in the hearts of all who would allow it. Faith comes from God, but like everything that God offers, man can either humbly receive it or obstinately refuse it. The Lord is always searching for hearts that will "receive with meekness the implanted Word."[6] In His parables, Jesus describes Himself as a Sower that scatters seed in every direction, casting His word upon all types of ground. But much like the seeds in this parable, the gift of faith will take root and grow only in hearts that provide good soil.

In his letter to the Romans, Paul writes:

> *For I say, through the grace given to me, to everyone who is among you, not to think of*

---

[6] James 1:21

himself more highly than he ought to think, but to think soberly, as God has dealt to each one a measure of faith.[7]

Here again we see that God Himself is the source of faith, and that being sober (Gr. of sound mind, sane, right-minded[8]) has to do with the measure of faith that is working in us. This measure that Paul mentions is not handed out arbitrarily, nor are Christians given a fixed allotment of faith at new birth and then stuck with that same measure for the remainder of their lives. Far from it! We are meant to grow strong in faith, becoming more and more rooted and grounded in the true knowledge of Christ. But the measure of faith that we experience working in our hearts corresponds to the liberty that the Lord finds in us to replace our view with His own. Only those who humble themselves and approach like children begin to receive His light. The Lord's perspective has always been "hidden from the wise and learned and revealed unto babes."[9] Paul tells us that when "a heart turns to the Lord, the veil is removed."[10] Faith comes when the eyes and ears of the soul turn to the living word of God[11] and offer it a place to reside and grow.

---

[7] Romans 12:3, LitV Translation, Jay P. Green
[8] Strong's # G4993 *sōphroneō* - to be of sound mind, that is, sane: - be in right mind, be sober (minded), soberly.
[9] Luke 10:21
[10] 2 Corinthians 3:16
[11] Faith works in us by a very specific kind of hearing or seeing. Paul calls it the "hearing of faith" (Galatians 3:2, 3:5), or the seeing of faith (Hebrews 11:13, 11:27). This isn't a natural hearing of God's written or spoken words, but a spiritual hearing of God's living Word. I believe this is the thought behind Romans 10:17 - "So then faith comes by hearing, and hearing by the word of God."

We need to remember that absolutely every aspect of our salvation is a participation in the resurrected life of Jesus Christ. Whether we are talking about righteousness, love, glory, or faith, nothing is given to us as ours, but all things are made available to us as His. God has placed us in His Son, and made Him to be all things of life and godliness unto us. Salvation is not an external transaction whereby God grants us a variety of spiritual things, abilities, and qualifications. Rather, salvation is a living union with Jesus Christ whereby we come to know and experience *Him* as the sum of all spiritual things. It is not our righteousness, but His. It is not our love, but His. It is not our wisdom, but His. We bring nothing of value to Him, but He gives us and works in us all that He is and has. By being joined to Him we inherit all things and we contribute nothing that comes from ourselves – not even our faith. Faith is His gift; it is His light. Though we receive it unto ourselves, and it works in us as our own spiritual view, still all true faith is "the faith of the Son of God."[12]

---

[12] This is the literal translation of **Galatians 2:20** - "...the life I now live in the flesh, I live by the faith of the Son of God." There are several other New Testament Scriptures that read the same way in a literal translation. For example, **Galatians 2:16** - "...man is not justified by the works of the law but by the faith of Jesus Christ, even we have believed in Christ Jesus, that we might be justified by the faith of Christ." **Galatians 3:22** - "...the promise by the faith of Jesus Christ might be given to the ones believing." **Philippians 3:9** - "...not having my own righteousness of Law, but through the faith of Christ." **Romans 3:22** - "...even the righteousness of God, through the faith of Jesus Christ." **Romans 3:26** - "...for Him to be just and the justifier of the one who is of the faith of Jesus." **James 2:1** - "My brethren, do not hold the faith of our Lord Jesus Christ, the Lord of glory, with partiality." **Ephesians 3:12** - "...in whom we have boldness and access with confidence by the faith of him." **Revelation 14:12** - "...the saints who are keeping the precepts of God and the faith of Jesus."

The Greatness of Faith

The author of Hebrews describes faith as "the substance of things hoped for and the evidence of things unseen"[13] because this is precisely how faith works in the believer's soul. As we grow in faith, we see and take hold of the spiritual reality behind every old covenant promise, prophecy, type, and shadow. We don't just agree that it is real, or hope to one day experience it. Faith is far greater than that. In perfect fulfillment of Abraham's experience, faith allows us to lift up our eyes, see where we are, and possess the land of our inheritance. Eternal life becomes a present and increasingly tangible reality to the inner man, even while we walk as strangers and pilgrims on earth in vessels of clay. In this way, true faith will actually prove the reality of unseen things, and become clear and conclusive evidence that the soul has become heir and partaker of God's promise through the gospel.

Even after receiving a bachelor's degree in religion and philosophy, I remember hoping that Christianity was based on something more substantial than correct beliefs and doctrines. After four years of study and searching for truth, I still couldn't help but wonder if I believed all the right things. What if I still hadn't come to the right conclusions or grasped what God expected me to understand? What if I had been persuaded by men, or wrongly influenced by my own presuppositions? There were so many interpretations and intelligent arguments. There were multitudes of biblically defendable positions. I tried to stand firm in the things I had been taught and believe the many true things that I had learned. But truth was a slip-

[13] Hebrews 11:1

pery thing for me in those days. Truth was an ever-morphing collection of personal beliefs that was held together by reason and persuasive arguments. And the information kept changing! There was always a book I hadn't yet read or an interpretation I hadn't considered. And while I continued my search to discover the truth, something inside of me began to wonder, "How can a true experience of Christianity depend upon man's ability to find and hold to correct ideas? How can something as important as eternal salvation be contingent upon mental agreement with creeds and concepts, or striving to believe the right spiritual things? There must be something greater than this! There must be something more dependable and real than human belief that determines man's experience of eternal life. Otherwise, I hope I choose the right beliefs before I die! I hope I find a church that explains the Bible the way it should be taught!"

Now I understand that knowing and experiencing spiritual life is based upon something infinitely more real, steadfast, and sure. I thank God that the gift of life is received, known, and experienced by faith. It is true that faith works in us and therefore can rightly be called *our* faith, but although we possess it, we do not produce it. It does not depend upon our education, upbringing, or intellect. It is not a work of the flesh or an accomplishment of the natural mind. Faith is the mind of the Lord being shared with His body. It stands firm in the power and perspective of God, not in the convictions of men.

If you think about it, belief is not even a foundation for meaningful human relationships. For example, I wouldn't say that I believe in my wife. I don't need to believe in her because I know her; I experience her on a daily basis.   Perhaps if I had only heard rumors of her existence – seen a few pencil sketches, or read tales of recent Jessie Henderson sightings – maybe then I would be left with only a belief.   But things being as they are between us, it never crosses my mind whether I should believe in my wife or not.   At this point in our marriage, knowing Jessie as a mere belief would be a significant downgrade in our relationship.   We already have something so much more real.

The Word Faith in the New Testament

As strange as it may sound, the Bible doesn't talk about human beliefs much at all!   In English Bibles, the Greek word for faith (*pistis*) is translated as both faith and belief.   When *pistis* appears as a noun in the New Testament, our translators usually use the English word faith. When the same word appears as a verb it is translated believe or believing.   We translate *pistis* as two different words because the English language lacks a verb form for the word faith.   In other words, nobody says "the man faithed in Christ," or "many people were faithing in Him." However, this is exactly how it reads in the original language.   For example, an extremely literal translation of John 20:31 would read, "These are written that you may *faith* that Jesus is the Christ, the Son of God, and that *faithing* you may have life in His name." Why does this matter?   It matters because belief and faith are two very different things.   Religion has to do with intellectual beliefs and external behaviors; Christianity has everything to do with a life that is lived by faith.[14]

As we read through the New Testament, we encounter descriptions of faith (*pistis*) that simply do not align with our familiar definitions. Although with some verses it may make sense to replace the word faith with belief, hope, or trust, there are plenty of verses that demand a much greater understanding of this word[15]. For example, the author of Hebrews says, "By faith we understand that the ages were framed by the Word of God, so that the things which are seen were not made of things which are visible."[16] Inserting belief or trust in the place of faith in this verse doesn't make sense. Nobody says, "By belief I *understand*..." But if faith, as we have argued, is a kind of seeing and apprehending that works in the soul by the Spirit of God, it is entirely reasonable that believers gain spiritual understanding by faith.

---

[14] Again, true Christianity affects behaviors as well, but external change is the byproduct of an internal transformation, a natural consequence of experiencing Christ's life and light.

[15] There are certainly occurrences in extra-biblical literature, and a few in Scripture as well (like James 2:19), where the Greek word *pistis* is used in a manner similar to our English word belief. I'm not really arguing about the dictionary definition of faith, but rather attempting to describe the way this word was used and, more importantly, *experienced* by the New Testament church. Regardless of what *pistis* might have meant to non-Christians, in the case of a believer, the reality and experience of faith is a God-given light that causes our hearts to share His perspective. The same could be said about almost any word in Scripture. Love, for example, certainly has countless human definitions and is used in a variety of ways throughout the Bible. But a true understanding of God's love is not gained through a written definition but rather through a living experience. In each case, the experience of the word brings its true meaning, definition, and reality to our hearts.

[16] Hebrews 11:3

Later in the same chapter of Hebrews the author explains, "By faith Moses forsook Egypt, not fearing the wrath of the king; for he endured as seeing Him who is invisible."[17] This is perhaps the clearest definition of faith in the Bible – the seeing of Him who is invisible. Not only Moses, but Noah, Abraham, Rahab, and all of the Old Testament saints were commended for having "died in faith, not having received the promises, but having seen them afar off were assured of them, embraced them, and confessed that they were strangers and pilgrims in the earth."[18] Theirs was a faith that saw from afar the things that were to come in Christ. Ours, in the new covenant, is a faith that sees and possesses that which has already come. In each case, faith is something far greater than the beliefs and hopes of the natural mind. It is the very perspective of God made real in the soul by the Spirit of Truth.

The same understanding of faith is evident in Paul's letters to the churches. One interesting example is found in Ephesians. Paul begins this letter commending the church for their faith and their love for the saints. Yet later in the same letter he tells these believers he is praying that they "be strengthened with might through His Spirit in the inner man, that Christ may dwell in your hearts through faith."[19] Someone might object saying, "But these are Christians! Christ is *already* in their hearts!" That is true. But Paul desired that Christ not only *be* in their hearts, but that He live, occupy and govern their hearts by an ever increasing faith.

---

[17] Hebrews 11:27
[18] Hebrews 11:13
[19] Ephesians 3:16-17

Another Scripture where the distinction between faith and belief can be clearly seen is Hebrews chapter four, where the author explains why Israel failed to enter into the Promised Land. He writes:

> *Therefore, since a promise remains of entering His rest, let us fear lest any of you seem to have come short of it. For indeed the gospel was preached to us as well as to them; but the word which they heard did not profit them, not being mixed with faith in those who heard it. For we who have believed [Lit. faithed] do enter that rest.* [20]

The "them" in this Scripture is a reference to the first generation of Israelites that were taken out of Egypt. What these men and women witnessed with their natural eyes is hard to even imagine. They saw ten supernatural plagues poured out upon the entire land of Egypt. They saw the Red Sea open up before their eyes, remain open as they passed through on foot, and then crash in upon an army of pursuing Egyptians. They saw water flow out of a rock, bread fall out of the sky, and a pillar of fire and smoke hover above their tabernacle by day and by night. They even saw the cloud of the Lord descend on Mt. Sinai and heard Him speak to them with a thunderous audible voice. It is estimated that three million Israelites left Egypt under the leadership of Moses, and there was surely not one unbeliever among them. Every man, woman, and child had seen God's glory, experienced His power, and learned that His words were faithful and sure. And yet, "the word

---

[20] Hebrews 4:1-3

which they heard did not profit them, *not being mixed with faith* in those who heard it." To the author of Hebrews, seeing, hearing, and believing in the God of Israel was obviously not the same as faith. They saw Him with their eyes but would not see Him with their hearts. And forty years later, all who witnessed these things perished in the wilderness, never experiencing the inheritance of the Lord that can only be possessed by faith.

Faith vs. Sight

In a very real sense, faith is to the spiritual realm what our five senses are to the natural world. With natural faculties we access, experience, and understand the earth. By faith, however, we access and walk in the reality of what God sees. Scripture speaks of walking by faith and not by sight and this means much more than we usually assume. Walking by faith is not when people live natural lives according to spiritual convictions. It is not simply trusting God for physical health or looking to Him for financial provision. We walk by faith when the light of God's view becomes the operating reality in our heart, and the world that faith sees becomes greater and more real than the world that is accessed by sight. Much of the Christian world is waiting for faith to one day turn into sight. God, however, desires that faith become to us a faculty far more powerful and tangible than sight could ever be.

In the diagram on page 275, the circle on the left represents the created, physical realm. The words in this circle belong to that realm. The circle on the right represents the spiritual and eternal world of Christ into which our souls are placed upon new birth. This circle too has its own list of words that belong to that realm. The overlap in the middle does not represent a blending or mixture between spiritual and natural, but rather the reality that man, for a time, belongs to both realms after being born of the Spirit. The soul of a believer is immediately joined to Christ and made a partaker of all that is real in Him. The body, however, continues on earth as the natural vessel in which we experience the treasure of Christ as our life.

What I am trying to demonstrate with this diagram is that sight sees the natural world of types and shadows on the left, whereas faith sees the world of spirit and truth on the right. As long as we are in these "tents,"[21] we continue to experience and interact with the natural world. We care for our families, work to pay our bills, brush our teeth, and buy groceries. But even during our time in the body, faith should be opening up a whole new world of reality to our soul. As the Spirit opens the eyes of our heart we learn to "fix our mind on things above,"[22] and "look not at those things which are seen, but those which are unseen."[23] By faith we live by the Spirit, walk in the light, dwell in the heavens, and abide in Christ. More and more, we see, comprehend, and possess all that God has accomplished through the cross. Again, faith doesn't merely believe in these things or hope to encounter them one day in the future. These are not doctrines in a Christian mind or Scriptures in a Christian book. These are present spiritual

[21] 2 Corinthians 5:1, 5:4; 2 Peter 1:13-14
[22] Colossians 3:2
[23] 2 Corinthians 4:18

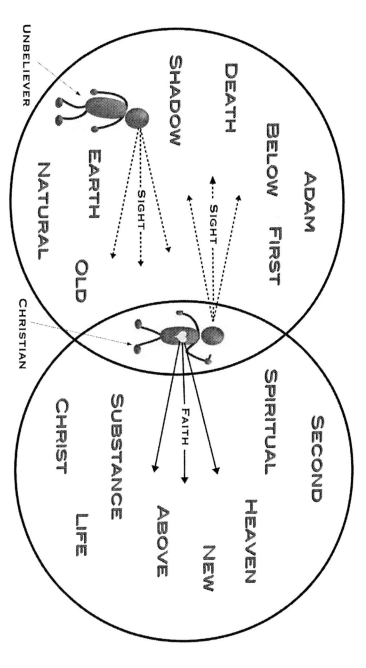

UNBELIEVER

SHADOW
DEATH
BELOW   FIRST
ADAM

NATURAL
EARTH
OLD

SIGHT
SIGHT

CHRISTIAN

FAITH

CHRIST
SUBSTANCE
LIFE
ABOVE

SPIRITUAL
HEAVEN
NEW

SECOND

275

realities that become living experiences to the soul that is growing in faith.

The man in the center of the diagram continues to experience and access the natural world for as long as he lives in a body. But in the meantime faith accesses all that God has given us in Christ. This is exactly what Paul the apostle explains to the church in Rome.

> *Therefore, having been justified by faith, we have peace with God through our Lord Jesus Christ, through whom also we have access by faith into this grace in which we stand, and rejoice in hope of the glory of God.*[24]

Notice both uses of the word faith in this verse. He begins by insisting that Christians are justified by faith. Faith is how our relationship with God begins, how we receive the finished work of the cross. By faith we are baptized into the death of Christ and are reconciled to God through His blood. But faith does not stop with justification. Paul goes on to explain that faith is also how we access the grace in which we stand.

What is grace? There are those in the church who would suggest that the greatness of grace is the forgiveness of sins or the fact that God does not hold us accountable for shortcomings. But grace is exceedingly abundantly greater than that! Grace means so much more than not being punished for acts of unrighteousness; it means the Person of righteousness is living in you! By grace Christians have been made heirs of all that Christ has done, all that He is, and all that He has. The grace that is ours in

---

[24] Romans 5:1-2, emphasis mine

Christ does not change the demands or desires of God, but it lavishes upon us and works in us all that is pleasing to Him. Through the work of the cross, we were crucified with Christ to the man of sin and set firmly in the One who has fulfilled God's desire and accomplished His eternal purpose. Christ can now work in us as the life of our soul, the light of our understanding, the nature that pleases God, the fountain of love and goodness and truth. All of these are aspects of God's grace. But how is it that Christians come to know and experience the immensity of this grace? How do we access all that God has finished and made available in His Son? Paul gives us a clear answer here in Romans – "we have access by faith into this grace in which we stand." He says very much the same thing to the church in Ephesus as well.

> *According to the eternal purpose <u>which He accomplished in Christ Jesus our Lord</u>, in whom we have boldness and <u>access with confidence through faith</u> in Him [Lit. the faith of Him].*[25]

God's "How" For Everything

In previous chapters we discussed the eternal purpose of God. We looked at the finished work of the cross and tried to describe what God has accomplished in His Son. These things have been well-explained by a great number of authors throughout the history of the church. However,

---

[25] Ephesians 3:11-12, emphasis mine

where some of these books fall short is in their description of *how* all that God has accomplished in Christ becomes a present reality and experience in us. Sometimes, after a wonderful presentation of the finished work of the cross and the indwelling life of Christ, authors conclude by offering little more than familiar religious life-applications that have to do with human discipline, behavior modification, and self-motivation. This is unfortunate because, while there is no fleshly method or program that can be offered to make all of this work,[26] there certainly is a way that all of this becomes very real in us. That way is faith – the light that works in the soul as a result of the revelation of Jesus Christ. Faith is the God-given way to see where we are and live in what God has already done. Faith is how we live in and work out all that was accomplished through the cross. Faith is God's *how* for everything.

The absence of true faith is the reason for nearly all of our spiritual confusion and frustration in the body of Christ. We say that we walk with the Lord, but we do not walk by faith. We say that we have received His righteousness, but that righteousness is not working in us by faith.[27] We know we should love our neighbor as we love our-

---

[26] Naturally speaking, we are just as blind and ignorant as to what *working* means to God as we are to any other spiritual thing. It is important to understand that true light will affect not only our understanding of the definition and process of spiritual growth, but the overall goal as well. In other words, in the light we realize that we were wrong about everything. We were wrong about the process of spiritual growth, and we were wrong about God's purpose for it. The reality of Christ revealed and formed in us is not just a better means to the same end or objective that we have always imagined. Only when we are seeing with new eyes do we begin to understand what *working* means to God.

[27] See Romans 1:17, 3:22, 4:13, Galatians 5:5, Philippians 3:9, Hebrews 11:7, 11:33

selves, but we do not know the love that operates by faith.[28] And to whatever extent we do not see and know these realities by faith, we naturally and automatically define each of them by sight – that is, by our natural ideas, experiences, and opinions.

I have heard faith defined as man's response to God's initiative. That has a pleasant sound to it, but it means that faith is entirely a natural thing. A definition like this means that Christians are the authors and finishers of faith, and that when we pass through difficult situations it is our responsibility to somehow muster up faith. When we are scared, angry, or plagued with doubts, the best we can do is call to mind beliefs and Bible verses and try to put hope in these things. Looking at the previous diagram, this version of faith is like living in the left circle while striving to believe in the circle on the right. While our hearts, identity, goals, and treasure all remain in the earth, difficult times make us long for something outside of our circle and we struggle to respond to God's initiative. When we feel stressed it is time to cast our cares over to the right side of the diagram. When we are scared it is time to believe in things that our hearts have never seen and claim things that have never felt real to us. When temptation or lust overwhelms our hearts, we attempt to reckon ourselves dead to sin and alive to God in the circle on the right. But this is not real faith, and it will not produce true fruit.

Paul indeed talks about reckoning ourselves dead to sin, but this reckoning is the natural and effortless consequence of seeing and knowing by faith. In fact, the use of

---

[28] See Galatians 5:6, Ephesians 3:17, Philippians 1:9, 2 Thessalonians 1:3

the word reckon in Romans 6:11 is presented to us as the result of the spiritual "knowing" that Paul mentions in the same passage. He first says, "Do you not *know* that as many of us as were baptized into Christ Jesus were baptized into His death?"[29]   Then a few verses later he writes, "*Knowing* this, that our old man was crucified with Him that the body of sin might be done away with."[30] Then again, he says, "*knowing* that Christ, having been raised from the dead, dies no more."[31] Only after making several references to this knowing does Paul speak of the reckoning that flows out from it – "Likewise you also, reckon yourselves to be dead indeed to sin, but alive to God in Christ Jesus our Lord."[32]

This word reckon has nothing to do with wishful thinking or claiming something that we don't really know. In fact, the Greek word for reckon is a word used in accounting. It has to do with drawing conclusions that are based upon having taken an inventory or having counted or weighed something. What we often don't understand as Christians is that we cannot reckon what we do not truly know. To illustrate our misunderstanding, suppose a man walks into McDonald's wanting to buy lunch but he has no idea if there is any money in his pockets. He waits in line for ten minutes, orders two cheeseburgers and a large fries, and is given the total by the cashier. When he hears the amount owed, he closes his eyes, reaches into his pockets, and begins reckoning upon a five dollar bill with all of his might. It is easy to see that this sort of reckoning is ridicu-

---

[29] Romans 6:3, emphasis mine

[30] Romans 6:6, emphasis mine

[31] Romans 6:9, emphasis mine

[32] Romans 6:11

lous and will obviously accomplish nothing. Reckoning doesn't create money out of nowhere; reckoning simply uses or relies upon the money we know to be available. But if this man had just been to the bank, withdrawn 100 dollars and placed it in his pocket, he could easily and effectively reckon upon the money he knew was there. Paying his bill would have nothing to do with hope or trust or positive thinking. It would be a simple matter of using what he knew to be his.

In a similar way, experiencing the greatness of our salvation has to do with a faith that clearly sees, reckons, and lives in all that God has given to us in Christ. We will never close our eyes, concentrate, and successfully reckon ourselves dead to sin and alive to God in Christ. Walking in this truth is not an effort of the flesh or a trick of the mind. It is the finished work of the cross that becomes a present experience of the soul through faith.

Faith Is For Living

It is unfortunate that so many teachers who emphasize faith in the body of Christ speak of it primarily as a means to secure physical healings or to lay claim to natural provision, prosperity, and blessing. With faith we try to grab hold of heavenly things and pull them down into our natural lives. Rarely, however, do you hear faith proclaimed as a way to escape the life and world below and abide in Christ above. The author of Hebrews boldly declares, "But you have come to Mount Zion and to the city

of the living God, the heavenly Jerusalem, to an innumerable company of angels, to the general assembly and
church of the firstborn who are registered in heaven."[33]
This is presented as a finished work and a present reality
for all new covenant believers. But who wants to see and
walk in these things? Instead of simply using faith to fix
our problems in the earth, who desires a faith that overcomes the world and causes us to live as citizens of
heaven? Jesus said: "These things I have spoken to you,
that in Me you may have peace. In the world you will have
tribulation; but be of good cheer, I have overcome the
world."[34]   Later, John explains how Christ's victory
becomes our experience: "For whatever is born of God
overcomes the world. And this is the victory that has
overcome the world—our faith."[35]

Faith doesn't always fix the earth, but it always shows
you another life and realm and lets your soul abide there.
It won't take away all natural problems or heal all natural
pain, but it will define and establish your heart in the truth
even before arriving at life's many difficulties. Human
beings face all sorts of tribulations and trials. There are
some who are familiar with even the greatest torments of
body and mind. But thanks be to God that faith is far
greater than our mind and more enduring than our bodies.
As a matter of fact, faith grants us the Lord's mind and
causes us to live as His body.

Hundreds of years before Christ, the prophet
Habakkuk spoke of a day when "the just shall live by

---

[33] Hebrews 12:22-23
[34] John 16:33
[35] 1 John 5:4

faith."[36] Paul quotes this Scripture three times in the New Testament.[37] Notice that Habakkuk did not write, "The just shall be saved by faith," or "The just shall be counted righteous by faith." Both of these statements would be true as well, but there is something more that we are meant to see in the words of the prophet. We are meant to see that faith is for *living*. In other words, true faith is how we abide in Christ's life, and how His life works in us.

It is evident in Scripture that Paul the apostle was a man that came to do all things by faith. Paul walked by faith, prayed by faith, taught by faith, and worked miracles by faith. This is just another way to say that Paul did all these things by the life of Christ operating in him. Notice again how Paul concludes his famous words to the Galatians.

> *I am crucified with Christ: nevertheless I live; yet not I, but Christ liveth in me: <u>and the life which I now live in the flesh I live by the faith of the Son of God</u>, who loved me, and gave himself for me.*[38]

Faith was the mind of Christ working in the apostle, and what a mighty work God was able to do in and through him! God triumphed in this man because he walked by faith and not by sight. Like Abraham his forefather, Paul "grew strong in faith, giving glory to God."[39] And it is for this very reason that Paul could say, "For me to live is

---

[36] Habakkuk 2:4
[37] Romans 1:17, Galatians 3:11, Hebrews 10:38
[38] Galatians 2:20 KJV, emphasis mine
[39] Romans 4:20 – This quote is spoken about Abraham

Christ, and to die is gain."[40]   When Paul walked by faith, Christ Himself was the life that governed his actions and constrained his soul.

---

[40] Philippians 1:21

Chapter XVII

Transformation of the Soul

After years of heart-felt prayer and fasting, dedicated ministry, and spiritual disciplines, one of the things that frustrated and confused me more than anything else was the conspicuous lack of change in my heart. This became more and more apparent as years went by. Discipline had made me a zealous Christian; Bible-study had made me familiar with Scripture; ministry had given me a reputation among other believers, but none of this had truly transformed my soul. When I was alone before the Lord, all of my masks, arguments, and excuses fell to the floor, and I had to admit that my heart was no different. I had no doubt that Jesus and His apostles preached a gospel for the *inner* man. There was no way to deny that the pages of the New Testament were filled with descriptions of inward transformation, "fountains of living water"[1] in the soul, the "cleansing of the conscience,"[2] and freedom from slavery to sin. I was familiar with all of these concepts but I knew I

---

[1]   John 4:14
[2]   Hebrews 9:14. See also Hebrews 9:9, 10:22

had not truly experienced them. In quiet times alone with God, I knew that my experience of Christianity had very little to do with being "conformed to the image of His Son."[3]

Freedom from Darkness

One of the primary reasons I devoted so much time to discussing spiritual sight, the revelation of Christ, walking by faith, etc. in previous chapters is because seeing with the Lord's light is the *only* way that any true change takes place in the human soul. Even though there are multitudes of verses that declare this very thing, Christians still struggle with this idea. For some believers, an emphasis on spiritual sight seems abstract or mystical. For others, it seems too simple, basic, or inactive. We are so used to human effort, action plans, and hard work that pays off. We like methods and models and organized steps that show measurable progress. It seems so impractical to just "stand still and see the salvation of the Lord."[4] How could something as elementary as knowing the truth really set us free from ourselves? But this is precisely what Jesus said – "If you abide in My word, you are My disciples indeed. And you shall know the truth, and the truth shall make you free."[5] Almost everyone in the church is familiar with this verse. Our problem is that we, like the Jews who heard Jesus speak these words, are unfamiliar with both the nature of our slavery and the kind of knowing that has this incredible effect in our soul.

---

[3] Romans 8:29
[4] Exodus 14:13
[5] John 8:31-32

Our slavery is to the nature of sin that governs the natural man, and in order to find freedom from our bondage we must first find a true exodus from Adam. We have seen that the cross is that exodus, and it is infinitely more real and liberating than the type and shadow seen in Israel's departure from Egypt. At the moment of new birth, we are translated out of the kingdom of Pharaoh and placed forever in the Son of God's love. The work is over, the land of sin and death is left behind, and we come out as one new man in covenant with God. But just like the Israelites that crossed the Red Sea so many years ago, we soon discover that it is one thing for God to take us out of Egypt and another thing altogether to allow Him to take Egypt out of us.

Moses' generation saw the mighty armies of Egypt wash up dead on the banks of the Red Sea. But even this did not stop them from looking back to that fallen kingdom all the days of their lives. Pharaoh was dead, but they still served him in their hearts. Slavery was over, but in ignorance and spiritual blindness they held tightly to their chains. God had forever separated them from that land of death and bondage, but Israel would not bear this division in their souls and count all former things as dung. Over and over they grumbled against God and cried out to Moses, "Why have you brought us up out of Egypt?"[6] "We remember the fish which we ate freely in Egypt, the cucumbers, the melons, the leeks, the onions, and the garlic;"[7] "Let us select a leader and return to Egypt."[8] Here we see why light is so necessary. In our hearts we live in

---

[6] Exodus 17:3
[7] Numbers 11:5
[8] Numbers 14:4

the darkness and vanity of the unrenewed mind until God's light begins to show us where we are and what He has done. Without a true revelation of our salvation, we wander aimlessly in the wilderness of our own ideas, living contrary to God's purpose and seeking to protect the adamic man – a man whom God has already judged and left behind. For better or for worse, we are a living expression of whatever is most real in our hearts.

Knowing the truth with true spiritual light transforms the soul because it puts out of your heart what God has already put away from Himself through the cross. In His light, what is dead to God becomes dead to you, and what is alive to God becomes the only life that you know. To illustrate, imagine that you are locked in a completely dark room where you are constantly tormented by a fear of crocodiles. You have obviously never seen a crocodile because there is absolutely no light in the room, but you have heard suspicious sounds and once or twice thought you felt something brush up against your leg. Days, weeks, perhaps months go by, but your fears will not subside. You continually reason with yourself saying, "Don't be silly, why would there be a crocodile in this room?" Or, "If there were really a crocodile in this room, it would have eaten me by now. I'm sure I'm quite safe." But all of the self-talk and intellectual reasoning has little effect on your emotions. Logical or not, you think what you think and you feel what you feel. One day, however, as you are curling up in a ball on the floor to escape an indistinct crocodile-like noise, your hand happens upon a box of matches. You frantically pull out a match, strike it on the side of the box, and a flame lights for a second and then goes out. For just one second you see the room in the dim light of a single match, and a wave of joy and relief strikes your heart. You couldn't see clearly, or for very long, but in that one flash of light there was definitely no crocodile in sight. Still fearful, but now at last with hope, you reach for the box and light another match. This one stays lit long enough for you to discover a shelf on the wall filled with candles which you excitedly light one by one. After only a few minutes, all the candles are lit and the entire room is flooded with light. It was true what you thought you saw in that initial flash of light – there are absolutely no crocodiles in the room and there apparently never have been. After so many months of fear and trauma it takes a while for your nerves to settle. But after sitting in the light for some hours and examining every square inch of the room, your emotions begin to calm, the fear fades away and becomes meaningless, and your heart at last begins to rest.

This analogy is helpful in a couple different ways. First, it illustrates to some degree what seeing or knowing the Lord feels like to the human heart. It is not an external light, an angelic voice, or a prophetic vision. It is like a new and foreign light that shines in our heart and brings something real into view. That is what all light does – it shows us what is real. Natural light has this immediate effect on our natural senses. In a flash of natural light we become conscious of our surroundings; we become aware of what is there. Like a flash of lightning on a pitch black night, suddenly the world around us comes into view. Spiritual light does very much the same thing, but it shines "in our hearts to give the light of the knowledge of the glory of God in the face of Jesus Christ."[9]   As the light of life flashes in our soul, we are brought to an ever increasing awareness of what is spiritually real.   It's not like a dream or vision that uses symbols or words to represent spiritual realities.   There are no figures that need to be interpreted or words that can be misunderstood.   It is as simple as seeing in the Lord's light what is true in Him.   It is like waking up from a long adamic dream, rubbing our eyes, and slowly recognizing what is real.

The second thing that this analogy illustrates well is that the natural byproduct of seeing what is real in Christ is a progressive liberty from all that is *not* real.   Just as the light made it impossible to continue fearing a crocodile that was not in the room, so too it becomes impossible for us to feel, think, and hold onto the fruits of darkness that have no place in Christ.   Light shows us where we are, what God has done in Christ, and all ideas and feelings contrary to the truth begin to fade away and lose their meaning.

In our analogy, the person quickly lit an entire shelf full of candles and the room was almost immediately filled with light.   Here is where our analogy falls short.   In our hearts, it doesn't happen in one perfect and permanent explosion of light.   It's more like the sun that slowly rises in the morning.   First there is just a glimmer on the horizon, but little by little the sun makes its way to the center of the sky where all shadows disappear.   Proverbs says, "But the path of the righteous is like the shining sun, that shines ever brighter unto the perfect day."[10]   And in our experience, there always seems to be more of His light to know

---

[9]   2 Corinthians 4:6
[10]   Proverbs 4:18

and more of our darkness to remove. It's important to realize, however, that the Lord does not need to do two separate things in our hearts – one being to teach us the truth and the other being to remove from us all that is false. Seeing Christ accomplishes both of these. In the natural realm, nobody attempts to remove darkness from a room by scooping it up and throwing it out a window. We understand that to remove darkness all we need is to turn on a light. The increase of the one becomes the decrease of the other. Speaking to his disciples about Jesus, John the Baptist said, "He must increase; I must decrease."[11] The order here is crucial. He did not say "I must decrease so that He can increase." Like light filling a dark room, the increase of Christ[12] *becomes* the decrease of everything else. I stress this because Christians of every denomination and background go to great lengths in their attempts to free themselves from fleshly acts and desires. But, although it is certainly appropriate at times to restrain

---

[11] John 3:30 I believe that John was speaking of more than just the decrease of his own personal ministry. John was the last of the old covenant prophets, and in a way summed up them all. Jesus said, "All of the prophets and the law prophesied until John." (Matt 11:13). In one way or another, all of the law and prophets spoke of Christ as their fulfillment. And John the Baptist, at the end of that age, was the very last piece of the testimony. Like all of the law and prophets before him, John stood in Israel, pointed to Christ, and said, "Behold the Lamb of God!" In saying "He must increase; I must decrease," John is speaking of the disappearing of the shadow now that the substance has finally arrived. The new had come, and it was time for the old to be put away.

[12] Whenever I speak about the increase of Christ, I am not talking about us getting more of Christ, but rather Christ getting more of us. The increase isn't ever a quantitative increase, as though we were receiving more and more of Christ over time. The increase is always the increase of His light and government working in our soul.

the adamic man,[13] true freedom and transformation are the fruits of Christ's kingdom taking ground in our soul and leaving room for nothing else.

It is essential to realize these things if we are going to understand how change happens in the human soul. The transformation of the soul has nothing to do with somehow making flesh[14] better. Transformation is not about fixing or improving the old, but rather experiencing and abiding in the new. The cross does not change Adam; it leaves him behind. It doesn't make a better version of you; it leaves the *you* that you've known in the grave and grants your soul the life of Another. Paul calls this "walking in newness of life"[15] because Christ's life is perfectly new in every conceivable way. Consequently, a careful search of the New Testament will turn up nothing that has to do with the restoration of the old man. In fact, Paul is quite clear that the change we experience involves "putting off the old man together with His deeds,"[16] or "putting off... the old man which grows corrupt according to deceitful lusts."[17] In order to experience freedom from Adam's lusts and deeds, the entire man must be put off from our hearts. This, he says, is the "circumcision without hands, in putting off the body of flesh by the circumcision of Christ."[18] It is first and

---

[13] For a greater explanation of this see the Frequently Asked Questions section at the end of the book.

[14] The word flesh is used in Scripture sometimes to speak of the natural body (i.e. Galatians 2:20) and other times to speak of the nature of Adam or sin that works in the natural man. I am referring to the latter meaning here.

[15] Romans 6:4

[16] Colossians 3:9

[17] Ephesians 4:22

[18] Colossians 2:11

foremost a finished work of God in Christ. But it becomes a present reality and experience in us to the measure that we see all things in the light of the truth.

Truth Makes its Own Application

One of the common misunderstandings in the body of Christ is the idea that spiritual reality is presented to us in the Bible to be read, remembered, and then applied to our lives. This would make sense if Christianity were a set of rules and values for living in a certain way. But since the goal of all spiritual learning is the knowing of a Person,[19] One who is also the life of our soul, then all application of truth is God's responsibility and His gift. Just like the person in our analogy experienced when he lit the candles and saw the room for the first time, truth applies itself to the soul when it is truly known. You see what's real and the reality affects you. It does not leave you there wondering how to make an application.

As we look through the pages of the New Testament, we read nothing of believers trying to apply spiritual facts to the natural man. Instead, we read of individuals who were confronted by, acquainted with, constrained by, and ultimately conformed to the reality that God was showing them. The following analogy may help to illustrate.

Imagine for a moment that after hiking up a mountain and eating a large picnic lunch, you fall sound asleep on

---

[19] In Jesus' words, "And this is eternal life, that they may know You, the only true God, and Jesus Christ whom You have sent." (John 17:3)

the edge of an enormous cliff. While you sleep, you happily dream of all of the plans you have for the day once you return home. You dream of walking your dog, reading a good book, painting the bedroom walls, etc. Your mind is filled with the afternoon's many possible activities. However, while you are still sound asleep, you accidentally roll off the edge of the cliff and begin a 2,000 foot plummet to the bottom of a deep ravine.

For the first 500 feet of the fall you remain asleep and are entirely unaware of what has happened. You continue to dream your dreams, make your afternoon plans, and smile in your heart with happy expectation, even as you fall faster and faster towards the earth. But all at once you awake, and notice the wind in your face, the mountain flying by, and the ground rapidly approaching. You quickly realize where you are and what is going on, and immediately all of your plans, ideas, and emotions begin to change. You may indeed have been intending to take a walk, but now that idea seems completely irrelevant. You may have had your heart set on painting your bedroom, but suddenly that is the furthest thing from your mind. Why the change? Because you have awakened to something that is already real and the truth of the situation is making its own application to you. Regardless of what you might like to believe, the reality that you see now is certain and inescapable, and the consequences are already upon you. Gravity is not an option. It is not Isaac Newton's opinion. It is an unchanging, inflexible law, and as such, is not open to discussion. You can reject it, but only by *pretending* that it is not real. Perhaps if you could somehow will yourself back into a dream, you might be able to deceive yourself into defeating gravity, but only until you hit the ground.

One weakness with this analogy is that the falling person is awaking to a horrible situation whereas the soul in Christ is awaking to a wonderful salvation. Nevertheless, the principle is the same – truth applies itself when it is seen. The Spirit of God opens the eyes of our heart in Christ and shows us what has already happened and we see that the consequences are already upon us. As He shows us what is real, there are soon so many ideas, realities, beliefs, goals, fears, and plans that cease to be alternatives. Faith discovers what God *has* accomplished in Christ and the power of His cross works in us because of what has already been completed by Him. In other words, in His light the reality of God's finished work begins to appear real and feel real to our soul.

The Renewing of the Mind

Every time the concept of transformation appears in the New Testament it is mentioned in the context of beholding the truth and experiencing a renewal of the mind. Consider the following verses:

> *And do not be conformed to this world, but <u>be transformed by the renewing of your mind</u>, that you may prove what is that good and acceptable and perfect will of God.*[20]

---

[20] Romans 12:2, emphasis mine

This I say, therefore, and testify in the Lord, that you should no longer walk as the rest of the Gentiles walk, in the futility of their mind... But you have not so learned Christ, if indeed you have heard Him and have been taught by Him, as the truth is in Jesus: that you put off, concerning your former conduct, the old man which grows corrupt according to the deceitful lusts, and <u>be renewed in the spirit of your mind</u>, and that you put on the new man which was created according to God, in true righteousness and holiness.[21]

Do not lie to one another, since you have put off the old man with his deeds, and have put on the new man who <u>is renewed in knowledge according to the image of Him who created him</u>, where there is neither Greek nor Jew, circumcised nor uncircumcised, barbarian, Scythian, slave nor free, but Christ is all and in all.[22]

But we all, with unveiled face, <u>beholding</u> as in a mirror the glory of the Lord, <u>are being transformed into the same image</u> from glory to glory, just as by the Spirit of the Lord.[23]

---

[21] Ephesians 4:17-24, emphasis mine
[22] Colossians 3:9-11, emphasis mine
[23] 2 Corinthians 3:18, emphasis mine

The common thread in all of these Scriptures is the reality that a genuine beholding of the truth results in conformity to the image of the Lord. Why does this happen? Again, it happens because we are seeing what is already finished and real. We are seeing the final product of a work of God and the implications and significance are thrust upon us in the light. We are transformed by the renewing of the mind because we are putting on what we already are, and learning to live in what God has already done.

Every born-again believer has received the fulness of Christ's life. But like many creatures in the natural realm, we were born blind. We need a work to be done in the mind[24] (spiritual understanding) that causes us to realize and align with the life that we now have. A renewed mind is simply a mind that matches or corresponds with the life that we have in Christ. An *un*renewed mind is a mind that is contrary to, or ignorant of, the new life that we received. In other words, the renewing of the mind is a process where the Holy Spirit causes spiritual understanding to catch up with spiritual reality. The Spirit awakens us to what God has already done, causing us to "know the things that have been freely given to us by God."[25] The result is not that we receive more of something we do not have, but that we are transformed into the image of what we do have.

Practically, this involves leaving behind one man and being found in Another. I repeat, this is not a changing of

---

[24] When Paul speaks of the renewing of the *mind,* he is not referring to the physical brain or natural intellect but rather the deeper faculty of understanding, perception, judgment, recognition, etc. in the inner man. I believe this is why he uses the language "be renewed in the spirit of your mind" in Ephesians 4:23.

[25] 1 Corinthians 2:12

the old man, but a great transition from one man, kind, and nature to another. The renewing of the mind is not the renewing of Adam; it is a Spirit-worked recognition that Adam is judged, dead, and removed from the camp. To the degree that we are seeing with God's light, Adam and his deeds are left behind and we move on with Christ onto resurrected ground.

The Kingdom of God

In two of the Scriptures quoted above, Paul explicitly says that the renewing of the spirit of the mind has the effect of putting off one man and putting on another. Another way to say the same thing is that the renewal of the mind causes the heart to experience the cross. It is always this way. Any true view of Christ is inevitably a confrontation with the judgment of the cross where something of the Lord is seen and established, and something of Adam is exposed and taken down.

We must understand that Christ and the cross are not really two distinct things. I don't mean that Jesus is two sticks of wood. Of course there is a distinction between Jesus the Nazarene and the wooden boards to which he was nailed. What I mean is that when we begin to know the Lord we will not know Him apart from the cross. Knowing Christ is knowing the One who is dead to sin, dead to Adam, and alive to God forevermore. Dying to sin is not just something Christ did; it is something He is. He is *still* dead to sin. In the same way, resurrection is not just something Christ did, it is something He is. And for us,

His body, truly knowing Christ will be an inward seeing and experience of being both dead to the old and alive to the new *in Him*. This is exactly how Paul described his experience of knowing the Lord.

> *Yet indeed I also count all things loss for the excellence of the knowledge of Christ Jesus my Lord, for whom I have suffered the loss of all things, and count them as rubbish, that I may gain Christ... That I may know Him and the power of His resurrection, and the fellowship of His sufferings, being conformed to His death, if, by any means, I may attain to the resurrection from the dead.*[26]

Knowing Christ is a continual experience of the cross. This may sound confusing at first, but it works in you as something very real and practical. Every time the light flashes in your heart, something of God's finished work in Christ becomes visible. You see Him in a new way and your view increases. But in this new light you see *both* sides of the cross; you see both what God has accepted and what God has judged and left behind. You see something true and wonderful and real, but you also recognize something that does not belong. Like Israel holding on to Egypt in their hearts, there are always things of the old, things of the flesh, that you have held onto in the darkness of the unrenewed mind. There are adamic thoughts, imaginations, lies, strongholds – things that the cross rejects, but that your heart has held onto in spiritual blind-

---

[26] Philippians 3:7-11

ness. Knowing the truth leaves no room for these things. One by one they are crowded out of your heart by the light of Christ's life. Notice Paul's description of Christ's victory over the darkness in us.

> *For though we walk in the flesh, we do not war according to the flesh. For the weapons of our warfare are not carnal but mighty in God for pulling down strongholds, casting down arguments and every high thing that exalts itself against the knowledge of God, bringing every thought into captivity to the obedience of Christ.*[27]

Contrary to some popular interpretations of these verses, Paul is not talking about casting demons out of cities or battling satanic forces in the world. Everything he mentions in these verses is taking place *within* the believer, and the enemies presented are strongholds of the mind, arguments, thoughts, and high things that exalt themselves against a true knowing of God. Furthermore, Paul is not making up this terminology. He is purposely borrowing the language used in the Old Testament stories that deal with the Kingdom of God conquering the idolatrous, uncircumcised land of Canaan. David went throughout the land pulling down strongholds, taking enemies captive, and removing the high places where the people worshipped according to their own imagination. Little by little, the land that God chose for His own dwelling place was purified of all things contrary to Him. The increase of

---

[27] 2 Corinthians 10:3

David's kingdom in the land became the decrease of every other rule and authority.

This is precisely what the Lord seeks to do in the land of our souls. We are now the land that He has purchased with blood and the place that He has chosen for His dwelling place and His kingdom. The renewing of the mind by the revelation of Christ is the way that He now enlarges the boundaries of His government in us. Our entire soul belongs to Him the moment we are born again. But by growing in the true knowledge of God, the land of our heart comes under glad subjection to its righteous King, and it progressively bears the image of His nature, purpose, and rule. This is true obedience. Many Christians strive every day to be outwardly obedient even while their hearts are still contrary to the nature and purpose of the Lord. But the renewing of the mind produces an inward obedience of the soul. By seeing Christ, our souls align with and conform to His indwelling life and we are transformed into the same image from glory to glory.[28]

All of this sounds wonderful as a mere concept. One might be tempted to say, "Who wouldn't want the light of Christ to displace the darkness that works in our hearts? Why wouldn't we let Him conquer every carnal stronghold in our soul?" But thoughts like these betray an ignorance of ourselves. When Christ's light shines in the heart it does not only remove the things that we don't like about ourselves, or the things we have identified as being contrary to Him. Christ's light will demand both what we call bad and what we call good. His light will vanquish both our tormenting lies and our favorite imaginations.

---

[28] 2 Corinthians 3:18

We all want the power of the cross to free us from the flesh that we hate, but our hearts build walls and fight to protect the flesh that we love, the flesh that we call our life.[29] We must remember that we *are* the flesh, the idolatry, the uncircumcision, and the rebellion in the land. We are by nature the thing that is resisting Christ's rule. We are the darkness that is displaced by His light. And it is rare to find a heart that is willing to bear the decrease that the truth demands.

Sooner or later, the Lord comes with His sword to every walled city of our hearts. He comes to destroy them like Jericho, and declare that they shall never again be rebuilt. These cities are the things in us that do not have Christ as their substance and source. They are things that the cross has crucified but we have thus far refused to bury out of our sight.[30] We have held onto them in the darkness

---

[29] King Saul was removed from his throne for precisely this reason. He kept what he considered the best of a kingdom that God had judged and given over to destruction. 1 Samuel 15:9 says, "But Saul and the people spared Agag and the best of the sheep, the oxen, the fatlings, the lambs, and all that was good, and were unwilling to utterly destroy them. But everything despised and worthless, that they utterly destroyed."

[30] In the natural realm, burial is how we remove from our sight something that is already dead. By burying somebody we are officially ending our relationship with them, removing them from our view, and giving their body back to the earth. Speaking of Sarah when she had died, Abraham said, "I am a foreigner and a visitor among you. Give me property for a burial place among you, that I may bury my dead out of my sight." The same principle applies when we experience the work of the cross in our hearts. God has crucified Adam together with his world, but now we must allow Him to bury the dead out of our sight. There is no point carrying around the dead old man, dressing him up, and trying to make him appear pleasing to God. The cross declared this man dead to God, so we must allow the Lord to remove him from our view and end our heart's relationship with him forever.

and ignorance of our soul, not realizing that they are foreign and uncircumcised seeds that have no right to remain in the Lord's land. Sometimes the light exposes strongholds of pride, religion, flesh, or lies. Other times what we see in the light feels even more devastating – invalidating ministries, nullifying life goals, destroying long-held beliefs, even exposing forty years of aimless wandering in the wilderness of man's ideas and opinions. But what are we going to do? Look away? Are we going to close our eyes and pretend it isn't true? I've seen people do this, but it doesn't change what's real. The only true option is to acknowledge what we see in His light, and let things come to be in our soul just as they are in Christ.

It was with a view to this inward working of the cross that Jesus spoke so much about losing our life, dying daily, and carrying our cross. Objectively speaking, the work of the cross is finished and perfect; it lacks nothing. Subjectively speaking, we lack the revelation of the truth that causes God's reality to become the reality that works in us. Make no mistake about it, knowing the truth will cost us what we've called our life. It will cause us to be "conformed to His death,"[31] and to "bear about in our body the dying of Jesus."[32] But even so, there will be no sense of loss. Quite to the contrary, we will happily "suffer the loss of all things, and count them as dung, that we may gain Christ."[33] In His marvelous light, we see and understand that the cross of Christ is the love of God for all who will receive it. Only through the cross could God give us "beauty for ashes, the oil of joy for mourning, the garment

---

[31] Philippians 3:10
[32] 2 Corinthians 4:10
[33] Philippians 3:8

of praise for the spirit of heaviness; that we may be called trees of righteousness, the planting of the LORD, that He may be glorified."[34]

---

[34] Isaiah 61:3

Appendix

Frequently Asked Questions

1. Where can I learn more?

Our website www.marketstreetfellowship.com has a large quantity of free teaching resources. Most of the subjects discussed in this book can be explored in greater depth through the resources provided there. There are hundreds of free audio sermons, Bible studies, and e-books that can be downloaded as audio and text files. Additionally, we offer all of our printed publications, softcover books, and CDs free upon request. There is absolutely no charge for products or for shipping. Visit our website for more information, or email msfprinting@gmail.com.

Additionally, please feel free to contact me with any questions or comments at my personal email address – henderjay@gmail.com.

2. What about good works?

Inevitably, when people begin to see and understand the finished work of the cross, questions arise about good works. If we have any history in the church, we have probably heard a great number of teachings that focus on behavior change and the need for Christians to produce good works. However, in light of all that God has accomplished through the cross of Christ and His clear declaration that in our flesh dwells no good thing,[1] how should we understand the good works mentioned in Scripture? What do we do with passages that seem to tell us to do good things?

To begin, it is wise to remind ourselves of God's eternal purpose. Wrong presuppositions always bring us to wrong conclusions. What does God truly want from the church? Once we have been born of His Spirit, what is His foremost expectation for the body of Christ? Many people wrongly assume that God is primarily seeking a certain kind of human behavior. After receiving the gift of salvation, it is often said that God expects us to try to act like Jesus, talk like Jesus, love like Jesus, and do the works that Jesus did. This may sound like a noble goal, but we've already demonstrated the fallacy of this assumption. If this were what God wanted, He could have simply left us under the law. If man could produce what God requires, the Old Covenant would have sufficed as an appropriate list of do's and don'ts.

The Scriptures unanimously testify that we were saved from sin and death in order to walk in a different kind of life, not merely a different kind of behavior. As Christians, our behavior certainly changes, but only because His life is given and our soul is transformed. We are meant to become recipients, participants, and living expressions of the life and glory of Jesus Christ. And every discussion about good works must stand securely upon this foundation.

---

[1] Romans 7:18. See also Romans 3:10-20, John 6:63

What are good works?

On one occasion a certain ruler approached Jesus and asked, "Good Teacher, what shall I do to inherit eternal life?" Jesus responded to him, "Why do you call me good? No one is good but One, that is God."[2] Obviously Jesus *was* good. In another Scripture He calls Himself the "good shepherd."[3] But this ruler had no business calling Jesus good unless He also knew Him to be God in the flesh. Jesus wanted this man to understand that goodness is not a word that should be used arbitrarily or connected to anything that does not have God as its source and substance. We do well to keep this in mind while we consider passages in the New Testament that speak of good works.

In order for our works to be good in any way, they must be the outworking of the indwelling Christ. Man tries to judge the goodness of an action or word based upon whether it seems nice or mean, friendly or grumpy, helpful or hurtful. God, however, recognizes the difference between Adam and Christ, which is also the difference between death and life. Goodness, from God's point of view, is not defined by the appearance of our work or by its effect in the natural realm, but rather by its source and function. Man praises the action itself; God sees through to the author and motivation. For a work to be truly good, it must be a work of the Lord through His own body. This is clearly stated in a number of Scriptures. For example:

---

[2] Luke 18:18-19
[3] John 10:11

For it is God who works in you both to will and to do for His good pleasure.[4]

For this purpose I labor, striving according to His power which mightily works in me.[5]

Now may the God of peace who brought up our Lord Jesus from the dead, that great Shepherd of the sheep, through the blood of the everlasting covenant, make you complete in every good work to do His will, <u>working in you what is well pleasing in His sight, through Jesus Christ,</u> to whom be glory forever and ever. Amen.[6]

And this is the condemnation, that the light has come into the world, and men loved darkness rather than light, because their deeds were evil. For everyone practicing evil hates the light and does not come to the light, lest his deeds should be exposed. But he who does the truth comes to the light, <u>that his deeds may be clearly seen, that they have been wrought in God</u>.[7]

Abide in Me, and I in you. As the branch cannot bear fruit of itself, unless it abides in the vine, neither can you, unless you abide in Me. I am the vine, you are the branches. He who abides in Me, and I in him, bears much fruit;

---

[4] Philippians 2:13
[5] Colossians 1:29
[6] Hebrews 13:20-21, emphasis mine
[7] John 3:19-21, emphasis mine

for without Me you can do nothing. If anyone does not abide in Me, he is cast out as a branch and is withered; and they gather them and throw them into the fire, and they are burned.[8]

In these verses, and many others that are similar, we see that believers are the vessels or branches though whom Christ works, but He is the author of every truly good work. Even Jesus, when He walked as a man, lived as a Branch that bore the righteous fruit of Another. He often explained, "The Father abiding in me does His works,"[9] or "I do nothing of My own initiative,"[10] or "The word which you hear is not Mine but the Father's who sent Me."[11] Jesus did not come to manifest His own life or His own name. As the Son of Man, His purpose in all things was to manifest the life, words, and works of His Father. Now, in the new covenant, it is we who are the branches and Christ is the Vine. And to the measure that Christ is formed in us, we too can say "The Son abiding in me does His works. The words I speak are not mine but His." Unless He is the One working in and through us, there is nothing we do that merits the word good.

We must remember that all of our works, good or bad, are expressions of a nature that works within us. As we have discussed, in Adam our works are effortless expressions of the nature of sin, the kingdom of darkness that governs the unbelieving soul. This is precisely what Jesus explained to the Jews.

---

8 John 15:4-6, emphasis mine
9 John 14:10
10 John 5:30
11 John 14:24

Why do you not understand My speech? Because you are not able to listen to My word. You are of your father the devil, and the desires of your father you want to do. He was a murderer from the beginning, and does not stand in the truth, because there is no truth in him. When he speaks a lie, he speaks from his own resources, for he is a liar and the father of it.[12]

By nature we are all expressions of "the spirit who works in the sons of disobedience."[13] We were born dead in sin and trespasses, and were "fulfilling the desires of the flesh and of the mind, and were by nature children of wrath."[14] It is only by receiving Christ as the new life of our soul that we become partakers of a new nature. Furthermore, it is only to the measure that His life works in us by faith that we become living expressions of His nature, a nature the Bible calls righteousness. For this reason, when Jesus was asked, "What shall we do, that we may work the works of God?" Jesus answered and said to them, "This is the work of God, that you believe (Lit. faith) in Him whom He sent."[15] Only by seeing and abiding in the life that we have received does the nature of Christ produce its fruit in and through us.

When Christians begin to see the finished work of the cross, the struggle and confusion that arises with the

---

[12] John 8:43-44

[13] Ephesians 2:2

[14] Ephesians 2:3

[15] John 6:28-29. As always, the word "believe" in this verse is the Greek word *pistis,* or faith. See chapter 16 for more on this.

phrase "good works" is due to our own presuppositions and misunderstandings. Almost automatically, when we happen across this phrase in the New Testament, our mind conjures up thoughts of works of the law or works of the flesh. Neither of these is ever what the New Testament authors had in mind.

In a sense, it is correct to say that Israel, under the old covenant, did good works by keeping the law. However, the goodness of their works was not truly in their hearts but rather in the specific actions and ceremonies that all represented Christ in one way or another. In other words, the sacrifices, offerings, behaviors, etc., of the law were good because they created types and shadows of the One who is good. They were good shadows and good testimonies. But we know from the prophets, the apostles, and from Christ Himself, that the heart of man under the old covenant was always contrary to the nature and mind of the Lord.

With regard to works of the flesh, there are many things that appear good to the natural eye or that indeed *are* good for the natural man. Helping an old lady across the street or volunteering at a soup kitchen are certainly nice things to do. And even when our hearts do these things begrudgingly or for attention and praise, they are still helpful, appropriate, and beneficial for society. But if these are indeed the works that God seeks, then the cross of Christ and the giving of the Spirit were entirely unnecessary. Atheists are just as capable as Christians of doing works in the flesh that are outwardly beneficial for mankind. But again, from God's point of view, goodness is not determined by the work itself or its temporary external effect, but by the source, life, and purpose behind the work, all of which must be Christ.[16] Truly good works are the fruit of His Spirit working in us according to His nature and towards His eternal purpose.

3. What about the do's and don'ts of the New Testament?

Before I began to understand something of the reality of the cross, I used to gravitate towards the verses in the New Testament that seemed to offer practical instructions on how to live a godly life. I didn't spend much time trying to understand what it meant to be baptized into Christ's death, or made dead to sin, or hidden with Christ in God. I knew these concepts were in the Bible, and I knew they had to have significance. They were beautiful Scriptures, but they seemed too lofty or deep to be practical. I wanted to find verses that were more concrete, ones that told me plainly what God wanted and how I could do it.

In those days, if I were going to pick up the Bible and read Ephesians, I would most likely begin reading in chapter four. If I were to read Romans, I would be drawn towards chapter twelve or thirteen. In Galatians, the prac-

---

[16] I would go as far as to say that the recipient of all good works mentioned in Scripture is also Christ, that is, His body the church. Though it is certainly appropriate for us to be kind and charitable towards all mankind, it seems to me that the phrase "good works" is reserved in Scripture for that which the mind of Christ works through the members of His body to the end that all "grow up in all things into Him who is the head, even Christ." (Ephesians 4:15)

tical instructions begin in chapter five. You will notice something about Paul's letters: he almost always begins by teaching, declaring, or reaffirming the finished work of the cross and the greatness of our union with Christ. He no doubt spent months or years discussing these things when he was with these churches in person. But later, being in prison or among some other group of believers, Paul still wrote to them describing these things by way of reminder. Following the often lengthy description of eternal, spiritual realities in Christ, Paul's letters often move on to deal with specific questions or issues related to the individual church.

In my ignorance, I assumed that the first chapters of Paul's letters were deep and important, but that the last chapters were far more helpful when it came to daily Christian living. I could not have been more wrong. The fact of the matter is that every natural or situational instruction found in the latter parts of his letters rests securely upon the foundational spiritual realities already established. In fact, one cannot avoid misunderstanding the apostles' do's and don'ts unless they have first seen and understood the foundational reality of the finished work of the cross. Unless the things described in the latter part of Paul's epistles are the result, outworking, or expression of the former foundational realities, then they will be nothing more than dead religion and works of man. Without a Spirit-given understanding that it is "no longer I, but Christ who lives in me," we will use the words of the New Testament to once again motivate the adamic man to live for God. As we have noted throughout this book, the letters of the New Testament are filled with statements that both exalt Christ as the only life acceptable to God, and expose the nature of Adam as enmity with God. The apostles would never describe these realities chapter after chapter only to immediately contradict themselves by requiring external religion and striving in the flesh.

Putting On and Putting Off

How then should we understand the verses that are often interpreted as the do's and don'ts of the New Testament? The answer, I believe, depends a lot upon the context. Despite how they are often interpreted, many of these verses are not do's and don'ts at all. For example, in the parts of Paul's letters where he speaks about putting on and putting off certain attributes or actions, these changes are not efforts of our flesh but rather consequences of putting on Christ and putting off the old man by the renewing of the mind. As we have already discussed,[17] a Spirit-given knowledge of the truth works in us to remove the old man together with his desires and deeds, and causes us to put on Christ. For example, notice the wording in Ephesians.

> *That you put off, concerning your former conduct, the old man which grows corrupt according to the deceitful lusts, and be renewed in the spirit of your mind, and that you put on the new man which was created according to God, in true righteousness and holiness. There-*

---

[17] See chapter 17 *The Transformation of The Soul*

*<u>fore</u>, putting away lying, let each one of you
speak the truth with his neighbor, <u>for we are</u>
members of one another.[18]*

The charge to "put away lying" is not just a behavioral
correction. Rather, it is Paul's expectation for the body of
Christ *because* the entire adamic man is being put away
from their soul. This is just one of many adamic fruits that
should begin to dry up and die because the cross has taken
the ax to the root of that tree. We see a very similar thing
in Colossians:

*Since you have put off the old man with his
deeds, and have put on the new man who is
renewed in knowledge according to the image
of Him who created him, where there is neither
Greek nor Jew, circumcised nor uncircumcised,
barbarian, Scythian, slave nor free, but Christ
is all and in all. <u>Therefore</u>, as the elect of God,
holy and beloved, put on tender mercies, kindness, humility, meekness, long-suffering.[19]*

Again, the list of virtues seen in this verse are not
fruits of adamic discipline, but rather fruits of the Spirit of
God that grow in us because of the new life we have been
given. To the measure that we are "renewed in knowledge
according to the image of Him who created us," the natural
result is a progressive "putting on" of the nature and character of Christ.

I believe there was an important reason why Paul gave
the church descriptions of both the adamic fruit that

---

[18] Ephesians 4:22-25, emphasis mine
[19] Colossians 3:9-12, emphasis mine

should be disappearing and the fruit of the Spirit that should be appearing in believers. There were many in his day (and many in ours as well) that were deceiving themselves, asserting that they knew the Lord and experienced the renewing of the mind, and yet there was no accompanying life transformation. Some of these people adhered to an ideology called Christian *Gnosticism.* Among other errant beliefs, Gnostics held that all matter, including the human body, was inherently evil, and that salvation was the result of coming to a kind of secret, enlightened knowledge of spiritual reality. It was popular among Gnostics to believe that, so long as this higher knowledge was achieved, it was irrelevant what one did or how one acted in the body. The body, they believed, was condemned to the evil material world and only the mind could be liberated. Therefore, it didn't matter whether these people continued to visit prostitutes, live their lives for worldly gain, treat others with contempt, etc. The only important thing was obtaining the so-called esoteric *gnosis.* This was a wrong but very popular idea in the early church. But whether Paul was contending with Gnostics or simply addressing Christians who had deceived themselves in other ways, he wanted all of his readers to understand that the true knowledge of Christ affects the entire man – body, soul, and spirit. The revelation of Christ indeed transforms the *inner* man, but this inward transformation affects all that we think, desire, and do. It affects how we relate to the world and to the church. So Paul provides his readers with descriptions of the "deeds of darkness" and the "fruit of light" to protect them from being misled.

This, I believe, was also James' intention in his

famous and often misunderstood comments about faith and works. Faith is the mind of Christ working in the soul of the believer. And wherever true faith is found, there will of necessity be the nature and fruit of His life. Faith is for living, and the man or woman that lives by faith grows up to become constrained by the truth in every aspect of their being. You cannot abide in Christ's light and continue to walk in darkness. Or as John says, you cannot walk in the light and hate your brother.[20] All true faith progressively works in us and out of us the life of Christ that we have received. So, once again, those who are growing in true faith should expect an increasing freedom from Adam's desires and deeds. Those who are "setting their mind on things above, not on things on the earth," will be thereby "putting to death our members which are on the earth: fornication, uncleanness, passion, evil desire, and covetousness, which is idolatry."[21]

Wisdom in Our Natural Vessel

Another category of so-called do's and don'ts in the New Testament are verses where the apostles are advising believers to make decisions in the body that are conducive to walking in the Spirit. This needs some explanation. We must first be clear that there is absolutely nothing that we can do to add to what God has finished and perfected through the cross of Jesus Christ. As believers, there is nothing that we must still receive from God that He has

---

[20] 1 John 2:9-11
[21] Colossians 3:3, 3:5

not already given. There is nothing we need to accomplish and nothing we need to prove. However, having understood this, we must also realize that there is still so much that God has accomplished and given that we do not yet know or experience. There is so much of Christ that we have not yet seen, understood, and lived. And this will not change unless our hearts are turned in the right direction, desiring to be the good soil that receives and permits an increase of His Seed. In other words, we can easily fall short of knowing and experiencing the greatness of our salvation if our affections, attention, time, and goals are all invested in the wrong world. We will grow very little in the truth if our hearts are fixed on the earth and continue to be governed by our own purposes and plans. Even as Christians, we can be those whose "god is their appetite, and whose glory is in their shame, and who set their mind on earthly things."[22]

Christ is in us by new birth. We have the fullness of salvation in one perfect Package. But Christ is revealed and formed in us according to the ground that we present to Him and the degree to which we are willing to experience the cross. With all of us, there is still much that we voluntarily give ourselves to that keeps us earthbound in our souls. And it is with this reality in mind that the apostles sometimes admonished believers with statements like: "Flee from youthful lusts,"[23] "Abstain from fleshly lusts which wage war against the soul,"[24] "Do not get drunk with wine, but be filled the Holy Spirit,"[25] "Set your

---

[22] Philippians 3:19
[23] 2 Timothy 2:22
[24] 1 Peter 2:11
[25] Ephesians 5:18

mind on things above, not on things which are on the earth,"[26] "Do not use your liberty as an occasion for the flesh,"[27] "Do not be unequally yoked with unbelievers,"[28] etc.

These kinds of statements are not instructions for how to please God. They are not new covenant laws that Christians are required to obey in the flesh. These are simply matters of wisdom or spiritual common sense that become appropriate and important for those who desire to grow up in Christ. While we are in the natural body and surrounded by a fallen adamic world, Paul says we should "walk circumspectly, not as fools but as wise, redeeming the time because the days are evil."[29] We have this treasure in earthen vessels, but if we are not careful to turn our hearts to the Lord the vessel will remain far more real to us than the treasure within. Again, nothing we do makes us *become* the precious Seed that God has planted. Nevertheless, there are wise or foolish decisions that we make during our time in the body that can affect the Seed's liberty to produce His fruit in us. For more on this subject, see questions five and six on discipline.

Natural Shadows of Spiritual Realities

Still another category of do's and don'ts in the New Testament are the verses where Jesus or the apostles expect the natural created order to align with and reflect

---

[26] Colossians 3:2
[27] Gálatas 5:13
[28] 2 Corinthians 6:14
[29] Ephesians 5:15

eternal spiritual reality. This too deserves some explanation. We have already discussed how the aspects of natural creation were intentionally designed and created by God to bear the image and likeness of His eternal purpose in Christ. Plants bend towards the light in order to grow; caterpillars enter into a tomb-like cocoon and then emerge as new creations; seeds fall into the ground and die, only to later bring forth an incredible increase of their kind. Night and day, birth and death, food, water, growth and increase, all of these created things have a spiritual and eternal counterpart.

The same can be said for the relationships, roles, and institutions that God established for mankind. For example, God created a permanent covenant called marriage where a man and women come together and live as one flesh. This relationship is specific and exclusive, and the result is an increase of their kind in the form of a family. Why did God set up human marriage this way? Because just like light and dark, the caterpillar and the seed, this human relationship gives physical expression to a spiritual union that is real in Christ. Paul tells us plainly that the relationship between Adam and Eve was an intentional picture of Christ and the church. The natural covenant and experience of marriage exists on earth because it first existed in the heart of God. This physical shadow was made to align with and bear the image of the spiritual relationship.

The same could be said for the relationship that exists between a parent and child. Long before there were human sons and daughters, there was an eternal Son who was known and chosen by His Father, and who defined the nature and purpose of the father-son relationship. This Son would one day enter the world, walk as a man, and accomplish the will of His Father without the slightest grumbling or rebellion. He would submit Himself in all things to the will of His Father, becoming obedient even unto death. Jesus Christ was the perfect Son, the One of whom the Father said, "This is My beloved Son, in whom I am well pleased."[30] And all father-son relationships were created in the earth to testify of this one eternal prototype.

In just the same way, before there was ever an earthly king in Israel, there was a perfect King foreknown and appointed by God. Jesus Christ was destined to become the true anointed King, the One who conquers all uncircumcised flesh and rules with a scepter of righteousness. The natural kings and kingdoms in Israel were meant to bear the image of the spiritual kingdom of God.

My point with all of this is that it is not for us to try to interpret or define these relationships and roles. These relationships were defined in the heart of God before there was ever a man on the earth. They were defined by the substance before there was a natural shadow. They were created to align with the pattern of God's eternal and unchangeable purpose in His Son. Shadows have no right and no ability to change whatever substance is casting the shadow. Very much to the contrary, shadows *receive* their form from the substance, and in every way they point back to their source.

Why is this important for us? It is important because it explains why it is not up to us to decide, for example, how many husbands a wife can have, or whether adultery

---

[30] Mark 1:11

is an acceptable option. These issues were defined and settled in the heart of God before man ever existed. It is not up to us to decide whether natural marriage should be a permanent relationship.[31] This too was decided by the truth that God purposed and knew from the very beginning. Furthermore, children are not free to decide whether or not to obey their parents, nor citizens meant to disobey the decrees of their king.[32] The nature of these relationships was determined before the creation of the world. And so, with this in view, when the apostles were responding to questions and problems about natural roles and relationships, they would sometimes instruct the churches to maintain in the earth the image and expression of the things in the heavens.

For example, wives are encouraged to submit to their husbands. Why? Because, as Paul explains, "The church is subject to Christ."[33] Husbands are told to love their wives as their own bodies. Why? Because "Christ also loved the church and gave Himself for her... For no one ever hated his own flesh, but nourishes and cherishes it, just as the Lord does the church."[34] Children are told to obey their parents in the Lord, and fathers are warned not to provoke their children to wrath. Why? Again, because these relationships were created in the earth according to the pattern

---

[31] I am speaking in general terms here. There are individual cases where, for a variety of reasons, it becomes appropriate for natural marriages to be terminated.

[32] Again, I am speaking in general terms. There are unfortunately some situations where it becomes very appropriate for children to disobey their parents, and for citizens to disobey the laws of the land, even as John and Peter did in Acts 4:19-20.

[33] Ephesians 5:24

[34] Ephesians 5:25, 29

of things in the heavens.

By instructing the church in this way, the apostles were correcting misunderstandings and preventing abuses that can result from failing to comprehend the nature of our liberty in Christ. For example, just because Christians have come to the fullness and fulfillment of the marriage relationship through their union with Christ, it does not then become acceptable to disregard or forsake our spouses in the flesh. Or just because we've received the perfect father-son relationship by becoming sons of God through Christ, it is not therefore acceptable to forsake the respect and obedience owed to our natural parents. The apostles say that such behavior is not "fitting"[35] or "right"[36] in the Lord's body. They had an expectation that, wherever possible, human relationships function according to their created design as shadows and testimonies of realities in Christ. This, however, does not mean that we should view these expectations as covenant laws, or think that by outward obedience to these things the natural man becomes acceptable to God.

Church Order

The final category of verses that are often thought to be religious do's and don'ts are the Scriptures that deal

---

[35] For example, "Wives, submit to your own husbands, as is fitting in the Lord." (Colossians 3:18) Or "But fornication and all uncleanness or covetousness, let it not even be named among you, as is fitting for the saints; neither filthiness, nor foolish talking, nor coarse jesting, which are not fitting, but rather giving of thanks." (Ephesians 5:3-4)

[36] For example, "Children, obey your parents in the Lord, for this is right." (Ephesians 6:1)

with church order. There are places in the New Testament, especially Paul's letters to Timothy and Titus, where much attention is given to the proper function of the Lord's body in the context of local fellowships. There are a few important things to keep in mind when we read passages of this kind. First and foremost, at no point in Paul's instructions with regard to church order does he contradict or nullify his consistent declaration of the finished work of the cross, Adam's crucifixion with Christ, Christ's position as the life of His body, the church, etc. Quite to the contrary, he continually reaffirms the gospel of the cross. The instructions given to Timothy and Titus are not intended to be methods of Adam improvement or recipes for pleasing God in the flesh. Rather, these letters deal with counsel, instruction, and warnings about what is conducive to fellowship, growth, and order in the Lord's body.

It is important to keep in mind that Paul traveled and ministered with Timothy and Titus for years, perhaps decades. In his letters to these men, Paul was dealing predominantly with the oversight of the church, with questions of wisdom in appointing elders, and with protecting believers from false teachings and teachers. With these men he would not have felt the need to re-explain the foundation of the cross, to define all of his terms, or to qualify all of his statements.[37] He spoke with them plainly and practically about issues of the church, not because God

---

[37] In other contexts, Paul is careful to qualify himself so as not to be misunderstood. For example, "I labored more abundantly than they all, yet not I, but the grace of God which was with me." (1 Corinthians 15:10). Or, "To this end I also labor, striving according to His working which works in me mightily." (Colossians 1:29)

required a very specific church model or structure, but because he wanted their fellowship to be an environment conducive for growing up in Christ. In some cases there were certain activities, people, or teachings that had become harmful, counterproductive, or distracting to members of the Lord's body, and Paul warns against such things. In other cases, Paul counseled the church to conduct themselves in ways that would not be unnecessarily offensive to unbelievers who were looking on. Whatever the case, the instruction was meant to *facilitate* true spiritual growth and not *produce* spiritual growth. As we have demonstrated, all true spiritual growth is the increase of Christ's reign in the soul, and "neither he who plants is anything, nor he who waters, but God who gives the increase."[38]

4. What does it mean to manifest or express Christ?

The phrase *manifestation of Christ* is one that can invite a lot of wrong ideas and imaginations. What comes to mind when Christians hear these words are often signs and wonders in the natural realm, power over demons or natural elements, spiritual gifts, words of profound wisdom, and other external manifestations. The Lord can certainly do all of these things through the members of His body, but there is a much greater manifestation of Christ that believers are meant to experience. The letters of the

---

[38] 1 Corinthians 3:7

apostles are far more concerned with the inward manifestation of Christ that transforms the soul and gives glory to
God. Notice the following Scripture in Paul's second letter
to the Corinthians:

> *[We are]... always carrying about in the body the
> dying of the Lord Jesus, that the life of Jesus also
> may be manifested in our body. For we who live
> are always delivered to death for Jesus' sake, that
> the life of Jesus also may be manifested in our
> mortal flesh.*[39]

In this Scripture, the manifestation of Jesus is said to
be working *in* us and not *through* us. These verses
describe the internal working of the cross that conforms us
to Christ's death and leaves us bearing the image of His
resurrection. The context of this entire chapter is not
external signs, wonders, and physical demonstrations of
power, but rather the greatness of the treasure that is
working within our earthen vessels.[40] Paul explains that,
"though our outward man is perishing, yet the inward man
is being renewed day by day."[41]

External and visible manifestations of power usually
fascinate us because of the role we get to play in
performing them. Even when we verbally give credit to
God for miracles and giftings, we love being the vessel
through whom God is acting in a noticeable way. However,
the greater manifestation of Christ, and the one that the
Father seeks, is an internal reality before it can ever be

---

[39] 2 Corinthians 4:10-11
[40] 2 Corinthians 4:7
[41] 2 Corinthians 4:16

something that has outward expression. It is something that God sees and recognizes before it is something that others appreciate. In fact, most often it is something that the world never does appreciate or understand. Notice again Paul's words to the Corinthians:

> *Now thanks be unto God, which always causeth us to triumph in Christ, and maketh manifest the savour of his knowledge by us in every place. For we are unto God a sweet savour of Christ, in them that are saved, and in them that perish: To the one we are the savour of death unto death; and to the other the savour of life unto life. And who is suffi-cient for these things?*[42]

This verse speaks of the fragrance of Christ being made manifest through us as we grow in the true know-ledge of the Lord. But there are two very important things to notice in this Scripture. First, God the Father is the primary recipient of this fragrance or expression of Christ. Similar to the fragrant aromas of offerings and incense that testified of Christ under the old covenant, the cross of Christ turns our soul into an altar where flesh is put away and the fragrance of Christ is presented to God. As Christ is put on and Adam is put off, we literally become living manifestations of His indwelling life.

The second thing to notice in this Scripture is that the very same fragrance or manifestation of Christ is an aroma of life to those being saved, but to those who are perishing it is an aroma of death. This shows us that, despite our

---

[42] 2 Corinthians 2:14-16 KJV

common assumptions, the unbelieving world is generally incapable of recognizing, appreciating, or understanding external expressions of the life of God. This often comes as a surprise to Christians. We imagine that any true manifestation of God's nature or power would leave onlookers shocked and amazed; but the truth is usually quite the opposite. Consider Jesus Christ. He was the perfect manifestation of God in all that He thought, said, and did, but the vast majority of Israel failed to recognize Him. Despite three and a half years of speaking words of life, performing countless miracles, and expressing God's selfless love, most of the Jews thought Him to be crazy or demon-possessed and consented to have Him crucified.

What is a manifestation of Christ? The temptation in the natural mind is to define this term by the actions and behaviors that we consider good, respectable, honorable, etc. We imagine that Jesus is expressed by honest, law-abiding citizens who have charming personalities and a friendly disposition towards their neighbors. But as we have already mentioned, there is a wide variety of things that can motivate humans to behave well, most of which have nothing at all to do with God. In one of his many books, T. Austin-Sparks jokes that, according to our most common and accepted definitions, it would be possible to create perfect Christians using the correct combination of training and prescription medication.

Christians are so consumed with outward expressions of spiritual life that can be seen and appreciated by others, but the greatest manifestations of Christ are the ways that His indwelling life influences, defines, motivates, and transforms the human soul. Long ago, the Spirit spoke through David saying that God "desires truth in the inward parts."[43] He desires that the inner man be conquered and governed by the King of kings, making us into instruments of His righteousness. Certainly, Christ's life working on the inside will also bring about a variety of outward expressions. There will be changes in our natural lives, our desires, behavior, and relationship with the world and the church. But these are generally the automatic byproducts of the inward manifestation of Christ. And although it runs contrary to our natural way of thinking, the primary fruit that God desires to harvest is the internal, spiritual, and eternal work of Christ in the hidden place of the human heart.

On one occasion, God testified audibly from heaven about Jesus Christ saying, "This is My beloved Son, in whom I am well pleased."[44] Christians are familiar with this statement, but it is interesting to notice *when* it was made. God did not declare His satisfaction with Christ after years of ministry and miracles, or after delivering the famous Sermon on the Mount. Rather, this declaration was made during His baptism in the Jordan River, before Jesus had even begun His public ministry. Christ had not yet performed one miracle or spoken one parable. God's satisfaction with His Son was bound up in the life that was at work within Him and not the various outward manifestations that followed. The same thing is also true of us.

I am not at all trying to minimize the greatness of Christ's spoken words or miraculous signs, nor am I

---

[43] Psalm 51:6
[44] Matthew 3:17

suggesting that the church does not function as the Lord's body in outward and visible ways. It certainly does and it must. I am simply trying to make two principal points, the first of which has already been stated: I believe that by far the greatest and most important manifestations of Christ are the ways that He inwardly defines and transforms the believer's soul. The second point is something of a warning: It is not a good idea to pursue or wait for outward manifestations of Christ. Although it may sound like a spiritual thing to do, it is just one more way that we end up fixing our attention on ourselves and on the earth. Assessing ourselves, trying to give ourselves a spiritual report card, looking for manifestations of Christ, and wondering when things will change, all of this keeps our hearts looking to the wrong man. It may sound strange because of our religious assumptions, but we never have to concern ourselves with the manifestation of Christ. We are *always* a manifestation of whatever is most real in our soul. And when it comes to the body of Christ, manifestation is not our business, it is His. He is the Head, we are the members. Our responsibility is to turn our hearts to know and abide in Him. His responsibility is "to work in us both to will and to do for His good pleasure."[45]

I remember a specific time in my life when I had started to see and experience the truth of the cross. So many things were changing in my heart but I was concerned that nobody could see or understand what the Lord was doing in me. And even more frustrating than those who failed to notice any change were the ones who thought I was changing for the worse. For one reason or

---

[45] Philippians 2:13

another, many were critical of the things I was sharing or the way I was suddenly obsessed with the cross of Christ. I wanted desperately for people to realize how real this was. And more than anything, I wanted them to appreciate the fruit of the Spirit that was for the first time beginning to grow in my heart.

It was at this time that the Lord began to deal with my heart about the manifestation of Christ and the fruit of His Spirit. I began to imagine a dark and ugly swamp in the middle of nowhere that was so wretched and foul-smelling that neither animals nor insects would make it their home. In fact, even the bushes and trees had all died with the exception of one enormous and flourishing apple tree that stood alone right in the center of the swamp. Every autumn this apple tree produced an amazing quantity of large, perfect, red apples that filled the branches, and hung there for weeks without a single creature to enjoy the fruit. This image came to my mind one day, followed by this question: When does fruit become fruit? Is it fruit only when somebody notices it? Does it become fruit when somebody picks and eats it? The answer was obvious – fruit is the increase of a seed, regardless of who sees or appreciates it.

As Christians we are reluctant to call something the fruit of the Spirit unless it is noticed and appreciated by others. Believers often evaluate the Lord's accomplish-ments based upon the number of people involved or the amount of attention or praise received. From God's perspective, however, the measure of His work in and through the church is not at all determined by man's understanding or appreciation. The Lord's work in His body is determined by the increase of His Seed. When it comes to assessing the growth of the church, God has only ever used one measure – "the measure of the stature of the fullness of Christ."[46]

5. Aren't you spiritualizing everything?

This is a common question that arises when we haven't clearly seen the incredible difference between "the first" and "the second,"[47] or the old and new covenants. The old covenant was the natural picture, promise, and prophecy; the new is the spiritual realization to which all of the old pointed.

Before anything else, we must remember that God is, and has always been, spirit. Long before He created natural testimonies and shadows of spiritual realities in a physical universe, the triune God was a spiritual being. The natural creation came out from the invisible, uncreated, spiritual reality within the Godhead, and in every way creation points back to its Source. The author of Hebrews says, "By faith we understand that the worlds were framed by the word of God, so that the things which are seen were not made of things which are visible."[48]

For us, since we are first born of the earth, natural things seem to be the most real. We think of the natural creation as more concrete and absolute, whereas spiritual things feel far less substantial. To God, however, the exact

[46] Ephesians 4:13
[47] See Chapter Four
[48] Hebrews 11:3

opposite is true. Spiritual reality is absolute and undeniable, and natural things are shadowy reflections. God's work through the cross accomplished a great transition from the shadow to the substance, the natural to the spiritual, the temporal to the eternal. Through the death, burial, and resurrection of Christ, God "put away the first and established the second."[49] This great transition is the centerpiece of the entire Bible and it is the essence of our own personal journey in Christ. We are baptized into Christ as the end of the old and we rise with Christ as partakers of the new. And in every way, we are making an exodus out of natural, temporal shadows, and learning to live in the eternal, spiritual substance.

When Nathaniel met Jesus for the first time, he was astounded that Jesus had seen him under the fig tree before Philip had even called him. But Jesus responded and said,

> *"Because I said to you, 'I saw you under the fig tree,' do you believe? You will see greater things than these." And He said to him, "Most assuredly, I say to you, hereafter you shall see heaven open, and the angels of God ascending and descending upon the Son of Man."*[50]

Jesus was speaking to Nathaniel about the fulfillment of what Jacob saw centuries before.[51] Far greater than a supernatural ability to see Nathaniel under a tree was the fact that Jesus was about to open the heavens through His

---

[49] Hebrews 10:9
[50] John 1:50-51
[51] Genesis 28:12

work on the cross and become the ladder out of one realm and into the other. Nathaniel need not marvel at a miracle in the earth when he was soon to see an exodus out of that entire realm and a way provided for human souls to be made alive, raised up, and seated with Christ in God.

In a sense you could say that the cross is the means by which Christ brings us back with Him to the spiritual reality and relationship that He shared with the Father before the foundation of the world. In fact, Jesus says this very thing while praying to His Father just prior to His crucifixion. He says, "And now Father, glorify Me with Yourself, with the glory which I had with You before the existence of the world."[52] And shortly after He adds, "Father, I desire that those whom You have given Me, that where I am, they may be with Me also, that they may behold My glory which You gave Me, because You loved Me before the foundation of the world."[53]

Once again, *our* beginnings are in the natural realm as members of the natural man, Adam. But the cross brings us up out of the fallen, natural shadows and immediately deposits our soul in the eternal, spiritual substance. For us, the order is always natural first and then spiritual. This is precisely what Paul describes in his first letter to the Corinthians.

> *And so it is written, "The first man Adam became a living soul." The last Adam became a life-giving spirit. However, the spiritual is not first, but the natural, and afterward the spiritual. The first man was of the earth, earthy;*

---

[52] John 17:5
[53] John 17:24

the second Man is the Lord from heaven. As was the earthy, so also are those who are earthy; and as is the heavenly Man, so also are those who are heavenly. And as we have borne the image of the earthly, we shall also bear the image of the heavenly Man. Now this I say, brethren, that flesh and blood cannot inherit the kingdom of God; nor does corruption inherit incorruption.[54]

Once our hearts begin to see this remarkable transition, it seems silly to think that we can over-spiritualize the gospel. Of course we can misunderstand or wrongly represent it because of the darkness of our natural mind. But God's salvation in Christ is a *spiritual* thing. Paul says, "He who is joined to the Lord is one spirit with Him."[55] And our experience of salvation is the incredible reality of being joined to the resurrected Christ and made partakers of all that He is and has with His Father. There was a time when God related to man through natural pictures and places and physical symbols and figures. But two thousand years ago Jesus said to the woman at the well, "But the hour is coming, and now is, when the true worshipers will worship the Father in spirit and truth; for the Father is seeking such to worship Him. God is Spirit, and those who worship Him must worship in spirit and truth."[56]

Over and over, throughout the entire New Testament, we are told that the physical and natural aspects of the first creation and covenant pointed to spiritual or heavenly

---

[54] 1 Corinthians 15:45-50, emphasis mine
[55] 1 Corinthians 6:17
[56] John 4:23-24

realities. For example, speaking of Sarah and Hagar Paul says, "These things are symbolic. For these are the two covenants."[57] The author of Hebrews explains that the levitical priests "served a copy and shadow of the heavenly things."[58] We are told that the tabernacle along with all of its furnishings and offerings are "copies of the true"[59] or "copies of the things in the heavens."[60] Hebrews chapter twelve insists that new covenant believers have not come to a natural "mountain that may be touched and burned with fire... and the sound of a trumpet and the voice of words."[61] Rather, we have come to the spiritual realization of all these physical pictures.

> But you <u>have come</u> to Mount Zion and to the city of the living God, the heavenly Jerusalem, to an innumerable company of angels, to the general assembly and church of the firstborn who are registered in heaven, to God the Judge of all, to the spirits of just men made perfect, to Jesus the Mediator of the new covenant, and to the blood of sprinkling that speaks better things than that of Abel.[62]

Countless other Scriptures demonstrate this very thing. Sadly, Christians are sometimes so unfamiliar with spiritual reality that statements like these seem confusing

---

[57] Galatians 4:24
[58] Hebrews 8:5
[59] Hebrews 9:24
[60] Hebrews 9:23
[61] Hebrew 12:18
[62] Hebrews 12:22-24, emphasis mine

or even disappointing. We are so wrapped up in and defined by the natural world that we don't have much use for spiritual things unless they seem beneficial to our natural lives. It sounds strange to say it, but the natural man actually dislikes spiritual things. We love calling things "spiritual," as long as those spiritual things are touching, fixing, blessing, or empowering natural things that are important to us. We love the idea of worshiping in the spirit as long as this remains something we can do for God through natural effort, gifting, time, or emotion. We love spiritual gifts, but only the ones that can be seen or experienced by the natural man. We love learning spiritual things as long as such knowledge makes us look wise in a natural world. We are fascinated by spiritual words and prophecies to the measure that they foretell things that will come to pass in the course of our natural lives. After all, we would say, how else could they be relevant?

None of this is a true appreciation for spiritual reality. We don't really like spiritual things; we only like how spiritual things touch the earth. And when you suggest to most Christians that the substance and reality of our salvation is a purely spiritual thing (that is, it is not intended to fix the earth, natural bodies, circumstances, etc.), such an idea seems entirely impractical. What's the good of a Bible verse that speaks of Christ and doesn't tell me what to do with my day? What's the good of a sermon that sheds light on the eternal purpose of God, but doesn't help me find my own purpose? Why read the prophets if they don't describe events that will happen in our lifetime? What's the point of a church if it is not serving the local community?

Too often we want a spiritual God, but one that leaves us in Egypt (the earth) and merely changes its conditions. We don't really want to go where He is, see what He sees, love what He loves, and all for His sake. Such a relationship with God is far too spiritual and foreign for our natural appetites. We're often very much like the Jews of the first century – we have very little interest in a Messiah that offers us a spiritual kingdom.

6. What about disciplining myself?

The purpose of self-discipline is another thing that drastically changes when we begin to see the reality of the cross. Once we see the otherness of Christ and the enormous gulf between the best of man and the beginnings of Christ, we realize that discipline could never make us something we are not. A disciplined Adam is still Adam, and this truth needs to strike us with some force. Until it does, Christians will always attempt to offer the Lord the best of a man that God has rejected. However, having seen and accepted the judgment of the cross, we can begin to understand the right place for discipline in the life of a believer.

When a person is born of the Spirit they continue to live *in* the world but they are no longer *of* the world. Speaking of His disciples, Jesus said, "I do not pray that You should take them out of the world, but that You should keep them from evil. They are not of the world, just as I am not of the world."[63]   But even though the cross has made our souls recipients and vessels of a heavenly life, we obviously still move around the earth for a time in natural vessels that are attached to the natural realm. This creates something of a struggle for all of us. On the one hand, "We have died and our life is hidden with Christ in God."[64] Yet, at the same time, we carry this spiritual treasure in natural bodies that continue to encounter and interact with the adamic world. We are new creations living as strangers in an old creation.

In a variety of ways, the authors of the New Testament admonish us to have little to do with the world we have left behind and everything to do with the world of Christ that we entered.   John says, "Do not love the world or the things in the world. If anyone loves the world, the love of the Father is not in him."[65] James' words are similar: "Do you not know that friendship with the world is enmity with God?"[66] Paul counsels the Colossians to "set your mind on things above, not on things on the earth. For you died, and your life is hidden with Christ in God."[67]   The apostles exhort believers with statements like these because they understand that, even after being born of the Spirit, the world continues to compete for our attention, affection, and identity.   Our experience of this struggle certainly changes to the measure that we grow in the true knowledge of Christ. But to some extent at least, while we live in these bodies "the flesh lusts against the spirit, and the spirit lusts

---

[63] John 17:15-16
[64] Colossians 3:3
[65] 1 John 2:15
[66] James 4:4
[67] Colossians 3:2-3

against the flesh, for these two are in opposition to one another."[68]

Here is where discipline comes in. Discipline is not how we earn God's approval, produce righteousness, or demonstrate our devotion. But discipline can play a role in protecting our hearts from the darkness and deadness of a world that is no longer our true home. In other words, some kinds of self-discipline can help us take our eyes off of the flesh now that we have been born of the Spirit.

In his letter to the Romans, Paul tells us to "put on the Lord Jesus Christ and make no provision for the flesh with regard to its lusts."[69] What does it mean to make no provision for the flesh? I believe this is a warning for believers not to feed the flesh, so to speak, after being made partakers of the divine nature. Don't stimulate and resuscitate what you are seeking to put away. Don't give your heart to things that are dead, or your time to things that will deceive you. Appropriate Christian discipline has to do with living in the earth in such a way as to protect yourself from all that hinders the increase of Christ in your soul. Paul tells the Ephesians to "walk circumspectly, not as fools but as wise."[70] Self-discipline does not earn life or produce life, but it can help protect life. It can help create and secure an environment that is conducive to the growth of God's Seed within you.

In the second chapter of this book, I used the analogy that involved a farmer, seed, and ground. God the Father is the farmer, Christ is the perfect seed, and we are the ground that is given the seed with a great expectation for

---

[68] Galatians 5:17

[69] Romans 13:14

[70] Ephesians 5:15

increase. The purpose of this analogy was to point out how confused we are about spiritual growth. Somehow we overlook the fact that the seed, not the dirt, is what is meant to grow and satisfy the farmer's expectation. Paul tells us plainly that "we are God's field" and that "God gives the increase."[71]

We can continue with this analogy to help us understand the function of discipline in the life of a believer. In the natural realm, we understand that a single seed somehow contains a plant's entire DNA, design, nature, capacities, etc. The seed possesses its own life, grows in its own specific way, and reaches its own predetermined potential. Any attempts to force growth would be counterproductive. For example, reaching down into the soil and attempting to stretch the seed up into a plant would most likely kill it. All that the seed requires is an environment that is suitable for it to do what it naturally does.

The same is true for the life of Christ that God has deposited in our soul. We cannot make it grow, and we do not have to. Christ desires His own increase and seeks the good soil that is conducive to an increase of His kingdom. There is no form of discipline that will produce growth, but there are certain things we can do and choices we can make that offer the seed of Christ a more fertile environment. Returning to the analogy of a farmer with his seed, discipline might be compared to a fence that keeps out birds and rabbits, or a greenhouse that protects seedlings from harsh weather conditions. Neither of these things *makes* growth happen, but they look after the seed and do what is possible to nurture its growth.

---

[71] 1 Corinthians 3:7, 9

I hesitate to give specific examples because we are quick to make rules and religion out of suggestions and warnings. But there is much that we can give our hearts to that works against God's purpose in us. Remember, the salvation of souls in itself is not God's purpose. Rather, we were saved *for* a purpose. And sometimes our choices, pursuits, and entanglements with the natural realm are detrimental to spiritual growth. Paul says, "No one engaged in warfare entangles himself with the affairs of this life, that he may please him who enlisted him as a soldier."[72] Paul is not referring solely to overt acts of sin and immorality. He's referring to anything and everything that proves to be an obstacle to growing up in Christ. Sometimes we find that we are watering the seed with one hand and poisoning it with the other. Or we realize we've spent ten minutes in the morning praying to see Christ and the next fourteen hours of the day passionately pursuing our own natural goals. The Lord will make the specifics clear to each of us as we continue in our journey of faith. But if, for example, He deals with our heart about cutting back the hours spent in front of the television, it is not because God hates all television or because watching less causes us to become more spiritual. It is simply because, as we see more of the heavens, it makes good sense to control or even cut some of our ties with the earth.

---

[72] 2 Timothy 2:4

7. What about spiritual disciplines?

There is absolutely nothing wrong with deliberately setting aside a specific time each day to read the Bible and pray. In fact, it is often appropriate and wise to do so. Problems arise, however, when we imagine that the amount of time spent in these activities corresponds to spiritual growth or maturity. It is common to hear statements like, "John is an amazing Christian; he spends two hours in prayer every day." But John's commitment to prayer doesn't necessarily have anything to do with spiritual life, growth, or understanding. I know this from experience.

There are lots of reasons why people devote themselves to spiritual or religious disciplines, and many of them have little to do with the truth. People often pray, fast, meditate, and study to feel better about themselves in one way or another. We like to think of ourselves as spiritual, knowledgeable, and wise, and we love to be respected and revered. Some may be attracted to spiritual disciplines because of religious pride, while others are motivated by guilt and shame. And some of the most disciplined men and women of prayer in the world are those whose devotion is wasted on false gods. Even within the church there are multitudes of Christians who regularly pray to and converse with a Jesus of their own imagination.[73]

---

[73] To some extent this is unavoidable. When we are born again we know only that Christ is our Savior, and we automatically fill in the innumerable blanks with imaginations, concepts, and ideas that we have heard. The real problem arises when we do not allow the Spirit of Truth to progressively cast down these imaginations and replace them with the true knowledge of the Lord.

The greatness of spiritual discipline is not defined by time or dedication. It is defined by true union and communion with the living God in spirit and truth. If the times that we have set aside to pray and read Scripture are not motivated by true hunger to "know Him and the power of His resurrection, and the fellowship of His sufferings, being conformed to His death,"[74] then all the discipline in the world will profit us very little.

8. If all were crucified with Christ, does that mean all now have life in Christ?

Sometimes when people begin to see that the entire Adamic man was judged in the death of Christ, they wrongly assume that all men are therefore made alive by Christ's resurrection. This is simply not true. There are a few verses in the New Testament that are sometimes used to support this idea. One such verse is 1 Corinthians 15:22 where Paul says, "For as in Adam all die, even so in Christ all shall be made alive." At first glance this verse may seem to be suggesting the universal salvation of all mankind. But there is something very wrong with this assumption. It is true that in Adam all die. And it is true that in Christ all are made alive. *But it is not true that all men are in Christ.* Paul is certainly describing two universal realities, but both condemnation and salvation are determined by the man in whom we are found. In other words, condemnation is universal for all who are in Adam and salvation is

---

[74] Philippians 3:10

universal for all who are in Christ, but in order to be in Christ we must be born again.

In the death of Christ, God crucified, judged, and separated Adam from Himself. In the words of Jesus, the cross was "the judgment of the world."[75] In the words of Paul, "If one died for all, then all died."[76] However, when Christ rose from the grave, all those who were dead in Adam did not automatically come alive in Him. In order to have life, man has to *receive* the One who is life. John says, "He who has the Son has life; he who does not have the Son of God does not have life."[77] Every human being is born "dead in sin and transgression."[78] But Jesus promised that "he who hears My word and believes in Him who sent me... has passed from death to life."[79] Only by faith do we receive the grace of God offered in Christ and are we "delivered from the dominion of darkness and translated into the kingdom of the Son of His love."[80] This reality is clearly stated in countless New Testament Scriptures. One of the clearest is in the gospel of John:

> *He came to His own, and His own did not receive Him. But <u>as many as received Him</u>, to them He gave the right to become children of God, <u>to those who believe in His name</u>: who were born, not of blood, nor of the will of the flesh, nor of the will of man, but of God.*[81]

---

[75] John 12:31
[76] 2 Corinthians 5:14
[77] 1 John 5:12
[78] Ephesians 2:1
[79] John 5:24
[80] Colossians 1:13
[81] John 1:11-13, emphasis mine

Here we are clearly shown that life comes through birth. We became partakers of Adam through birth, and we are made partakers of Christ through new birth. Jesus said, "That which is born of flesh is flesh, and that which is born of Spirit is spirit."[82]

Therefore, although the judgment of the world in the body of Christ is a reality (known or unknown) for all mankind, resurrection life is a reality only for those who by faith are born of God's Spirit. In a sense, every person in the world could rightly say, "I have been crucified with Christ." But only believers could truly say, "Nevertheless I live, yet not I but Christ lives in me." And then, only those who are growing in the revelation of Christ could continue the verse and say, "And the life I now live in the flesh I live by the faith of the Son of God."[83]

9. Why does Paul say "imitate me"?

There are a few Scriptures where Paul admonishes his readers to "imitate me" or "become imitators of Christ."[84] These verses sometimes cause confusion in Christians who are realizing that Christianity is so much more than external behavior modification. Why would Paul encourage believers to imitate him? The problem we have with these verses comes from our understanding of the word *imitate*. Generally, when we think of an imitation,

---

[82] John 3:6
[83] Galatians 2:20 .
[84] 1 Corinthians 4:16, 11:1, Hebrews 6:12

what comes to mind is an external copying or mimicking of something we have seen. But this is clearly not what Paul had in mind. First of all, the Greek word used in these verses has to do with viewing something as a model, or following in another's footsteps. In fact, the KJV translates this word *follower* instead of imitator. But more importantly, Paul's point is not that he wants his readers to mimic his words and actions, but rather to learn to live as he was living. How did Paul live? In every way, Paul was becoming a branch that lived by the life of the Vine. He made statements like, "For me to live is Christ,"[85] and "Nevertheless I live, yet not I, but Christ lives in me."[86] Jesus too, when He walked as a Man, lived in and by the life of His Father. Of course He was the eternal Son of God, but as the Son of Man He did nothing of His own initiative. His works and His words were not His own, but the Father's who had sent Him.

In each of Paul's letters, a great emphasis is placed on the necessity for every believer to experience in themselves the revelation, formation, and glorification of the Lord Jesus Christ. He wrote to the Galatians, "My little children, for whom I labor in birth again until Christ is formed in you."[87] When using imitation terminology, Paul is certainly not challenging the heart of his gospel and settling for a cheap external impersonation. Far from it. Paul's greatest hope was that all men come to know and experience the reality of Christ crucified in the exact same way that he had. Standing trial before King Agrippa, Paul cried out, "I would wish to God... that not only you, but

---

[85] Philippians 1:21
[86] Galatians 2:20
[87] Galatians 4:19

also all who hear me this day, might become such as I am, except for these chains."[88]

10. How do I know if it is Christ or me?

This is a common question for those who begin to understand the difference between Adam and Christ, but it quickly disappears when the soul sees more of the otherness of Christ. The more we see of Him, the more we are able to clearly recognize what *isn't* Him. In the light of Christ, the flesh (not only as actions, but as a nature) begins to stand out as a conspicuous, contrary, and self-serving thing. With a bit of the Lord's perspective working in a believer's heart, Adam's ideas, desires, religion, and actions all begin to look the same. They all come from the same source and aim towards the same goal.

For those who are struggling with this question, I think Watchman Nee's advice from *The Normal Christian Life* is helpful. He says, "Trying to look within, to differentiate, to discriminate, to analyze, themselves only brings them into deeper bondage. True inward knowledge will never be reached along the barren path of self-analysis."[89] His conclusion is simply that "In His light, we see light."[90] The flurry of questions in our natural mind begin to disintegrate as the light of the Lord continues to define our understanding.

---

[88] Acts 26:29 NASB

[89] Watchman Nee, *The Normal Christian Life,* Chapter 12 Tyndale House Publishers, Inc.

[90] Psalm 36:9

Although it has been mentioned elsewhere, it deserves repeating that this kind of self-analysis and evaluation usually only functions to get our eyes fixed on ourselves. The fruit of self-assessment is usually one of two things – pride or condemnation, depending upon our opinion of ourselves. In this journey, I have found it to be so much more helpful to concern myself with "fixing my eyes on Jesus, the author and finisher of faith."[91] It is just like the carnal and religious mind of Adam to imagine what progress should look like and then judge himself by imaginary criteria. We have our own ideas about what our problems are, what God wants to change, and how it should all take place. And in our blindness we end up praising ourselves for works of the flesh and condemning ourselves for what God has already condemned. Again, the natural man lacks the light to discern what progress, growth, and transformation really are. We begin to understand these things only as we look away from ourselves and see with new light.

11. How do we teach this to children?

Parents who begin to see the finished work of the cross often wonder how to teach this to their kids. They don't want to put their children under the law, or raise them up with religious legalism and bondage. They want their children to genuinely know Christ and experience His

---

life. How do you go about sharing things like the renewing of the mind, abiding in Christ, and freedom from sin to a child? Having four children myself, this is something I have pondered a lot. Although I am far from being an expert on children's ministry, I can share a few things that have become clear to me over the years.

The first thing is a little saying that has proven helpful in understanding how to deal with my children: *self-control is necessary when self is still in control.* In other words, if the fleshly nature of Adam is all that a person knows (whether child or adult), then it is very appropriate for that person to learn and exercise self-control. We obviously cannot let our children run wild and live by the impulses of the flesh simply because they are too young to learn Christ. Kids are wonderful, precious, and cute, but they are little bundles of selfishness that need to be guided and disciplined. And if flesh is all that they know, it seems entirely appropriate to instruct them according to God's written requirements with the expectation that they at least *know* what is good and right, and do their best to submit to it and to relate to others according to what is right. Is this law? Yes, but law is necessary when man lives in the flesh. Paul says, "The law has jurisdiction over a man as long as he lives."[92] We have shown that law does not bring about true righteousness or transform the inner man, but law is not a bad thing. In fact, it is "holy and just and good."[93] The law is the righteousness of Christ described in words and commandments, and until the soul knows and aligns with a greater law and a greater

---

[92] Romans 7:1, emphasis mine
[93] Romans 7:12

righteousness (both of which are Christ Himself living from within) it is good to impose law on the natural man.

The same thing could be said with regard to the civil laws of the land. A Christian might ask, "Why should we try to legislate good behavior? If righteousness is a Person, then what are we accomplishing by forcing people to act better than they really are?" There is some truth in this argument. Obeying civil laws is certainly not the same as true righteousness, and is most definitely not God's objective for mankind. Nevertheless, for the sake of society, safety, relationships, commerce, etc., it is obviously not appropriate to let the adamic man live according to the whims of the flesh without boundaries or consequences. Again, outward subjection to law should never be confused with righteousness. But law is a necessity when man lives in the flesh.

Therefore, with our children, I believe it is necessary to teach them right from wrong, enforce right behavior and discipline wrong behavior, even though these things will never truly produce the righteousness that God desires. Written and spoken laws can never create in us what they demand from us, but they can work in our favor. As Paul explains, law can become to us a ministry of condemnation that exposes our need for another *kind* of life. And when our children are old enough or interested enough to listen, we can share with them the truth of what God offers us in His Son. Much more than just forgiveness for sin or heavenly direction through life's difficult situations, God offers us Jesus Christ Himself as the life and light of our soul.

One other important thing that I have come to realize is that parents cannot truly teach Christ to children any more than they can teach Christ to friends or neighbors. Morals, values, and Bible stories can be passed along to children, but the only Person who can teach Christ to the human soul is the Spirit of God, and He does so whenever hearts turn to Him. Often parents assume total responsibility for their children's spiritual life. We long for our children to know the Lord in the same way that we do. This is a normal and appropriate desire, but we need to understand our limitations. Religion can be taught; life must be born. Even Jesus Himself could do nothing more than scatter seeds of life. The increase depended entirely upon the ground on which the seeds landed.

As parents, I believe we should openly share with our children the truth that we are seeing and experiencing in Christ. We can also provide them an environment where they see how real the Lord is to us, and where they feel comfortable talking and asking questions about spiritual life. But ultimately, in order to truly know the Lord, each individual heart has to turn to the Lord motivated by its own hunger for truth and life.

12. So... how do I do this?

Some people reach the end of a book like this and say to themselves, "Ok, it all sounds great. Now how do I do it?" This is an extremely common question, and I've tried to deal with it to some extent already. The problem with this question is that it makes no spiritual sense. I don't say this to be rude or condescending. I had the exact same question myself, and it drove me crazy for a while. But the question itself is a misunderstanding; it is an expression of the darkness and confusion that works in our natural minds.

The whole point of everything we have mentioned in this book is that God has done everything because man was powerless to do anything, and that now God seeks to reveal and work in you all that He has accomplished through Christ. To ask how *we* do this is a contradiction to the cross. The cross was not only the forgiveness for man's innumerable failed attempts, but also the crucifixion and elimination of the adamic man himself. The cross stands firm as the eternal boundary between Adam and Christ and forever declares, "Nothing of the first man can cross this line!" In Christ, the question of spiritual growth is not dependent upon man's effort, intellect, gifting, zeal, or discipline. The pivotal issue is the true knowledge of the One who is our life. Peter says:

> *Grace and peace be multiplied to you in the knowledge of God and of Jesus our Lord, as His divine power <u>has given to us all things that pertain to life and godliness, through the knowledge of Him</u> who called us to His own glory and virtue.*[94]

Nobody likes it at first when I say this, but *the how is actually a Who.* Or I could say that the how is the knowing of the Who. Statements like this sound abstract or strange until we begin to see just how true they are. God has "accomplished His eternal purpose in Jesus Christ our

---

[94] 2 Peter 1:2-3, emphasis mine

Lord."[95] There is nothing for you to add or contribute. You are not finishing what Christ started or waiting for some future consummation. Your role as a member of Christ's body is simply to know and be transformed into the image of His perfect and finished work.

When it comes to pursuing the true knowledge of God, there are issues of personal hunger and wisdom (discussed previously in this appendix) that are factors in our spiritual growth, but there are no ladders to climb or steps to follow. Again, the how is a Who. You cannot learn to be like Him. You must learn Him as the life of your soul. And to the measure that He is seen and known in truth, He becomes the light by which we see, the life that constrains us, and the nature behind all that we want and do. If this response seems disappointing or unsatisfactory to you, give it some time, and keep turning your heart to know Him. With a little more light, this will become clear, and will be a reason for rejoicing in your heart.

13. If Adam is born dead, why did he need to be crucified with Christ?

Realizing that the adamic man is born dead in sin and transgressions, some believers wonder why it was necessary, or what it means, for him to be crucified with Christ. This question, like many others, begins to make more sense when we understand how Scripture uses terms like death and judgment.

---

[95] Ephesians 3:11

It is certainly true that Adam was separated from the Tree of Life in the Garden of Eden, and that his seed has always been spiritually dead, that is, lacking spiritual life. The crucifixion of the corporate adamic man in the body of Jesus Christ did not change this one bit. The cross didn't actually kill the adamic man physically or spiritually. Rather, the cross judged Adam and separated him from God. The distinction is important.

For thousands of years God had a relationship with the natural man through the old covenant.[96] During that age, He related to mankind through a variety of specific types and shadows of Christ. However, even though offerings and sacrifices were always among the covenant types and shadows, it was "not possible that the blood of bulls and goats could take away sins."[97] Animal sacrifices painted natural pictures of the righteousness of God and the removal of sin, but they never truly accomplished that of which they testified. Only at the cross of Christ did God truly manifest His righteousness, settle all debts with sinners, end His relationship with the adamic man, and initiate a new relationship (a new covenant) with "one new

---

[96] There were actually several covenants that God made with man prior to the coming of Christ. The Mosaic Covenant is generally referred to as the old covenant because it receives by far the most attention in the Old Testament Scriptures. It is not wrong, however, to consider all of the former covenants (established with Noah, Abraham, Moses, Phinehas, David, etc.) to be aspects of the one old covenant. Contrary to common misunderstandings in the church, these covenants should not be viewed as separate and unrelated relationships between God and man that changed over the course of time. Rather, each of these covenants provide distinct and important pictures, shadows, and promises of the *one* eternal and spiritual covenant that was coming in and as Jesus Christ.

[97] Hebrews 10:4

man,"[98] the body of Christ. Notice Paul's explanation of
these things to the church in Rome.

> *For all have sinned and fall short of the glory of
> God, being justified freely by His grace through
> the redemption that is in Christ Jesus, whom
> God set forth as a propitiation by His blood,
> through faith, to demonstrate His righteous-
> ness, because in His forbearance God <u>had
> passed over the sins that were previously
> committed, to demonstrate at the present time
> His righteousness, that He might be just and
> the justifier of the one who has faith in Jesus</u>.*[99]

What did the cross accomplish for man? It judged
both sin and sinner in the body of Christ, satisfying the
righteousness of God. Why is that important for those who
are born in Adam? It is important because, having dealt
with sin and death fully and for all time, God could open a
door for us to follow Christ[100] out of the old and into the
new. In other words, Adam's spiritual status was not
affected by the cross – he was spiritually dead before the
cross and equally dead afterwards. But only after the cross
of Christ did the Red Sea open and become a highway out

---

[98] Ephesians 2:15

[99] Romans 3:23-26, emphasis mine

[100] When Jesus invited believers to follow Him, He didn't just desire
that they walk with him through the cities and towns of Israel.
Following Jesus, then and now, has to do with leaving behind the
old man, creation, and covenant, and following Him through the
cross onto resurrected ground. For this reason He said, "take up
your cross and follow Me" (Matthew 16:24, Mark 8:34, 10:21,
Luke 9:23). There is only one place to go with a cross on your
back.

of Adam for all who had painted His blood on their door. Only after the cross did all who were *dead in sin* have the opportunity to become *dead to sin* in the resurrected Lord. God now relates to all who believe as "dead indeed to sin, but alive to God in Jesus Christ our Lord."[101] In this way, God becomes both "just and the justifier of the one who has faith in Jesus."

14. If Christ is my life, does that mean I no longer sin?

In a word, the answer to this question is no. To see why, we need to start with an understanding of what sin really is. Most understand sin to be the overtly bad or wrong things that humanity generally looks down upon. This is far from God's understanding of sin. From the Lord's perspective sin has less to do with *what* is being done, and more to do with *who* is doing it. Sin is every-thing that has missed the mark, everything that has come up short of the glory of God, and therefore it is everything that has Adam as its source and substance. In the mind of God, there are only two categories – righteousness and sin. Righteousness is the person and nature of Christ that works in the soul by faith. Sin is the nature of Satan that works in the soul through darkness.

When a person is born of the Spirit, we are immedi-ately taken out of the dominion of darkness and translated into the kingdom of Christ. Our soul is handed over to a

---

[101] Romans 6:11

new government, and Christ now has every right to fill us with His rule and make us an expression of Himself. Nevertheless, even after new birth, there is much that still takes place in us that is not an expression of our new King. A clear picture of how this works can be seen when the land of Canaan was given to Israel as a possession. In its natural state, the Promised Land was filled with idolatry, uncircumcised flesh, and abominations of every kind. And even though all the land belonged to Israel, it continued to manifest another nature and government until every city was conquered by the sword of David. We too, having been purchased by the blood of Christ for His own glory, begin our journey of faith still filled with strongholds, high places, idols, and enmity with God. And unless the judgment of the cross spreads through the land of our heart by the revelation of Christ, we continue to manifest the nature of our first birth.

If somebody were to ask me if I still commit sin, my answer would be that, by nature, I *am* sin. And everything that comes from me as a man is an expression of what I am. Righteousness is the nature and expression of Christ alone, and only to the degree that He is revealed and formed in me am I capable of expressing anything other than the sinful adamic man. On the other hand, to whatever measure the nature of Christ is working in me, there I do not sin. This, I believe, is the meaning of John's words, "Whoever is remaining in Him is not sinning."[102]

Having said this, however, it is important to point out that, if we are in Christ, God no longer relates to us in sin. Sin is what we were by nature, sin is what we manifest to

---

[102] 1 John 3:6 (Concordant Literal Translation)

the degree that we walk in the flesh, but sin is not how God relates to us or recognizes us in His Son. God sees all things from the perspective of the finished work of the cross, and in Christ there is absolutely nothing left to condemn. This is by no means a reason to continue in sin, as Paul argues in his letter to the Romans, and only the spiritually blind would interpret it as such. But the truth remains that, whether we understand His incredible gift or not, God "made Him who knew no sin to be sin for us, that we might become the righteousness of God in Him."[103]

15. Why isn't this more popular?

I remember sitting in a mostly empty auditorium and hearing somebody preach the true message of the cross for the first time. I had attended many Christian conferences over the years and this one was by far the smallest. At the time, my eyes were just beginning to open and the reality of the cross was striking my heart with incredible force. I remember sitting there, among only fifteen or twenty other people, wondering why crowds of Christians were not banging down the doors and climbing in the windows to hear what I was hearing.

The unfortunate truth is that religion has always been more popular than the gospel of life. Religion offers so much to the natural man, whereas the true gospel offers him a cross. Man loves religion because it allows him to stay right where he wants to be – in the center of his own

---

[103] 2 Corinthians 5:21

universe, using God as a means to his own end and glory. In our many and varied religious ideas (inside and outside of the church,) we create and worship a concept of God that is beneficial to the flesh.   Some use religion for comfort and security while others use it for power, influence, and personal greatness. Some find in religion a way to gain respect from others, to be considered wise and revered as spiritual. Others simply want to feel good about themselves, to alleviate guilt, to feel like a moral, upstanding citizen. Religion is very useful for the adamic man, but not so the true gospel of the cross. The cross has always been an offense and a stumbling block to the natural man because "when Christ calls a man, He bids him come and die."[104]

When you look through the history of the Lord's dealings with man, there has always been a relatively small number who walk with God by faith. Two or three million Israelites came out of Egypt and walked through the Red Sea.   Only Joshua and Caleb, however, wanted to see the greatness of their Salvation.   In the days of King Jehoshaphat, four hundred prophets of God were gathered together to prophesy before the king, but only Micaiah had the word of the Lord.[105]   Stories like these abound in the Old Testament, and in them are examples of what Jesus said to the Jews:

> *Enter by the narrow gate; for wide is the gate*
> *and broad is the way that leads to destruction,*
> *and there are many who go in by it. Because*

---

[104] Dietrich Bonhoeffer, *The Cost of Discipleship* (London: SCM Press, 1948/2001), pg. 44.
[105] 1 Kings 22

narrow is the gate and difficult is the way which leads to life, and there are few who find it.[106]

When it comes to churches and ministries, the number of people involved is not a telltale sign of anything. And just as large crowds are never a sure sign of God's approval, neither are small gatherings or home groups an indication of the Lord's activity. There are both enormous and tiny religious organizations that have little or nothing to do with God's revelation of Christ. But there is no doubt in my mind that there have always been, at every time and in every generation, those who have come to the end of themselves and turned to see the Life that God offers mankind in His Son.

---

[106] Matthew 7:13-14